From Cotton Field to Schoolhouse

CHRISTOPHER M. SPAN

From Cotton Field

to Schoolhouse

AFRICAN AMERICAN EDUCATION

IN MISSISSIPPI, 1862–1875

THE UNIVERSITY OF NORTH CAROLINA PRESS · CHAPEL HILL

Designed by Courtney Leigh Baker and set in Dante and
Archive Autograph Script by Tseng Information Systems, Inc.
Manufactured in the United States of America

. . .

The paper in this book meets the guidelines for permanence
and durability of the Committee on Production Guidelines
for Book Longevity of the Council on Library Resources.

. . .

The University of North Carolina Press has been a
member of the Green Press Initiative since 2003.

. . .

Library of Congress Cataloging-in-Publication Data
Span, Christopher M.
From cotton field to schoolhouse : African American
education in Mississippi, 1862–1875 / Christopher M. Span. — 1st ed.
p. cm.
Includes bibliographical references and index.
ISBN 978-0-8078-3290-5 (cloth : alk. paper)
1. African Americans — Education — Mississippi —
History — 19th century. 2. Freedmen — Mississippi — History.
3. Education — Mississippi — History — 19th century.
4. Education and state — Mississippi — History — 19th century.
5. Mississippi — Race relations — History — 19th century.
6. Mississippi — Politics and government — 1865–1950. I. Title.
LC2802.M7S65 2009
371.829'96073076209034 — DC22
2008052517

. . .

13 12 11 10 09   5 4 3 2 1

TO MY PARENTS

. . .

Samuel Spann and Judith Jenkins

Slaves yesterday, to-day free: What shall they be to-morrow?

—WILLIAM WELLS BROWN,

The Negro in the American Rebellion (1867)

CONTENTS

Acknowledgments · xiii   *Introduction* · 3

PART ONE · 1862–1870

· · ·

1 · LIBERATION THROUGH LITERACY · 23

2 · EDUCATED LABOR · 49

3 · EDUCATION FOR SERVITUDE · 84

PART TWO · 1870–1875

· · ·

4 · UNIVERSAL SCHOOLING · 117

5 · PUBLIC SCHOOLS, 1871–1875 · 153

Epilogue · 177

APPENDIX · KNOWN AFRICAN AMERICAN

POLITICIANS AND LEGISLATORS IN MISSISSIPPI DURING

RECONSTRUCTION, 1870–1875 · 181

Notes · 185   *Bibliography* · 223   *Index* · 237

MAP AND TABLES

MAP
. . .
Mississippi, 1870 · 2

TABLES
. . .

1 · Schools Reported by the Freedmen's Bureau as Sustained
Wholly or in Part by Freedpeople, 1867–1870 · 42

2 · Schools for Freedpeople Taught by Northerners, Early 1865 · 62

3 · Schools Consolidated by the Freedmen's Bureau
for Freedpeople, January 1867–May 1870 · 70

4 · School Population, Enrollment, and Average Attendance
of Educable Children, 1870–1871 · 134

5 · School Population, Enrollment, and Average Attendance of Black and
White Youth in Fifteen Majority-Black Counties, 1870–1871 · 136

6 · Enrollment, Number of Public Schools, and Number of Enrolled
Pupils per School in Fifteen Majority-Black Counties, 1870–1871 · 137

7 · School Population, Enrollment Percentage, and Average Attendance Percentage of Black and White Youth in Fifteen Majority-Black Counties, 1870–1871 · 139

8 · Number of Public Schools for Enrolled Black and White Youth in Fifteen Majority-Black Counties, by Type, 1870–1871 · 140

9 · School Population, Enrollment, and Average Attendance of Black and White Youth in Fifteen Majority-White Counties, 1870–1871 · 144

10 · School Population, Enrollment Percentage, and Average Attendance Percentage of Black and White Youth in Fifteen Majority-White Counties, 1870–1871 · 145

11 · Enrollment, Number of Public Schools, and Number of Enrolled Pupils per School in Fifteen Majority-White Counties, 1870–1871 · 146

12 · Number of Public and Private Schools for Black and White Educable Youth in the Black and White Counties Analyzed, 1870–1871 · 148

13 · Number of Public Schools for Enrolled Black and White Youth in Fifteen Majority-White Counties, by Type, 1870–1871 · 150

14 · School Population, Enrollment, and Average Attendance of Educable Children, 1870–1871 and 1876–1877 · 168

15 · Enrollment, Number of Schools, and Number of Enrolled Pupils per School in Fifteen Majority-Black Counties, 1876–1877 · 170

16 · Enrollment, Number of Schools, and Number of Enrolled Pupils per School in Fifteen Majority-White Counties, 1876–1877 · 171

ACKNOWLEDGMENTS

I wish to extend my gratitude to everyone who assisted and encouraged me as I completed this book project. I particularly want to acknowledge the people who read all or parts of my book and offered me invaluable suggestions that improved its content. My gratitude extends first and foremost to my colleagues at the University of Illinois: Vernon O. Burton, Sundiata Cha Jua, Ralph Page, Larry Parker, David R. Roediger, William T. Trent, and particularly my fellow historians of education, James D. Anderson and Yoon K. Pak, whose conversations, jokes, and continual support make work in the academy a blessing and not a curse. My appreciation also extends to my colleagues and role models in the field: Ronald E. Butchart, Dionne Danns, V. P. Franklin, Linda M. Perkins, Vanessa Siddle Walker, Fanon Che Wilkens, and Jason R. Young, who have offered their time, eyes, energies, and wisdom to ensure I provided the best narrative possible.

In addition, I would like to acknowledge the staff at the Mississippi Department of History and Archives in Jackson for their commitment to excellence, their patience with my many queries, and their graciousness in making my many research trips to Jackson as painless as possible. Special thanks should be given to the staff at the University of Illinois Interlibrary Loan Department for their patience and efficiency in addressing my countless requests over the years. I want to thank my college and department for continually encouraging and supporting me from my doctoral days to now. Similar gratitude goes to the staff at the University of North Carolina Press for all their assistance. I want to thank the Center for Democracy in a Multiracial Society at the University of Illinois for the faculty fellowship they awarded me. It gave me the uninterrupted time needed to research and revise this book. Last, I want to acknowledge two more mentors, Dean

Michael Jeffries and Dr. Priscilla Fortier, for every ounce of support and every memory they have given me throughout my career. To all others, who have gone unintentionally unnoticed, I humbly say thank you.

. . .

I want to conclude these acknowledgments by relating a conversation I had with my son and offering a few additional dedications. Lollipops. One day while I was working on the edits of this book, my almost-three-year-old son, Langston, asked me what I was doing. I told him that I was writing a book and he inquisitively asked, "Is it about lollipops?" I said no, it is about the first schooling opportunities of a people a long time ago, and he paused, look at my computer, then looked back at me, and said, "You should write a book about lollipops." His smile and comments instantly reminded me of why I was working so hard to write and tell this story, and while it is not about lollipops, I hope my son — one day — will come to understand why this story is so important. In many ways this book is an introduction for him to the history of his people. All of my father's family and a significant majority of my wife's family have roots in Mississippi. Retelling the educational experiences of African Americans who emerged from slavery in Mississippi, in many ways, is the chronicling to my son of the lived experiences of his ancestors and what they did to ensure that the next generation of black men and women in the family would have a life better than they had themselves.

I could not have written this history without their stories, their hopes, their spirit, and their support. So this work is dedicated to so many people. It is dedicated to my late mother and father, Judith Jenkins and Samuel Spann, my grandparents, aunts and uncles, brothers and sisters, in-laws, nieces, nephews, and cousins. It is dedicated to my friends, especially Jason Weathington, Felton (Kenny) Maxie, Ronald Wiley Jr., Boyd Reynolds, and Jason Young, for all their encouragement and ability to keep me humble. It is dedicated to my mentors, James D. Anderson and the late Paul C. Violas, for giving me the confidence, wherewithal, and skills to continue their legacy. It is dedicated to my doctoral students — Chamara Kwakye, Jon Hale, Tamara Hoff, Olanipekun Laosebikan, Paul Mathewson, Ishwanzya Rivers, David Roof, Dwania Turner, Duronne Walker, and Kim Walker — for their patience as I completed this project. It is dedicated to my ancestors — Mr. Teet and Miss Holly, Mr. Victor, Miss Emma, Great-Grandma Mattie, Great-Uncle Herman and Great-Aunt Lilly Mae, Great-Aunt Ester, Great-Uncle Tony, Great-Aunt Carrie, Grandma Arvelia and Grandpa Jimmy — whose blood, sweat, and tears led me to tell this story and guided my weary mind and pen when I felt like giving up. Their dreams, born, whispered, and cast aside on cotton plantations in Bolton, Clinton, and Jackson, Mississippi, live on in this story, and in me. Never in my life have I owed so much to so many at one time.

Last but not least, this book is dedicated to my loving wife, Kaamilyah Abdullah-Span, and our beloved son, Langston Akil Abdullah Span. I could not have completed this labor of love without their unwavering support, tireless encouragement, limitless patience, and boundless love for me. I count my blessings twice every day for having them in my life. Thank you so very much.

From Cotton Field to Schoolhouse

Mississippi, 1870

· · ·

TENNESSEE

ARKANSAS

LOUISIANA

ALABAMA

GULF OF MEXICO

DeSoto
Benton
Alcorn
Marshall
Tishomingo
Tippah
Tunica
Tate
Prentiss
Union
Panola
Lafayette
Coahoma
Pontotoc
Lee
Itawamba
Quitman
Yalobusha
Calhoun
Chickasaw
Monroe
Tallahatchie
Bolivar
Grenada
Webster
Clay
Leflore
Montgomery
Sunflower
Carroll
Choctaw
Oktibbeha
Lowndes
Washington
Humphreys
Holmes
Attala
Winston
Noxubee
Issaquena
Sharkey
Yazoo
Leake
Neshoba
Kemper
Madison
Warren
Scott
Newton
Lauderdale
Jackson ★
Rankin
Hinds
Smith
Jasper
Clarke
Claiborne
Copiah
Simpson
Jefferson
Covington
Jones
Wayne
Lincoln
Jefferson
Davis
Adams
Franklin
Lawrence
Wilkinson
Amite
Pike
Marion
Forrest
Perry
Greene
Walthall
Lamar
Pearl River
Stone
George
Harrison
Jackson
Hancock

INTRODUCTION

Before the Civil War there wasn't a free school in the state, but
under the Reconstruction government, we built them in every county. . . .
We paid to have every child, Negro and white, schooled equally.
Today, they've cut down on the educational program, and
discriminated against the Negro children, so that out of every
educational dollar, the Negro child gets only 30 cents.
—GEORGE WASHINGTON ALBRIGHT, *The Daily Worker*, 1937

In June 1937, at the age of ninety-one, an ex-slave from Holly Springs, Mississippi, by the name of George Washington Albright was interviewed by the
Daily Worker regarding his legislative and educational activities during and
after the Civil War.[1] Albright proffered the above statement, and his inten-
tions seemed unmistakable. Cognizant of Mississippi blacks' existing educational opportunities and their vulnerable and denigrated status, he wanted
to inform the public of the important contributions African Americans—in
particular former slaves—played in the establishment of Mississippi's first
comprehensive tax-supported public school system. Albright knew firsthand
that the status of African Americans in the decade following slavery and in
contemporary Jim Crow Mississippi were markedly different. Prior to the end
of the Reconstruction era and the rise of de jure segregation, African Americans in Mississippi viewed the initial years of emancipation optimistically
and had rights that extended beyond second-class citizenship.[2] For nearly a
decade after the war, they voted, attended school, became landowners, determined and negotiated their working conditions, and were leaders and
contributors in their local communities, counties, state, and nation.

As an active agent in the processes promoting education in postwar Mississippi, Albright recalled the foremost public school initiatives he and the

other black delegates in attendance at the state's 1868 constitutional convention wanted for Mississippi. Public schools in Mississippi were to be free, all-inclusive, and, most important, equitable, irrespective of a child's gender, race, class, or previous condition of servitude.[3] In attempting to achieve this aim, Albright was convinced that African Americans of his generation— through their determination, appreciation of the value of education, and limited resources—collectively laid the groundwork for the rise of universal education in postwar Mississippi. They provided the financial resources and "sweat equity" for the establishment and continuation of the first schools for African Americans, served as teachers, solicited northern-born teachers to migrate to Mississippi, and pressured state legislators to consider their educational ambitions and needs as newly freed citizens. During the war, Albright, himself barely literate and no more than eighteen years old, served as one of the first teachers for formerly enslaved African Americans. As the Civil War commenced, Albright taught his first class under a shade tree in Holly Springs, then in an abandoned barn, and thereafter in a church. "The state had no teachers," he contended, "until we brought in teachers from the North, men and women, white and Negro."[4] To Albright, this generation of formerly enslaved African Americans was not a powerless citizenry forced, like their descendants, to accept the laws and dehumanizing status quo of Jim Crow Mississippi. On the contrary, formerly enslaved African Americans in Mississippi were an empowered group that contributed to the pursuit of education not only on their own behalf but for all children in postbellum Mississippi.

The editors of the *Daily Worker* virtually dismissed Albright's recollections of his and his generation's activities in the first decade after slavery. While the Communist editors thought Albright's commentary to be quite animated, they questioned the accuracy of his memories, especially regarding the legislative and educational impact former slaves had had on Mississippi's postbellum political economy.[5] However, Albright's retrospection concerning the influence formerly enslaved African Americans had on public education in Mississippi—despite his occasional lapses in memory—was sharply accurate. It epitomized W. E. B. Du Bois's assertion that "the first great mass movement for public education at the expense of the state, in the South, came from Negroes" and that "public education for all at public expense, was, in the South, a Negro idea."[6]

Contemporary scholarship indicates that during and after the Civil War, educational opportunities for African Americans throughout the South arose primarily from the efforts and enthusiasm of African Americans themselves.[7] This was especially true in Mississippi. Prior to the end of the war, before the concerted arrival of northern religious or freedmen aid organizations, such as the American Missionary Association or the Bureau of Freedmen, Refugees, and Abandoned Lands (better known as the Freedmen's Bureau), African Americans in Mississippi began organizing schools, wherever possible, and educating themselves. As early as 1862, free, freed, fleeing, and enslaved African Americans established churches and schoolhouses for individual and collective improvement. Literate free and freed African Americans in Mississippi served as these schools' first teachers, and previously enslaved African Americans—young and old, male and female—were their pupils. By 1868, countless missionary organizations, teachers, and government and military officials had migrated to Mississippi intent upon educating, uplifting, and protecting former slaves. These grassroots initiatives proved to be the origins of universal education for African Americans in Mississippi as well as the catalyst for the state's first comprehensive tax-supported public school system, inaugurated in the autumn of 1870.

Despite the proactive demeanor of formerly enslaved African Americans, their educational history in post–Civil War Mississippi and their contributions amid this development remain virtually untold. In 1979, historian William Leon Woods deduced that "historians who have concerned themselves with Mississippi during Reconstruction have written very little about black education in the state."[8] Neither James Garner, nor Vernon Lane Wharton, nor William C. Harris—the state's foremost postbellum historians—devoted much attention to the evolution of African American education following the Civil War. Garner and Wharton were more concerned with the political and economic affairs African Americans and whites in Mississippi wrestled with following the Civil War than with the probable role education played in dealing with these affairs. William C. Harris, being more selective, focused on the political battles waged among President Andrew Johnson, Congress, and Mississippi's postwar legislatures over the readmission of Mississippi into the Union. In his immense 1979 publication, *The Day of the Carpetbagger: Republican Reconstruction in Mississippi*, Harris did include a chapter on the rise of public schools in the early 1870s under Republican rule. This account, however, did not specifically consider the educational history of African Americans in Mississippi and, similarly to his earlier publications, made very little mention of how acquiring an education, or even desiring its rudiments, assisted formerly enslaved black Mississippians in their postbellum experiences.[9]

Nevertheless, moderate but meaningful scholarship does exist concerning the origins and history of schools for African Americans in postbellum Mississippi. In 1918, Stuart Grayson Noble wrote the first, and to this date only, history of African American education in postbellum Mississippi, entitled *Forty Years of the Public Schools in Mississippi: With Special Reference to the Education of the Negro*.[10] His work chiefly described the educational policy considerations associated with the rise of public schools for African Americans between 1870 and 1910. Noble's educational history accompanied numerous early twentieth-century monographs to make mention of schools established for formerly enslaved African Americans in Mississippi during this era; the majority of these publications can be found in the periodical *Publications of the Mississippi Historical Society*, edited by Franklin L. Riley. These early histories of Reconstruction provide piecemeal analysis and evidence regarding the policies and persons endeavoring in Mississippi in the name of African American education. They also provide, in much greater detail, information on the persons and organizations utterly opposed to African American education—such as local officials and the Ku Klux Klan—and the tactics they used to deter, and in some cases eradicate, schools established for former slaves and their children.

Whereas these early histories are informative, they are also loaded with glaring and immediate problems that diminish the reliability of their analysis and assessment of the Reconstruction era and the origins of schools for African Americans in Mississippi. All are outdated—some over eighty years old—but more important, the interpretations presented in the vast majority would be deemed patronizingly racist, or at the bare minimum antiblack, by contemporary standards. Evident throughout these histories are personal biases against African Americans and a staunch disapproval of the opportunities that African Americans gained with the downfall of slavery and the overall reconstruction of the South. They praised the tactics, even the violence, used to prevent African Americans from purchasing land, voting, becoming statesmen, or attending school; they penned their discontent of black self-sufficiency, the Freedmen's Bureau, northern-born teachers, and the Republican Party; and they belittled the policies, practices, and ideologies that seemed to challenge the doctrine of white supremacy and the etiquette and power structure upon which the white South was built. Authors of these early histories articulated their own personal cynicism regarding African Americans. They were certain formerly enslaved African Americans were inherently unable to govern themselves as freedpeople. Few expressed this sentiment more vehemently than W. H. Hardy in his 1904 Reconstruction history of east and southeast Mississippi. While he felt the law should protect African Americans' personal rights, property, and happiness, Hardy was convinced that this could only be achieved under the leadership and guiding hand of southern whites because of the "inherent" limitations of blacks.

> The negro has *no fitness for wise* self-government, and the thirty-five years of freedom and education that has *intervened* show that *he cannot be fitted* to share with the white man in governing a republic. . . . The negro *will never* be permitted to share in governing the white people or his own people because he *is not capable* of governing, and *centuries may elapse before he reaches that stage of evolution* which will fit him for self-government. [italics added][11]

Under the editorship of Franklin L. Riley, the publications of the Mississippi Historical Society offered a very pejorative portrayal of African Americans in Mississippi and of those engaged in the process of educating or assisting them. The historians represented formerly enslaved African Americans as little more than passive, indiscriminate recipients of a corrupt school system imposed upon them by underhanded Republicans and overzealous northern-born missionary schoolmarms.[12] To state the obvious, such illustrations of the era, and of the legislative and educational contributions of Mississippi blacks following the war, were quite different from the recollections proffered by George Washington Albright.

Late nineteenth- and early twentieth-century historians of this era and region felt it their duty to construct a past that rationalized the actions—no matter how inhumane or unjustifiable—of white southerners and the overall subjugation of African Americans within an oppressive system of segregation known as Jim Crow. Historian Leon Litwack deduced that this generation of Reconstruction traditionalists and historians "rummaged in the past to find a history that would best serve the needs of the present, and professors and teachers went on to miseducate the next several generations in a prescribed version of reality."[13] These "histories," or "propagandas of history" as W. E. B. Du Bois aptly described them, served to validate the rigid, brutal, and dehumanizing practices that the doctrine of white supremacy espoused and maintained so efficiently: de jure segregation and African American subservience well into the twentieth century.[14]

Few of these studies from the turn of the century presented an accurate description of the processes and persons that shaped southern Reconstruction or the rise of universal education for African Americans in Mississippi. As in other southern states following the Civil War, newly freed African Americans in Mississippi saw the earliest years of emancipation as a time of great promise and opportunity, including the chance to gain and exercise full citizenship—the legal right to vote, own land, and participate in all the duties, rights, and privileges afforded to civilians in society. They characterized education in similar fashion, and determined its acquisition to be essential in their pursuit of becoming citizens and obtaining equality and self-sufficiency. In *Trouble in Mind*, Leon Litwack—with precision and literary expertise—captured this collective sentiment among previously enslaved African Americans.

> When black Southerners in 1865 staked out their claims to becoming a free people, they aspired to a better life than they had known, to a life once thought impossible to contemplate. They wanted what they had seen whites enjoy—the vote, schools, churches, legal marriages, judicial equity, and the chance not only to work on their own plots of land but to retain the rewards of their labor. During Reconstruction, they seized the opportunity to make these goals a reality, to re-order the post-bellum South. It was a time of unparalleled hope, laden with possibility, when black men and women acted to shape their own destiny.[15]

Albeit ignored or overlooked in much of the previous analysis, such drive, determination, and initiative established the first schools for African Americans—free or freed—in Mississippi, and were instrumental in assuring their continuation throughout the Reconstruction era. It challenged white Mississippians—especially the state's planter and ex-slaveholding class—to re-assess, even alter, their treatment and expectations of African Americans in slavery's aftermath as schools for African Americans became an ever-increasing feature in the state's landscape—grassroots schools at first, then public and private ones later on—and as African Americans, native born and otherwise, quickly became lead officials in Mississippi's postbellum political economy.

Amid the events that ultimately shaped the rise of universal education for African Americans in Mississippi, ubiquitous tensions were deeply entwined in the racial segmentation of the state's political economy. Central to the rise of universal education for African Americans, not just in Mississippi, but throughout the postbellum South, was the question of what purpose schools for African Americans served, and as important, who would control them: southern blacks, southern whites, migrant northerners, or some combination of each group? As in the political and economic arenas, the perennial question "What shall we do with the Negro?" took center stage in the earliest formation of schools for African Americans in the South and became more pressing as the schools became more permanent. In Mississippi, this new "Negro problem" consumed the thoughts of all involved in the establishment of schools for African Americans and in the overall transition of slaves into freedpeople and citizens.

Between 1862 and 1875—the formative years of schools for African Americans in Mississippi—tensions over the general purpose of these schools and who would control them ran deep. Where most African Americans envisioned schools established by and for them as a chief means of achieving independence, equality, political empowerment, and some degree of social and economic mobility—in essence, full citizenship—there were many northerners assisting them who saw such expectations as unrealistic. Where Mississippi freedpeople further expected to live as independent landowners and possibly receive compensation for years of forced and unpaid labor, again most northerners among them assumed otherwise and expected African Americans to continue laboring for those who had previously enslaved them and their families, only this time as citizens laboring in a free market economy. These northern-born emissaries sought to control the first educational experiences of freed Mississippi blacks, convinced that former slaves were not capable of maintaining themselves. They envisioned the type of learning freed African Americans received would entail the moral and literacy lessons necessary for them to subsist and understand their new status as freedmen and freedwomen in a post–slave economy South.

White Mississippians, in general, disapproved of schools for African Americans and despised the new status and opportunities afforded to former slaves. Slavery was dead, but its legacy, and white Mississippians' refusal to acknowledge African Americans as anything other than slaves, lived on. Black Mississippians attending school challenged this way of thinking and the expectations most Mississippi whites had of reviving the status quo and labor system of the antebellum era. Still there was an "unalterable conviction" among most white southerners about blacks attending school. Many were convinced "Negroes could not and would not learn," that "education of the Negroes would be labor lost," that schools for African Americans encouraged social and racial equality, and that schooling, in itself, "ruined niggers."[16] Even so, many whites in Mississippi felt a certain responsibility to monitor the progress of schools for African Americans following the Civil War. As a general rule, they sought to govern these schools in order to control the thoughts and actions of African Americans and to best ensure that the type of instruction in these schools adhered to the etiquette, labor demands, and overall expectations of southern whites. Whites in Oxford, for example, were among the first to understand the role southern whites in general needed to play in the education of freed blacks. In the summer of 1866, a concerned few went to considerable lengths to explain this to their disgruntled brethren. Their rationale was straightforward and took into consideration the imminent future of the post–Civil War South. "If it ever was good policy to keep them ignorant, it certainly is no longer so, but the very reverse. The right of suffrage will, in all probability, be given to this people at some future day. If we don't teach them some one [sic] else will, and whoever thus benefits them will win an influence over them which will control their votes."[17]

According to Reconstruction traditionalist and historian Walter L. Fleming, "No more important problems were left by the Civil War for future settlement than those relating to the churches and to education in the former slave states."[18] Few remarks gauged better the crisis brewing over the establishment and purpose of schools for African Americans in Mississippi. In 1865, when the Civil War officially ended, a new war, one of ideas and policies, was being waged in Mississippi over who would ultimately control the future of these schools, a battle that would continue beyond the Reconstruction era and well into the twentieth century. However, the educational policy involving the augmentation and perpetuation of schools for African Americans in Mississippi was never more heated and contested than in its first decade of development, as migrant northerners and black and white

Mississippians vied with each other over the educational future and overall livelihood of former slaves and their children.

Neither blacks nor whites in Mississippi seemed willing to budge. African Americans were determined to have schools, so they built them, with or without the assistance of others. Conversely, whites in Mississippi were determined to see the educational initiatives and opportunities of formerly enslaved blacks fail. On the whole, Mississippi whites both tacitly and violently resisted schools for African Americans, not so much because these schools challenged a fervent belief that African American children were racially inferior or ineducable as for quite the opposite reason. Schools for African Americans in Mississippi proved to be a triumph in not only teaching freedpeople the rudiments of learning, but also in affording them the aspirations and skills necessary to become self-sufficient citizens deserving of equal status and opportunities. They aided African Americans in voting, in negotiating labor agreements, in becoming landowners, in managing their own everyday affairs, and in obtaining independence. They challenged the leverage and expectations of the state's planter class by putting black children in schoolhouses rather than cotton fields and inspiring them to be more than a cotton picker for someone else's profit. Schools were incubating a new generation of African Americans in Mississippi, a generation of black men and women who could for the first time in the state's history conceivably alter their life opportunities and societal status by becoming literate. To black and white Mississippians alike, schools for African Americans conveyed the message that equality was truly attainable.

Schools for African Americans in postbellum Mississippi had even greater implications, however, because the transition between slavery and freedom was a dangerous and critical one. They challenged the ideological underpinnings of a white supremacist doctrine that rationalized American slavery and black subjugation, and determined African Americans to be, by nature, inferior. More important, if left to the control and considerations of black Mississippians, or those favorably assisting them, schooling threatened to uproot the very foundation of the state's social system and economy. If schools taught that anything was possible with an education, was it not plausible that black children would aspire to be more than what whites expected? Couple this prospect with the reality that Mississippi's black majority population, by 1868, was its voting majority, and that most freed African Americans desired to become landowners, and the origins and purpose of schools for African

Americans assumed even greater significance. The type of schooling black children in Mississippi received determined not only the status of and opportunities for future generations of African Americans, but also, indubitably, the future way of life for white Mississippians as well. If allotted the time and resources needed to promote the agenda of the ex-slave, schools for African Americans in Mississippi had the potential of being a democratizing force; they had the power to transform Mississippi society, a society whose very existence both before and after the war depended upon the subjugation and labor of black people. Subsequently, the question of whether schools for formerly enslaved African Americans in Mississippi would be established to produce full-fledged citizens or free but subordinate laborers (or some combination of the two) was a question of extreme importance in the first decade after the Civil War.

. . .

This book details how this history unfolded. It documents the origins and purposes of schooling for African Americans in Mississippi between 1862 and 1875, from the first reported schools for African Americans in the state to the end of Reconstruction in Mississippi. But this book is much more. It is the story of how African Americans in Mississippi—the overwhelming majority of whom were formerly enslaved—attempted to acquire an education in order to improve themselves and achieve equality and citizenship, of what they confronted, and of how they struggled and endured in a state resistant to their aspirations. It is the story of what opportunities, obstacles, friends, and foes black Mississippians met head-on in their pursuit of an education in slavery's aftermath. It is the story of what formerly enslaved African Americans in Mississippi thought schools would do for them. Whenever possible the narrative is drawn from the perspectives and experiences of formerly enslaved African Americans. When this is not possible, the book is largely drawn from the correspondence of northern-born emissaries laboring in Mississippi and from other archival sources such as diaries, labor contracts, newspapers, organizational records, census data, governmental reports, monthly school reports, educational statistics, and municipal records. In their own right, each of these types of archival data offers invaluable information on the origin and social purposes of schools for African Americans during this period.

The book is divided into two parts. Part I (chapters 1, 2, and 3) illustrates the grassroots initiatives and activities that established the first educational opportunities for formerly enslaved blacks in Mississippi between 1862 and 1870. Chapter 1 initiates this discussion and documents the role freed blacks played in establishing the first schools for African Americans throughout the South, but in particular in Mississippi. In 1862, before the arrival of northern-born missionary or freedmen aid organizations, or the Freedmen's Bureau, African Americans in Mississippi had already started the process of educating themselves and their children for personal and professional self-improvement. These schools were created and maintained almost exclusively by the self-determination, limited resources, and educational enthusiasm of former slaves. Their objective was to use schooling as a means to transform themselves and other formerly enslaved men and women into citizens and as a pathway to securing and maintaining freedom.

Chapter 2 complements chapter 1. It illustrates the influence migrant northern-born teachers and their agencies, in particular the various missionary and freedmen aid associations, the Union army, and the Freedmen's Bureau, had on the development of grassroots schools for African Americans in Mississippi. It documents the social purposes that teachers and emissaries from the North assumed schools for African Americans in Mississippi would serve following the Civil War. The schools established by northerners sought to prepare Mississippi freedpeople for life and work after enslavement and concomitantly "educate" landowning and ex-slaveholding white Mississippians in regard to the necessity of supporting schools for their former bondsmen. In many ways the actions and expectations of these migrant northerners conflicted with the ambitions of freed black Mississippians. Even so, the arrival of teachers from the North assisted black Mississippians in their pursuit of establishing a system of schools for themselves and their children. From 1863 until mid-1870 these northerners diligently labored in Mississippi, intent upon educating and uplifting former slaves. Northern teachers and the schools they established proved to be successful, despite their limited resources, the discrepancies they had with many black Mississippians over the purpose and future leadership of these schools, and the hostility they regularly encountered from antagonistic whites. Grassroots schools set up by them gave former slaves a rudimentary education; they served as the foundation and model for Mississippi's postbellum public school system;

and they provided African Americans with the protection and the material, human, and financial resources much needed in their quest to ensure greater freedoms and a system of schooling for themselves and their children.

Chapter 3 details the various responses of white Mississippians to the establishment of grassroots schools by and for African Americans. While some Mississippi whites supported and even started schools for African Americans, most were wholly opposed to the thought. Schools were antithetical to their long-held beliefs and expectations of African Americans. The white elite, in particular, expected black men and women to continue laboring for them and expected African Americans — in every manner possible — to remain subservient and accepting of this societal expectation. The war may have abolished slavery, but it did not do away with these deep-rooted beliefs held by most white southerners, not just whites in Mississippi. Chapter 3 chronicles these developments and explores, in depth, the political economy of postbellum Mississippi, the expectations white Mississippians had of former slaves after the war, and what purposes schools for African Americans — if they were to exist at all — served in the minds of Mississippi whites.

The two chapters in Part II document the origin and purposes of public schools for African Americans in Mississippi from 1870 to 1875, the year white Democrats and landowners frustrated with the never-ending costs of Reconstruction, the state's public school expenditures, and the newfound political empowerment of black Mississippians, used the racial tensions ever present in the state as a springboard to launch a political campaign of violence and terror. The end result of this violence and terror was to shift control of all affairs in Mississippi away from loyalists and northern migrants into the hands of the state's pro-Confederate white elite, upend Republicanism and Reconstruction in postbellum Mississippi, and thwart many of the advancements formerly enslaved African Americans had struggled to achieve since emancipation.

Chapter 4 concentrates on the inaugural year of public schools in the state and on the politics, policies, and debates concerning the creation of these schools. Key events would take place between 1869 and 1871 that invariably influenced the direction and overall purposes of schools for African Americans. Most significant were the departure of the Freedmen's Bureau and the formal establishment of a comprehensive system of tax-supported public schools inclusive of all Mississippi children. Like their grassroots predecessors, public schools assisted Mississippi blacks in their pursuit of equal access and consideration as citizens. Previous analysis has adequately addressed the rise of public schools in postbellum Mississippi, but lost in the discussion is the role—legislative and otherwise—African Americans played in the debate and establishment of a public school system in the state. The push for public schools arose from the collective expectations and the grassroots and legislative efforts of formerly enslaved black Mississippians.

An analysis of educational parity between schools for black and white children in Mississippi is presented and data that illustrates pupil enrollment, daily attendance, duration of school terms, and types of schools are examined to highlight the type of schooling African Americans were offered and what purposes they served. Never before the rise of public schools had African Americans in the state had greater access to an education, but the number of schools and the type of instruction available to them were severely limited. Public schools for African American children rarely could accommodate the pupils enrolled, let alone the many more that desired to attend, because of limited capacity. In some locales, private schools assisted in meeting the educational ambitions of African Americans, but they too faced many of the same problems. The schools were always overcrowded, understaffed, low on resources, and poorly equipped, and most offered little more than elementary instruction.

All the same, the decision to establish a comprehensive system of public schools in Mississippi inclusive of former slaves was not without controversy. Countless whites staunchly opposed the measure, certain the approved school bill advocated racial equality and produced an undue burden of taxation upon white property owners. They were most outspoken about three measures in particular: first, that the school bill guaranteed African Americans a legal entitlement to attend school; second, that it required whites to contribute a part of their income or wealth toward the finance and upkeep of schools for African Americans; and last, and perhaps most important, that it did not call for the racial segregation of public schools.[19] To quell white fears on the latter point, state legislators established a dual system of public schools, one for "colored" children and one for white children—a decision that challenged the expectations of most Mississippi blacks seeking equal educational opportunities, and one that would dramatically alter the livelihoods and educational future of black children in Mississippi.

Chapter 5 considers the schooling opportunities available to African

American children in the years immediately following the inauguration of public schools, 1871–75. It highlights the responses of Mississippi whites to public schools for African Americans during this time period. By the close of 1871, most whites seemed to tolerate the establishment of a separate system of public schools for African Americans in Mississippi, but a significant minority simply could not. To this latter group, schools for African Americans—like many of the advancements blacks had made since emancipation—served as a reminder of slavery's abolition and the dramatic changes that befell the state after the war. During the inaugural year, public schools in general, but schools for African Americans in particular became a prime target of intimidation and violence by disapproving whites. Schools were set ablaze; teachers were whipped and run out of town; and black children and their parents were frightened, tortured, and, in some cases, murdered for attempting to attend school.

Accordingly, how schools for African Americans fared in the year preceding the overthrow of Republicanism and the virtual disfranchisement of African Americans in Mississippi is the primary focus of this chapter. It contends that by the close of 1873 schools for African Americans in Mississippi, despite their newness and apparent limitations, were achieving the aims of former slaves and having a direct effect on the overall development of the state's political economy. Schools were preparing African Americans in Mississippi for opportunities that challenged the status quo and societal expectations whites had for blacks. This chapter argues that schools for Mississippi blacks were preparing them to live and exercise their rights as full-fledged citizens. Voting is one example. By early 1874, blacks in Mississippi held three major state offices—lieutenant governor, secretary of state, and superintendent of education—and countless county and local positions, and the nation's only black senator hailed from Mississippi.[20] Ironically, the relative gains made by African Americans in Mississippi, in both school and life, would be used against them by white Democrats and landowners during the elections of 1875. These whites, eager to regain control of the state's overall affairs, used the progress made by African Americans in previous elections and years as a rallying cry for white solidarity and supremacy. By the close of 1875, Mississippi would have a state legislature composed primarily of old-line Democrats and a legislature considerably less sympathetic to the needs and concerns of former slaves and their descendants.

. . .

By examining the origin and purpose of schools for African Americans in Mississippi, *From Cotton Field to Schoolhouse* seeks to broaden one's understanding of the ideas and activities—educational and otherwise—of formerly enslaved African Americans in Mississippi. But this book is more than an educational or revisionist history addressing a gap in the historiography of African American education by offering a narrative specific to a state altogether overlooked in previous analysis. It is a history that informs its readers about the decisions and policies that shaped the earliest educational opportunities for former slaves in the first decade following the Civil War. It raises important questions about what purposes schools for formerly enslaved African Americans served in one of the leading and largest states in the postbellum South and what impact schools had on Mississippi society—and vice versa—during one of the most trying epochs in American history.

Both before and after the Civil War, Mississippi was an economic and social trailblazer south of the Mason-Dixon line. Prior to the war, it was one of the richest states in the Union, not just in the slave South. For nearly three generations its very existence was built upon the cultivation and exportation of cotton by slave labor, and its slaveholding aristocracy defined the culture and expectations of the general masses of whites throughout the South. Of all the states in the South on the eve of the Civil War, Mississippi was one of the few where cotton was truly king. It boasted one of the region's highest slave and slaveholder populations, only Georgia and Virginia having more slaves; it was the chief producer and exporter of cotton in the South; and it was a leading advocate for secession and the creation of an independent slave-sanctioning confederacy.[21] When the Confederacy was formed in the spring of 1861, it looked to Mississippi for its first leader and president. Jefferson Davis, a resident of Vicksburg and one of the largest cotton planters in Mississippi, proudly accepted the honor and responsibility. Until the Confederacy's surrender in 1865, Davis faithfully served as president of the "southern cause" for independence and the right to maintain slavery; Mississippi embodied this southern cause.

After the Civil War, Mississippi was still seen as a leading state in the South, only this time for the amount of resistance it posed to the actions of Congress and the processes shaping emancipation, schools for African Americans, and Reconstruction. It was among the first to refuse to adopt the

Thirteenth Amendment, which abolished slavery; it was the first southern state to institute a series of black codes to restrict the opportunities and overall livelihoods of freed African Americans; and it was one of the states that opposed emancipation and black suffrage most violently. During the postwar and post-Reconstruction years, many southern states would once again look to Mississippi because of its ability to effectively secure and regulate cheap black labor, its ability to stifle the political and economic aspirations of African Americans, and its ability to maintain a system of schools for black children conducive to the state's economic demands and the deferential expectations of whites.[22]

The themes and focus of this book challenge a longstanding presumption about the future life opportunities of formerly enslaved African Americans and their progeny, especially in Mississippi. It questions the general acceptance in the historiography that former slaves, from the onset of emancipation, were to some extent destined to endure a life of subjugated second-class citizenship in a segregated South. This position was contemplated more than a century ago and arguably for the first time by W. E. B. Du Bois, initially in an 1897 monograph published in *Atlantic Monthly*, and again six years later in the first chapter of his monumental publication, *The Souls of Black Folk*.

> The first decade [of emancipation] was merely a prolongation of the vain search for freedom, the boon that seemed ever barely to elude their [former slaves'] grasp,—like a tantalizing will-o'-the-wisp, maddening and misleading the headless host. The holocaust of war, the terrors of the Kuklux Klan, the lies of carpet-baggers, the disorganization of industry, and the contradictory advice of friends and foes left the bewildered serf with no new watchword beyond the old cry for freedom.[23]

Early in his career, a young Du Bois expressed this critique of the first decade of freedom, and his generalized assessment of the times and of the bleak future of formerly enslaved African Americans has ever since defined generations of historical inquiry.

But Du Bois's analysis, despite his keen understanding of the times and appreciation of the efforts realized by this generation of previously enslaved African Americans, conflicts in important ways with the recollections and actions of George Washington Albright and the recollections of countless others who witnessed firsthand freed black Mississippians in active pursuit of the benefits of freedom. If the words and efforts of Albright and his fellow contemporaries are to be believed, the actions of black Mississippians in the first decade of emancipation cannot be seen as a vain search for freedom. What their postbellum demeanor and actions suggest is that it was not a foreseen reality that formerly enslaved African Americans in Mississippi would endure life as subjugated second-class citizens in a society that would legally segregate them and deny them their most basic fundamental rights; that they did not envision freedom being a short-lived experience; that it was not foreseen that blacks in Mississippi, prior to the violence and abrupt actions that determined the outcome of the elections of 1875, would be systematically disfranchised and compelled to work under conditions very reminiscent of slavery; or that the schools they built and attended for freedom and citizenship would within the next twenty years primarily educate them for servitude. The demeanor and actions of formerly enslaved African Americans in Mississippi between 1862 and 1875, especially regarding their educational efforts and expectations, suggest that they envisioned a very different outcome.

PART ONE

. . .

1862–1870

I · LIBERATION THROUGH LITERACY

Only those who have watched and guided the faltering feet the misty
minds, the dull understandings of the dark pupils of these schools know
how faithfully, how piteously, this people strove to learn.
—W. E. B. DU BOIS, *Atlantic Monthly*, 1897

. . .

If I nebber does do nothing more while I live, I shall give my children a
chance to go to school, for I considers edecation next best ting to liberty.
—MISSISSIPPI FREEDMAN, 1869

. . .

Our job was to go to school and learn all we could.
—IDA B. WELLS, native of Holly Springs, Mississippi

Freedom and education for African Americans begin in and around Holly
Springs. In a symbolic sense, they begin around the birth of one slave child
in particular. Amid the devastation of a nation at war and a turbulent Mississippi society, a future crusader for justice and the rights of African Americans
was born a slave on a cotton plantation in Holly Springs; her name was Ida
Bell Wells. The timing of Wells's birth—July 16, 1862—with regard to the
rise of emancipation in Mississippi was without question coincidental, but,
given the times, it was significant. Ida, the future crusader for the rights and
advancement of African Americans in the late nineteenth and early twentieth centuries, was born at the crossroads of American history, at a time when
enslaved African Americans throughout the South were suddenly realizing
their freedom. She was born in the dawn of a new era when black men and
women could at last raise their children to be free and upstanding citizens
rather than deferential slaves.

Around the time of Wells's birth, the benefits and frustrations of freedom were just weeks away for enslaved African Americans in Holly Springs. Not until two weeks prior to her birth, around the Fourth of July, had Holly Springs seen its first noteworthy skirmish between Union and Confederate soldiers. Shortly afterward, Union General Ulysses S. Grant would oust the Confederate armies from northern Mississippi and place the region under military rule. He would make Holly Springs his temporary headquarters and have his army chaplain, John Eaton Jr., establish a camp specifically for the countless enslaved African Americans who opted to emancipate themselves and flee to Union lines. "Eaton chose Grand Junction, Tennessee, as the camp's location—just across the state line from Holly Springs."[1] For the Mississippi, Alabama, and Tennessee blacks who entered the camp, freedom had finally arrived, and most seemed determined to take full advantage of it. Some, for example, enlisted as soldiers and nurses in the army, many worked within the camp for the betterment of themselves and others, and the vast majority attempted to attend the makeshift school established by northern-born missionaries following the Union army into Mississippi. Despite the immediate advantages to be enjoyed at Grand Junction, Ida's parents chose to stay in Holly Springs. To them, Holly Springs was home. But as the war continued, freedom in Holly Springs always seemed to be in jeopardy. The city would be "captured and recaptured by the two armies, changing hands at least fifty-nine times during the war."[2] The challenges Holly Springs faced during the war foreshadow the struggles that awaited most African Americans in search of freedom and its rewards after the war. Even so, it was in and around Holly Springs that freedom first came to enslaved African Americans in Mississippi; it was here that Ida B. Wells, born a slave, would begin her remarkable life and career; and it was here that one of the earliest schools for formerly enslaved African Americans would take root.

William Edward Burghardt Du Bois was also born at this turning point in American history, and much like Wells, he too would devote his entire career to advocating civil rights and social equality for black people through his research and activism. This noted sociologist and historian was one of the first to chronicle the rise of freedom and education for formerly enslaved African Americans in the South. In his seminal 1935 publication, *Black Reconstruction*, Du Bois, at age sixty-seven, would reiterate a point he had contended for more than thirty years, that "the first educational efforts" for formerly enslaved African Americans "came from Negroes."[3] Few scholars—then or now—understood better than Du Bois the yearnings freed black men and women had for learning and the steps they took to acquire an education in the earliest years of emancipation. His perceptiveness was due in part to his firsthand experiences with former slaves and their teachers. As a young college student at Fisk University, an eighteen-year-old Du Bois eked out part of his college tuition as a teacher for former slaves and their children in the summertime in rural Tennessee.[4] This early experience shaped his research pursuits and gave him an appreciation for and understanding of the expectations and uses formerly enslaved African Americans had for schools and knowledge. Black folk, Du Bois steadfastly contended, equated knowledge with power; they recognized that literacy and education could transform lives and society, that they were vehicles for social change and uplift, and that they created opportunities. The collective determination and regard formerly enslaved African Americans had for education thoroughly impressed Du Bois. He was certain that no oppressed people in the history of mankind had made greater strides to educate themselves in the dawn of emancipation than the freedpeople in the post–Civil War South.

. . .

The enthusiasm and initiative that freedpeople in Mississippi had for education epitomized Du Bois's assessment. These qualities are illustrated by the fact that the state's first schools for African Americans originated with ex-slaves. As with liberated blacks throughout the South, African Americans in Mississippi, both during and after the Civil War, demonstrated their lifelong desire for acquiring an education by building and attending schools as soon as they could. Their goal was to use schooling as a means to obtain liberation and citizenship through literacy. Accordingly, before the outcome of the war was determined, before the mass migration of teachers and missionaries from the North, before the official establishment of the Freedmen's Bureau, and before crude temporary schools would take root in Union garrisons and camps, African Americans started organizing schools and educating themselves wherever possible. Throughout the state, free and freed African Americans, as early as 1862, established churches and schoolhouses for individual and collective improvement. Literate and barely literate blacks would serve as these schools' first teachers, and freedpeople—young, old, male, and female—were their first pupils. Years later Ida B. Wells would recount childhood memories of this mass movement for liberty and literacy in Holly Springs and other parts of northern Mississippi. When she and her siblings came of age in the early years of emancipation, their "job," she professed, "was to go to school and learn all we could."[5]

To be sure, the educational activities and initiatives of Mississippi freed-people were not isolated occurrences. Schools independently established by and for freedpeople arose in every locale. They commenced in the South's most prominent cities, such as Charleston, Nashville, Richmond, New Orleans, Savannah, and Little Rock as well as in the backwoods and on the most secluded cotton, rice, sugar, and tobacco plantations; some even had antebellum roots. One of the first schools to open for freedpeople at the expense of southern blacks during the Civil War was in Alexandria, Virginia.[6] On September 1, 1861, Mary Chase and an unnamed freedwoman opened a pay school for wartime runaways. Less than a month later, one of them joined Mary Smith Peake, daughter of a white Englishman and a free black woman who had taught at an antebellum school in Hampton, Virginia. Together they opened a second school for contrabands at Fortress Monroe, Virginia.[7] The actions of these three black women preceded those of northern white missionaries by nearly a year. In fact, by the time northern white teachers engaged in the education of freedpeople in Virginia, African Americans in Alexandria had already opened three other schools.

The Freedmen's Inquiry Commission, an agency established by President Lincoln to investigate the needs of former slaves, was quick to note the activities of freed blacks in Alexandria. "One of the first acts of the negroes when they found themselves free," the commission declared, "was to establish schools at their own expense."[8] Union army Lieutenant C. B. Wilder was astonished at the pace former slaves and their children learned in these grassroots Virginia schools. "Scarcely one could be found who could read as they came in," Wilder admitted. "Now very few but can read some, and all are getting books and with or without teachers are striving to learn themselves and one and another."[9] By 1867, the push for schooling among Virginia freedpeople was truly a spectacle. One white Virginian promptly recognized this upon his visit of a school attended by free and freed black children in Norfolk. "We cannot express," the observer reasoned, "our satisfaction more fully than by saying that we were literally astonished at the display of intelligence by the pupils. Abstruse questions in arithmetic were promptly answered, difficult problems solved, the reading beautifully rhetorical, and the singing charming." Given the pace of learning among former slave children, the onlooker concluded, "More encouragement must be given by our city council to our public schools to prevent white children from being outstripped in the race for intelligence by their sable competitors."[10]

Around the time schools for freedpeople taught by northerners arose in Virginia, it was reported by Union army officials that free and contraband blacks in Nashville, Tennessee, had already independently established a number of schools for more than eight hundred children. The impetus for this educational push in Nashville came from ex-slaves themselves and from Daniel Watkins, an antebellum free black, who had maintained, for nearly a decade, a school for the children of free blacks. By summer's end 1864, several schools managed and taught by African Americans in Nashville had "sprung up," and black children outnumbered white children in school attendance.[11] By 1869, freed African Americans in Tennessee had established a total of twenty-two private schools throughout the state and were financially assisting northern benevolent societies and the Freedmen's Bureau in maintaining fifty-nine other schools. As C. E. Compton, a brevet lieutenant colonel and the superintendent of education for Tennessee's freedpeople, observed, the private schools established were "wholly supported by the freedmen without any aid from the bureau, State, or from benevolent societies."[12]

Equally impressive private efforts were exhibited elsewhere, particularly in Baltimore, Washington, D.C., Delaware, and Little Rock, Arkansas. By the winter of 1865, the Philadelphia-based Society of Friends, or Quakers, and the New York–based American Missionary Association (AMA), in collaboration with Baltimore blacks, established sixteen schools with nearly two thousand pupils. The city's black population, however, promoted the push for schools even further and independently established and managed seven additional schools for freedpeople, two of which had already been in existence for more than a decade. The latter schools were "supported from a legacy given by Nelson Willis, a colored man."[13] A capstone to these efforts came in January 1866, when freeborn and formerly enslaved African Americans in Maryland hosted a state convention in Baltimore to assess and address their overall needs. An advisory board convened and urged each and every Maryland black to "use every exertion to contradict the predictions of [their] enemies, which were uttered previous to the emancipation of the States that if the slaves were freed they would become a pest to society."[14]

They advised formerly enslaved African Americans to feel and act like they were free and independent, to be industrious, to purchase land, and to acquire an education. Specifically, the assembly advised black Marylanders to educate their children for equality, self-sufficiency, and citizenship. "Educate your children and give them trades, thereby making them equal for any position in life, for if ever we are raised to the elevated summit in life for which we strive, it must be done by our own industry and exertion. . . . No one can do it for us," they concluded.[15]

Several schools in and around Washington, D.C., were established by and for newly emancipated blacks with similar vigor. For example, the African Civilization Society of New York, founded in 1858 to promote the colonization of African Americans to Africa, reconstituted itself during the Civil War as a freedmen's aid society. Between 1864 and 1867, the organization, with the assistance of former slaves, opened six schools for African Americans. Freeborn African American Catholics devoted to their parish, *Blessed Martin de Porras*, in the nation's capital also founded five schools for the area's freedpeople, and an additional twenty-two African Americans "individually started private schools for contrabands" and other blacks during the 1860s.[16]

The same was true in Delaware. While Delaware did not have a large slave population, we still see the proactive demeanor of former slaves with regard to education. By mid-1867, there were a total of twenty schools in Delaware, of which all were sustained, either fully or in part, by the freedpeople themselves. Moreover, Delaware blacks owned eight of the twenty schoolhouses, and were sixteen of the twenty teachers.[17]

In Little Rock, Arkansas, freed African Americans—in addition to establishing schools for their children—formed the Freedmen's School Society in March 1865, intent upon collecting monies for educational purposes. "By their own exertions," reported John Eaton Jr., liberated blacks "made the city schools free for the rest of the year," an astonishing feat considering the relative impoverishment of a people just removed from enslavement. To the best of his knowledge, Eaton estimated that "these were the first free schools in Arkansas—whether for whites or blacks—to subscribe and pay in full the compensation of the teachers."[18] By November 1865, many of these same freed blacks and others reconvened in Little Rock to demand that state legislators acknowledge them as citizens and recognize their labor as invaluable to the progress of the state, as well as to appeal to elected representatives to provide a system of schools for their children. "We do most earnestly desire and pray," their request read,

> that you clothe us with the power of self protection, by giving us our equality before the law and the right of suffrage, so we may become *bona fide* citizens of the State in which we live. . . . Believing, as we do, that we are destined in the future, as in the past, to cultivate your cotton fields, we claim for Arkansas the first to deal justly and equitably for her laborers. . . . That we are the substrata, the foundation on which the future power and wealth of the State of Arkansas must be built . . . we respectfully ask the Legislature to provide for the education of our children.[19]

The decree offered by freedpeople in Arkansas was solemn and straightforward, and it characterized the general understanding and feelings of emancipated African Americans throughout the South. It articulated the expectations freedpeople had of enjoying equality, the vote, civic duties and privileges, and the right to an education after enslavement; it expressed their understanding of the South's dependency on the labor of African Americans, as well as the role black folk would need to play in the rebuilding and economic restoration of the region. The appeal offered by African Americans in Arkansas can be likened to a nonnegotiable manifesto: Give to us our rights and recognition as citizens, treat us equitably, and provide a system of schools for our children, and, in accordance, we will *continue* to give to you great wealth and prosperity from our labor.

Amid this mass movement for liberty through literacy and schooling, few missionary or military personalities from the North recognized and appreciated the zeal of the South's freedpeople better than the superintendent of education for the Freedmen's Bureau, John W. Alvord. Alvord was appointed to this commission in July 1865 and made it his first priority to tour the region to assess its needs. He observed firsthand the strides and sacrifices former slaves had made to acquire an education, even if it was only rudimentary instruction. Everywhere Alvord traveled he discovered, with surprise, "a class of schools" in which he identified as "native schools." These independent or self-sustaining schools were managed and "taught by colored people, rude and imperfect, but still groups of peoples, old and young, *trying* to learn" (emphasis in original). In the first of ten semiannual reports, Alvord estimated that at least five hundred of these independent black schools existed throughout the South, the vast majority never before visited by a white person. Flabbergasted by the educational motivations and activities of the South's freedpeople, Alvord made it a point to pen his observations. He wrote, "Throughout the entire south an effort is being made by the colored people to educate themselves. . . . [And] in the absence of other teachings they are determined to be self-taught."[20] Given the current state of affairs, the collective resolve of formerly enslaved African Americans energized and shocked Alvord, especially with regard to the role freedpeople seemed willing to play in their own advancement and the importance they placed on schools. Alvord continued enthusiastically,

> This is a wonderful state of things. We have just emerged from a terrific war; peace is not yet declared. There is scarcely the beginning of reorganized society at the south; and yet here is a people long imbruted by slavery, and the most despised of any on earth, whose chains are no sooner broken than they spring to their feet and start up an exceeding great army, clothing themselves with intelligence. What other people on earth have ever shown, while in their ignorance, such a passion for education?[21]

By 1867, two years after emancipation, Alvord was even more convinced that education was deemed a priority among freed African Americans. Again everywhere he traveled, African Americans—young and old—were engaged in study, with, quite often, recently schooled black children serving as teachers to parents and grandparents in the home. These private and very personal acts of instruction were a profound testament to the reverence enslaved people had for literacy. That the old sought instruction from the young in many ways demonstrates an extension of the loving and nurturing kinship bonds created during slavery and then expressed by the black family upon emancipation. Parents and grandparents deprived of learning because of enslavement wanted to learn, and children and grandchildren attending school because of emancipation wanted to teach. These private acts of "home schooling" to Alvord were remarkable, because they not only demonstrated the enthusiasm freedpeople had toward learning, they also assisted in reducing the rates of illiteracy among formerly enslaved African Americans. Alvord, with both pride and sarcasm, conjectured:

The study of books, miscellaneously by the freedmen, to which we have alluded in previous reports, was never so widespread as at the present time. . . . Thousands of children who have become advanced are teaching parents and older members of the family; so that nearly every freedman's home in the land is a school-house, and instead of scenes of sorrow or stupidity, perhaps of brainless mirth, whole families have become pupils. . . . To say that half a million of these poor people are now studying the spelling-book, or advanced readers, including the New Testament, who were but lately degraded victims of slavery, would be a low estimate.[22]

Alvord's commentary concerning the initiatives of the South's freed-people is without question praiseworthy, but it is also enlightening, espe-cially of the demeanor of formerly enslaved African Africans and of the as-sumptions and fears many northern whites, eager to migrate southward, had of southern blacks and the South in general. His words assured agents and teachers from the North that their energies were needed and would not be spent in vain; they revealed that freed African Americans, the primary beneficiaries of northern assistance, desired self-reliance and were willing not only to receive support but also to give assistance whenever and wher-ever possible; and Alvord's observations illustrated that freedpeople had un-conditionally deemed education an essential acquisition in slavery's after-math and were committed to obtaining it, with or without the assistance of others. To Alvord, the freedpeople of the South were building and attending school to attain liberty and citizenship through literacy.

. . .

This was never truer than in Mississippi, a state that had approximately 437,000 enslaved blacks and only 773 free blacks on the eve of the Civil War. Long denied the opportunities of schooling and instruction because of en-slavement and antiliteracy sentiment and laws, African Americans seized the opportunity as the war progressed to emancipate both themselves and loved ones and to collectively pursue the means of obtaining an education. Upon his arrival to Mississippi in 1865, Alvord immediately noticed the educational ambitions of freed African Americans. In his mind, former slaveholders and planters would have been wise not to resist the efforts and exertions of freed-people to obtain an education; it was a battle, Alvord assumed, they simply could not win. Whites, he jested, "would find it harder fighting the alphabet and spelling-book than ~~they did Grant and Sherman~~."[23] But in Alvord's humor was a recognition of a conflict already in action: on one side, black Mississippians strode toward an education for the sake of full citizenship, while on the other side, a white populace resisted them.

Nevertheless, ex-slaves, through their own initiative and resources, in Grenada, Canton, Aberdeen, Corinth, Meridian, Natchez, Vicksburg, and elsewhere, were determined to acquire an education. They independently built schools and raised, collected, and spent money for educational purposes. Freedpeople served as lead officials and advocates in many of their educational endeavors and not just as the primary laborers for the construction of their schools. At the close of the Civil War, for example, emancipated blacks in Natchez, over a two-year span, raised about forty dollars per month to support their schools' expenditures and pay teachers' salaries.[24] In Raymond a group of formerly enslaved African Americans purchased a plot of land and erected a building to function as both a schoolhouse and a church.[25] One hundred and thirty miles to the north, freed African Americans in Grenada similarly built a church that doubled as a schoolhouse. Despite their impoverished condition, they also paid the "board and washing costs" for the town's two northern-born teachers.[26] In Vicksburg, Natchez, and Meridian, African Americans imposed additional taxes upon themselves for educational purposes and formed all-black boards of directors that oversaw the erection of a number of schoolhouses and churches. Members of such boards were responsible for assessing and collecting the funds to be used for schools. At the same time, formerly enslaved African Americans formed various political, social, and religious associations to advance their pursuit of citizenship and universal education.[27]

Equally impressive strides occurred on the secluded, abandoned cotton plantations of Mississippi. Before the war ended, African Americans on these plantations had converted parts of the "big houses" into their own private schoolhouses. By 1864, these educational initiatives had become commonplace, so much so that northern missionaries and Union officials discovered that many former slaves had already begun to learn to read and write. These schools were virtually independent, relying on the resources—usually a Bible, a few books or primers, and a teacher—gathered by the African Americans attending or serving the school; and they were the epitome of the "native schools" that Alvord observed and wrote about in his first semiannual report. James Yeatman, who was appointed the sanitary commissioner of the lower Mississippi River valley by the St. Louis–based Western Sanitary Commission, encountered several of these native schools as he moved through the countryside documenting the general health conditions of the state's wartime inhabitants. "There is at Groshon's plantation," remarked Yeatman, a school of about forty to fifty students, young and old, taught by Rosa Anna, "a colored girl."[28] Up the road on the Savage plantation, a local black man conducted a school for at least thirty pupils.[29] On the Goodrich plantation, Yeatman continued, a former slave known to many as "Uncle Jack" taught a school with over eighty students. "William McCuthehen, a colored man," as identified by Yeatman, "commenced a school on the Currie place" and taught at least sixty students.[30] McCuthehen served as the school's teacher despite having only one arm; the other arm, Yeatman learned, was severed in a cotton gin accident during enslavement.

Yeatman's and Alvord's observations illustrated more than the creation and maintenance of a network of virtually independent schools established by ex-slaves. Their discovery of these schools conclusively validated the existence of a handful of enslaved African Americans who — despite the prohibition on their education and legal restraints against them — had acquired some degree of literacy prior to their emancipation and were willing to share their learning with those eager to be taught. Great enthusiasm for learning and sharing knowledge characterized these early schools for Mississippi freedpeople. Illiterate men and women, young and old, wanted to learn, and literate friends and relatives wanted to teach them. This was precisely how George Washington Albright — a former slave who during and after the Civil War became a teacher and leading political official in Holly Springs — began his school. After picking up a rudimentary education from his mother during enslavement, Albright's first objective as a freedman was to establish a school. He taught his classes wherever he could: under a shade tree during the war, then in an abandoned building, and then in a church shortly after the war.

The same was true of Belle Caruthers, also from Holly Springs. She too had learned to read while enslaved. "The baby had alphabet blocks," she stated, "and I learned my letters while she learned hers."[31] Caruthers later found an old Webster blueback speller and one day was so preoccupied with its contents that she did not notice her master catching her in the act of studying the book. She recalled, "Master caught me studying it, and struck me hard with his muddy boot." The assault frightened Caruthers, but it did not deter her from continuing her learning. "I found a Hymn book one day," Caruthers continued, "and spelled out, 'When I Can Read My Title Clear.' I was so happy when I saw that I could really read that I ran around telling all the other slaves."[32] When emancipation came, Caruthers taught—whenever and wherever possible—newly freed blacks what she had learned and continued her education at a school started by the AMA. Soon thereafter, she became a schoolteacher of blacks in and around Holly Springs. She taught for nearly thirty years and wrote a column pertaining to African American issues in the county newspaper. For Albright, Caruthers, and many others who started their own schools, pedagogical training, makeshift classrooms, and limited financial and material resources were secondary concerns, and, arguably in many circumstances, inconsequential. With imagination, resourcefulness, and some degree of flexibility in what constituted a "school" or a "teacher," freedpeople in Mississippi relied on their collective desire and respect for learning and made good use of what was available.

In addition to the writings and testimonies left by formerly enslaved African Americans, testimonies from military, missionary, and governmental representatives further reveal the existence of a number of private grassroots schools created and sustained by Mississippi freedpeople. In 1862, for example, when the Union army secured the northernmost city of Corinth, officials were surprised to see African Americans already attending schools and churches that they had established for themselves.[33] Arguably, these schools were the first reported schools in the state for African Americans—enslaved or free. In his mid-twentieth-century study on the Freedmen's Bureau in Mississippi, historian Clifford Ganus Jr. asserted that key Union victories in Mississippi provided the first real opportunities for African Americans to independently establish some "form of academic training" for themselves and their children.[34] Ganus's assertion, despite limited data, proved to be correct. As Union troops seized control of the western Confederate mainstay—the mighty Mississippi River—and eliminated all hopes of a continued defense of Mississippi, locations indispensable for Confederate success, such as Tunica, Davis Bend, Vicksburg, and Natchez, acknowledged defeat, and as in Corinth and Holly Springs, an outgrowth of black educational activities soon occurred thereafter.

The war waged on Mississippi's fertile soil, however, stirred up more than the opportunity for African Americans to express their educational enthusiasm. The war hurled to the forefront the unseen horrors and destitution of chattel slavery, as I discuss in greater detail in chapter 2. Destitute African American refugees gathered in Union-occupied areas by the thousands, nearly all having "left food, clothing and other goods" behind.[35] Many of these refugees, especially the women, were "very poorly clad" and "half-naked" upon their arrival at camps established by the Union army. Despite their destitution, Samuel Shipley, an emissary of the Friends' Association of Philadelphia, saw they had no regret in their change from slaves to freedmen and freedwomen. Rather, Shipley proclaimed, "They regard their deliverance from bondage as a special work of the Almighty and are willing to trust in His continued care over them."[36]

The war also brought about the transformation of some of the most luxurious manors in Mississippi. Because of their sheer size many were partitioned and turned into orphanages, hospitals, billets, or schools. The Blake plantation, just outside of Vicksburg, was an excellent example of this transformation. The plantation was enormous, comprising over ten thousand arable acres and several hundred slaves. Upon its abandonment, the plantation was transformed into a freedmen camp and military outpost for the state's newly created black regiments. As one observer commented on the manor's new appearance, "It was a strange sight to see the Negro pickets surrounding the quarters of this once luxurious icon of the old feudal days."[37] Davis Bend, a small town that housed, among others, the plantations of Confederate President Jefferson Davis and his brother Joseph, was similarly altered. The wealth and prestige associated with "the Bend," located on the outskirts of Vicksburg, represented, before the war, the ideal for every southern man working cotton fields with slaves. After its occupation, its large manors and spacious grounds seemed to illustrate the South's defeated cause as its plantations were converted into outposts for soldiers and destitute blacks and whites.[38]

Whitelaw Reid, who toured the South during and after the Civil War, was quick to note the apparent changes and "strange irony" on the two Davis plantations. Reid commented, "Negro soldiers were now doing duty on the landing whence cotton had been shipped," and "runaway niggers" were tilling Davis's fertile fields, only now "on their own account" and not as slaves for the profit of another.[39] When Reid arrived at the front door of the manor of Joseph Davis, he was not greeted by the owner, but by two northern-born teachers engaged in the process of teaching former slaves. "A couple of Yankee school-mistresses were within," stated Reid, "and they were the teachers of the boys and girls of Mr. Davis' slaves, and of the runaways from plantations in the interior."[40] Reid noted that most of the furnishings in the house had been looted; what remained were a few pieces of furniture and some scattered books. To Reid, the books symbolized the times: scattered about were "tactics for Northern soldiers and spelling books for slaves," and among these were "defenses of the divine right of slavery and constitutional arguments in favor of repudiation and secession."[41] The nation's civil war and enduring struggle over slavery lay scattered in tracts and pamphlets on the floor of Joseph Davis's house, the brother of the Confederacy's president, lay scattered for former slaves and their children to acquire the rudiments of literacy for citizenship, not servitude. The proslavery arguments in these books apparently did not matter much to a people eager to learn to read and write. Ironically, tracts that defended the "divine right of slavery" were the first texts studied by Mississippi freedpeople.

A year earlier, in 1864, the missionary commissioner of the Cincinnati Contraband Relief Commission, Henry Rowntree, witnessed similar "alterations" when he arrived at Davis Bend. Like Reid, Rowntree also found freed African Americans engaged in study. He reported with immense satisfaction "a large school of 260 children" on the Bend, and two other "large schools" outside the Bend on the former cotton plantations of Mills and Lovell.[42] From Rowntree's standpoint, these schools would not have been possible without the selfless efforts and resources of former slaves. Despite the establishment of the schools, Rowntree was still utterly dumbfounded by the educational enthusiasm and progress of the freedpeople given their infirm and destitute status. He recalled:

> On my way to the Lovell place, adjoining to the estate of the Davis's
> I called at a cattle shed without any siding, there huddled together
> were 35 poor wretchedly helpless [N]egroes, one man who had lost
> one eye entirely, and the sight of the other fast going . . . five women all
> mothers, and the residue of 29 children, all small and under 12 years of
> age. One woman had the small pox, her face a perfect mass of scabs. . . .
> They had no bedding, two quilts, and a soldier's old worn out blanket
> comprised the whole for 35 human beings.[43]

Rowntree's description typified the hardships African Americans faced as war besieged Mississippi. Perplexed by the educational zeal of these freed blacks amid such grim circumstances, Rowntree dismissed his own logic and personal convictions and concluded that it was "very gratifying to witness how eager they are to obtain learning."[44]

The war also further hurled to the forefront schools secretly taught by African Americans during the antebellum era, and additional schools privately established by African Americans as the war drew to a close in Mississippi. Upon the abolition of slavery in 1865, many of the founders of these schools would consolidate their efforts with the various missionary societies that frequented the state. At least one school in Natchez, as identified by historian Randy Sparks, secretly began in the slave quarters. Lily A. Grandison, a former slave, "had taught among her fellow slaves for many years" and recalled having to do so by "night and stealth" because the teaching of slaves was strictly prohibited.[45] Once emancipated, Grandison became one of "three native black female teachers" to open a school and charge a one- to two-dollar monthly tuition amid the city's wartime disorder.[46] When interviewed by the Works Progress Administration (WPA) during the late 1930s, former slave Mandy Jones of Lyman recalled having a "bright mulatto man," Henry Gunn, for a teacher when she first attended school after the war. Mandy was thirteen years old when she started school and professed to her interviewer that her first and only teacher "got his learnin' in a school taught in a cave durin' slavery days, un be knownst to the white folks."[47] "Way out in de woods," Jones explained, "de slaves would slip out o' de Quarters at night, an go to dese pits, and some niggah dat had some learnin' would have a school."[48] Gunn, got his learning from his father, who acquired his learning from the child of his slaveowner. Some enslaved blacks, however, did not have to "slip out of the quarters" to be schooled. Clara Young, though she was ninety-five years old when she was interviewed by the WPA, vividly remembered being taught by an African American during slavery. "Dey had a nigger woman to teach all de house darkies how to read an' write an' I larned how to sign my name an' got as fur as b-a-k-e-r in de Blue Back Speller."[49] Noah Rogers, who served in the Union army after the fall of Vicksburg, acquired his first lessons differently. As a child he learned to read, write, and do simple arithmetic from the son of his master. He remembered that "the white folks didn't approve" of him learning to read and write, "but they considered it cute to teach a Negro" and "show up" their son's ability.[50]

Similarly to Grandison, Josephine Nicks opened a school and an unnamed woman maintained a school in Natchez during and immediately after the war. Upon visiting Nicks's school, AMA Reverend J. P. Bardwell reported never visiting a "school room that was kept in better order & no school that appeared to be under better discipline."[51] Before 1867, both Nicks and Grandison would consolidate their schools with the AMA. In fact, the majority of African Americans in Mississippi who established an independent or private school during or immediately after the war would consolidate their efforts with a northern agency such as the AMA or the Freedmen's Bureau. Economic necessity was the primary reason.

All the same, there were many Mississippi blacks who resisted consolidation and persisted in maintaining virtually self-sufficient schools. George Johnson from Davis Bend, for example, became a prosperous landowner and founded the Johnson School and Church.[52] Jackson Habersham, a resident of Natchez, taught school out of a rented house and charged one to two dollars a month for tuition. He was reported as teaching a "room full though he could only read & write."[53] He wasn't alone. By the war's end, Natchez's black community had created at least "six schools of their own taught by colored teachers . . . and by 1867, ten private schools with black teachers."[54] One of Alvord's officers, Reverend William K. Douglas, made mention of these schools in his annual report. As Alvord noted,

> Douglas was appointed to traverse the State and urge upon the people
> the necessity of taking into their own hands the education of the
> freedmen, as the best and only means by which amity and prosperity
> can be restored, and to establish schools when possible. The first point
> visited was Natchez, where he found ten schools in operation, as private
> enterprises, embracing from three to five hundred children, all taught
> by *intelligent colored persons*. The books, method of instruction, and
> discipline correspond very nearly with those of the white schools in
> the city. [emphasis in original][55]

Natchez was about the only locale in Mississippi that could establish this many private black schools in slavery's immediate aftermath. On the eve of the Civil War, the city possessed the highest number of free blacks (approximately 220), which in itself was a feat because of Mississippi's harsh stance on free blacks. Very little is known about these people, but presumably they educated their children privately to understand the rigors of living in a slave-sanctioning society prior to the war. After the war, it is conceivable that these same free blacks would become some of the first teachers of freedpeople. Whereas the acquisition or display of literacy was staunchly prohibited prior to the war, literate African Americans—free and freed—in Natchez after the war exercised their new freedoms and openly expressed their privately learned skills by teaching their formerly enslaved brethren what they knew.

Natchez may have yielded the highest number of self-supporting schools for Mississippi freedpeople, but it was not alone. Between 1863 and 1870, a small number of relatively successful private schools for freed children were established elsewhere. In late 1865, when Joseph Warren of the Freedmen's Bureau became the state's first educational superintendent, he, like so many before him, was surprised to find schools independently established by formerly enslaved African Americans. One private school, in particular, that caught his attention was taught by a young African American woman in Vicksburg. "For some time," Warren wrote, "a private school, taught by a young colored woman" has existed "in which several of the more wealthy people send their children."[56] It appeared that this school was among a handful that successfully competed with schools consolidated under the auspices of the Freedmen's Bureau for tuition-paying pupils. By November 1865, Warren reported at least ten additional private schools outside the cities of Natchez and Vicksburg, some with pupils that numbered in the hundreds.[57] These schools, Warren deduced, were established, maintained, and controlled by free and freed African Americans in Mississippi. He wrote,

> A school with a colored teacher can be found at Aberdeen. At Canton, one or two schools have been established [for] some time. At Brandon an interesting school of nearly 40 scholars was being taught by a young colored woman [who migrated] from Mobile. At Forrest, a colored sergeant was teaching a small number of scholars. At Meridian two schools were in operation taught by colored men . . . each with about 30 scholars. At Columbus 3 colored schools are in operation taught by colored men poorly qualified with a total of about 100 scholars . . . [and] an evening school is taught by a colored man at Corinth.[58]

Warren informed his superiors that the majority of these schools identified were unwilling to report to him as a bureau school, "lest it should be construed into an acknowledgment of an authority." In other words, these schools sought to cooperate in some ways with the bureau, but wished to remain virtually autonomous. This was a request, Warren reported, he had no desire to grant."[59] Available monthly reports gathered by Warren and others validate the existence of these schools. They indicate that most private schools for freed children were reported as "an open school," but unlike schools that consolidated with the Freedmen's Bureau, these schools did not provide information on topics such as a pupil's age, gender, courses of instruction, and progress.

The stance freedpeople took to maintain some degree of autonomy in their educational advancement during and after the Civil War simultaneously amazed and frustrated most northerners who migrated southward to "uplift" slaves into freed men and women. Frustrations occurred when it became apparent many freed African Americans were not interested in the assistance and uplifting agenda of their northern-born teachers. Arguably one of the most surprising qualities of formerly enslaved African Americans was their commitment and ability to financially support schools for themselves and their children. Alvord commented that everyone seemed willing to give. "Even the lower class of free blacks and the slaves," stated Alvord, who had, before and during the war, hidden or laid aside small sums of money, "cheerfully" donated what they collected for their race's education.[60] These contributions and the tuition paid by former slaves were the primary source of funding for schools intended for freedpeople. Despite their landless and poverty stricken status, the great majority of freedpeople willingly contributed to their group's overall educational development. As one northern-born teacher noted in Columbus, "They show a commendable spirit of independence and desire to provide for themselves. . . . Many of them working as laborers are willing to pay one-dollar tuition per month for their children's education."[61] In Vicksburg, "by the advice of the more intelligent of the colored people," African Americans agreed to charge a tuition of sixty cents per month per pupil to defray some of the educational costs.[62] Moreover, they instituted imposed taxes upon themselves to assure that the schools in operation were available to all black children in the city.

Black militiamen and day laborers, mostly transient workers in the early years of emancipation, also contributed to the cause of black education. Many used their first salaries to clothe, feed, house, and educate themselves, their families, and the most destitute among them.[63] Between 1863 and 1865, a number of African Americans—with some assistance from the Union army—leased plots of land on confiscated or abandoned plantations and were very successful in harvesting cotton and corn for themselves for a small profit. While very little is known of their efforts, trials, or successes, historians do know that former slaves, like Granville Green, Tom Taylor,

Luke Johnson, Solomon Richardson, and many others, produced hundreds of bales of cotton, which was purchased by the government and northern industries, and used the remainder to clothe, aid, and educate dependent freedpeople and children in Union camps and refugee asylums.[64]

In many instances, the financial contributions to educational activities by and for freedpeople were not always monetary. Throughout the state, many paid their teachers with food, clothing, laundry, local transportation, and shelter when resentful and antagonistic whites refused to accept the teachers' patronage or assist them because of their activities with former slaves. Likewise, most of the labor needed for the erection of these schools was provided by the freedpeople. Throughout the state these forms of material and physical assistance were essential contributions to both the salaries and safety of the northerners laboring among freedpeople for the advancement of black education. The sweat equity offered by the freedpeople in Mississippi assisted in paying the travel, housing, and material and provisional needs of their teachers. Simultaneously, it demonstrated the self-determinist attitudes and practices of black Mississippians in pursuit of educational, social, and economic advancement. One formerly enslaved and illiterate African American summed up this position well when asked by Alvord why freedpeople were so adamant about sustaining a system of schools for their children. The former slave affirmed, "If I nebber does do nothing more while I live, I shall give my children a chance to go to school, for I considers education next best ting to liberty."[65] This affirmation characterizes the general sentiment of most freed African Americans throughout the South; it unconditionally demonstrates the firm determination freedpeople had to use schooling as a means of achieving citizenship and liberty.

The financial contributions of free and freed African Americans also provided a significant portion of the funds to establish a network of grassroots educational institutions. Clifford Ganus Jr. calculated that the reported tuition paid by Mississippi freedpeople between August 1866 and June 1870 was $23,976.10, or almost $6,000 a year.[66] This contribution amounted to almost 34 percent of the total known revenue collected and expended for educational activities sponsored by the Freedmen's Bureau and the various missionary societies in Mississippi. Equally important, this reported monetary contribution was not inclusive of the time, energy, and resources that freedpeople provided, or the additional funds contributed to the growing number of relatively independent black schools in the state. As table 1 dem-

TABLE 1. Schools Reported by the Freedmen's Bureau as Sustained Wholly or in Part by Freedpeople, 1867–1870

Date	Number of Schools in the South	Number of Schools Sustained by Freedpeople in the South	Number of Schools in Mississippi	Number of Schools Sustained by Freedpeople in Mississippi
January 1867	1,207	623 (51.6%)	42	3 (7.1%)
July 1867	1,839	1,056 (57.4%)	66	51 (77.2%)
January 1868	1,486	1,000 (67.3%)	76	54 (71%)
July 1868	1,831	1,325 (72.3%)	127	93 (73.2%)
January 1869	1,600	1,323 (82.7%)	92	77 (83.7%)
July 1869	2,118	1,581 (74.6%)	81	68 (84%)
January 1870	1,881	1,094 (58.1%)	72	56 (77%)
July 1870	2,039	1,324 (65%)	65	56 (86.1%)

Source: Adapted from John Alvord, Semi-Annual Reports, 1–10 (Washington, D.C.: Government Printing Office, 1866–70).

onstrates, during the five years following the Civil War, bureau schools for black Mississippi children constituted at most 6.9 percent of the total number of schools established throughout the South, which occurred in July 1868. Meanwhile, freedpeople sustained, for the most part, at least three-quarters of the schools established between 1867 and 1870 in Mississippi. Given these statistics, schools established for freedpeople would have been far fewer had it not been for the financial and other contributions of Mississippi blacks.

Adding to the significance of such contributions was the fact that these collective efforts were sustained at a time when few freedpeople were receiving a living wage and the state suffered two years of devastating crop failures. During the crop failure in 1866–67 few black farm workers were paid for their labors, and most were displaced from the plantations where they labored all year.[67] At the same time, employed African Americans were taxed by the state's local authorities to assist in the care of dependent freedpeople. The Freedmen's Pauper Tax Law, as it was known, authorized the police of each county to levy a poll tax on "each and every freedmen, free Negro, and

Mulatto between the ages of eighteen and sixty not to exceed one dollar annually."[68] No such tax was levied on Mississippi whites, even for the care of dependent or disabled Confederate veterans or their families. In some counties the freedmen's pauper tax amounted to as much as $20,000 and as low as $5,000 per year. However, as historian William Leon Woods revealed, "much discrimination was practiced at collection intervals and instead of providing a livelihood for destitute blacks" the funds were used to enrich corrupt civil authorities.[69]

· · ·

But why the rush to build or attend schools, and why the demand for education? What purposes did schooling serve in the minds of formerly enslaved African Americans in the South in general, and Mississippi in particular? Most freedpeople regarded literacy and schools as pathways to freedom. Unquestionably, that children of formerly enslaved African Americans were in school indicated the times had changed. This fact signified a new social order in the South, in which black parents, not slaveholders, controlled and managed the time and futures of their children. Black children were in school to become something more than a cotton picker or menial laborer for another's profit. They were in school to gain knowledge of and access to a broader world, to gain greater opportunities, to acquire skills, and to achieve a status systematically denied to their parents and grandparents. They were in school to learn how to be something other than a slave.

Literacy as such equated to possibilities and opportunities, options that were limited during enslavement and denied during emancipation to an illiterate freed person. Becoming literate proved to be as much a psychological victory for many freedpeople as it was an intellectual one. Illiteracy was a vestige of slavery, a reminder of the blatant denial of one's rights to self-advancement; it served as a badge of inferiority and societal impotence. To become literate challenged this status. Still, some could never forgive those who held them in perpetual bondage and who had denied them their most basic human rights. "There is one sin," ex-slave James W. C. Pennington professed, "that slavery committed against me which I can never forgive. It robbed me of my education." Even as a free man, "the injury is irreparable," Pennington continued.

I feel the embarrassment more seriously now than I ever did before. It cost me two years hard labour, after I fled, to unshackle my mind; it was three years before I had purged my language of slavery's idioms; it was four years before I had thrown off the crouching aspect of slavery; and now the evil that besets me is a great lack of that general information, the foundation of which is most effectually laid in that part of life which I served as a slave. When I consider how much now, more than ever, depends upon sound and thorough education among coloured men, I am grievously overwhelmed with a sense of my deficiency.[70]

Pennington arguably voiced the frustrations of most African Americans who struggled to obtain liberty and literacy for citizenship following emancipation. His testimony illustrates the personal woes and endeavors of freedpeople in their transition from slavery to freedom and establishes a very important point, which is that neither freedom nor literacy upended slavery and its effects. Slavery may have legally ended in Mississippi with Lincoln's announcement of the Emancipation Proclamation in 1863, and was universally abolished soon thereafter with the passage of the Thirteenth Amendment in 1865, but its overall impact lived on. In the minds and actions of those who had been enslaved, overcoming even the most rudimentary ill effects of slavery was a long and arduous process. For Pennington it took him nearly a half decade to learn the basics of literacy; it took him even longer to feel comfortable enough speaking and living as a freedman. He lost out on time, resources, job opportunities, social mobility, and personal pursuits and comforts; in essence, he lost an important part of his life because of the psychological and educational debt of slavery. Even after such diligent attention to his educational development, Pennington, like so many others before and after him, still felt inadequate as a free person because of his enslavement. This feeling of inadequacy came from the fact that he had not acquired the rudiments of learning at an early age or learned as a child that his role in life could be something other than a slave. Slavery, that "vile monster," Pennington concluded, "hast hindered my usefulness, by robbing me of my early education. . . . Oh! what might I have been now, but for this robbery perpetuated upon me as soon as I saw the light."[71]

Historians who have studied the specifics of this mass movement for liberty and literacy through schooling during and after the Civil War agree that formerly enslaved African Americans throughout the South considered education a paramount and invaluable acquisition. One of the most noted contemporary historians on African American education in the postslavery era, James D. Anderson, is correct in asserting that freedpeople in general "emerged from slavery with a strong belief in the desirability of learning to read and write." "This belief," Anderson continued, "was expressed in the pride in which they talked of other ex-slaves who learned to read and write in slavery and in the esteem in which they held literate blacks."[72] For both individual and collective reasons, liberated blacks sought an education because it represented previously prohibited means of control, empowerment, and autonomy, as well as practical means of personal and professional improvement. The enthusiasm and expectations formerly enslaved African Americans placed on education and its usefulness cannot be underestimated. Practically every contemporary, friend or foe, of ex-slaves witnessed their determination in acquiring an education for themselves and their children. "In its universality and intensity," one New England Freedmen Aid Society missionary recounted, "they [formerly enslaved African Americans] believe that reading and writing are to bring with them inestimable advantages."[73] To freedpeople, education was perceived as a means to progress and societal uplift; it was seen as an investment, an insurance of a better day for themselves and their children. It was considered a priority, a necessary expenditure for citizenship and the advancement of the race.

Such aspiration for learning was a deeply entrenched cultural value in the African American experience, and was virtually universal in the ex-slave community. It sharply differed from the value that poor southern whites placed on education. Where poor whites, according to W. E. B. Du Bois, viewed schooling as a "luxury connected to wealth" and did not demand an opportunity to acquire it, African Americans—both during and after slavery—demanded it. Du Bois concluded that formerly enslaved African Americans firmly "believed that education was a stepping-stone to wealth and respect, and that wealth, without education, crippled" a person's prospects of attaining equality, self-reliance, landownership, the vote, and citizenship.[74] Had he been aware of Du Bois's contention, former slave Charles Whiteside most likely would have agreed. The very day Whiteside's owner informed him that he was free, he also informed Whiteside that his freedom was "essentially meaningless" and that he "would always remain a slave," because he had "no education." "Education," the former slaveowner decreed was "what makes a man free." Concerned, but not discouraged, by the words of the man who hitherto held him in bondage, Whiteside made up his mind, then and there, to ensure that his children received the type of education he was systematically denied. He sent each of his thirteen children to school, determined, as he said, "to make them free."[75]

Still, it is highly likely that the prohibition in the "old slave codes" against "learning to read and write," had a great deal to do with the adamant determination former slaves had to become literate, as suggested by Mississippi historian Vernon Lane Wharton.[76] In 1823, Mississippi did create a statute that deemed it unlawful for African Americans — enslaved or freeborn — to learn how to read or write or meet for the purpose of being schooled. The punishment for violating this statute was thirty-nine lashes.[77] The systematic denial of schooling or the fear and excitement whites demonstrated at the thought of a slave becoming literate could have motivated many emancipated African Americans to find out for themselves what all the fuss over being able to read and write was about. Or it could have been as John Alvord observed and as W. E. B. Du Bois speculated, that perhaps the very fact so many enslaved African Americans in Mississippi had "seen the wealthy slaveholders at close range" and assumed that their ability to read and write aided them in prosperity, that this understanding led to the "extraordinary mass demand" for education by liberated blacks.[78] Historian Leon Litwack has argued a similar point. "If black people needed to be persuaded of the compelling importance of learning," Litwack deduced, "they had only to look around them. Power, influence, and wealth were associated with literacy and monopolized by the better-educated class of southern whites."[79]

In any case, prohibition in the antebellum South against the education of blacks — enslaved or freeborn — and its corresponding vigilance against it did not by themselves motivate formerly enslaved African Americans in Mississippi to seek out schooling. As a skill literacy had numerous social purposes and was central to freedpeople's definitions of freedom, progress, success, self-identity, and views about the nature of citizenship. Acquiring any amount of education in slavery's aftermath represented a dual progression to Mississippi's black community. It represented a step toward shedding an imposed slave status as well as a step toward obtaining greater freedoms as prospective citizens. To be educated was to be respected; to be educated was to be a citizen. Accordingly, countless black Mississippians willingly sought out schooling, viewing it as the foundation for self-improvement and one means for attaining social and economic parity in slavery's aftermath.

The primary motivation for black Mississippians' educational enthusiasm stemmed from their beliefs about what being literate represented in their

daily life. Upon emancipation, African Americans valued literacy for a number of reasons, such as being able to the read the Bible and teach it to the
young, to understanding their legal rights, to negotiating labor contracts,
to buying or leasing land. Nothing exemplified the convictions formerly
enslaved African Americans had toward learning than the private discus-
sions they had with their teachers, many of whom were New England- and
Midwestern-born white women. When one northern-born teacher timo-
rously asked an unnamed eighty-five-year-old ex-slave from Vicksburg what
good it would do her to learn to read, she sincerely replied, "I must learn
now or not at all . . . so I can read the Bible and teach the young."[80] Similarly
in Natchez, another elderly former slave was convinced that learning to read
and write would help him establish his own business. When his educational
motivations were questioned, he informed his teacher, "I want to learn to
cipher so I can do business."[81] After some members of the Friends' Association of Philadelphia arrived in Vicksburg, one of its teachers recalled how
one poor and very old ex-slave woman "clang" to her Bible "as her dearest
possession." The freedwomen told the teacher of her agonizing experiences
as a slave, how all nineteen of her children were sold away from her during
enslavement, and how before she died she yearned to learn to read her only
remaining possession, her Bible, so she could understand the words of God
for herself.[82]

In the greater scheme of things, however, education also protected formerly enslaved black Mississippians from the vices of whites who despised
their new status. The hostile treatment of African Americans by whites
quickly reinforced the ex-slave's belief that being literate was a necessity.
Arguably nothing reinforced this conviction more than when it came time
to negotiate a labor contract or "settle up" at the end of the harvest. Literacy
ensured that one could not be easily cheated or deceived when it came to the
duration, wages, and expectations of a contractual agreement. When planters used their political and economic leverage to induce the state legislature
to pass a number of laws—black codes—to explicitly control how freedpeople could express their newly earned freedom, becoming literate took on
added significance. Black codes defined the legal rights of the state's former
slaves and free blacks. Parts of the codes were "positive." For instance, some
sections determined African Americans had the right to acquire and own
property, marry, file legal suits, testify in court decisions involving members of their own race, and establish contractual arrangements.[83] All these

activities necessitated, if not required, some degree of literacy. Yet Mississippi's black codes also served as a restrictive legal stratagem to reinforce and perpetuate the landowning gentry's supremacy and control over the economic, political, and social opportunities of Mississippi blacks. Overall, the codes protected the interests of Mississippi's landowners and defined African Americans as a permanent underclass. In 1865, when the codes went into effect, even only a rudimentary education served as a useful possession and practical means of self-protection. While literacy did not guarantee equality, protection from violence, or even a direct path to advancement in a hostile, segregated society, it was assumed a literate person could protect him or herself against possible reenslavement or societal trickery better than someone who was illiterate.

Perhaps more than anything else, however, the collective desire and expectations African Americans in Mississippi had for education served as the inspiration needed to erect the first schools for themselves, their children, and fellow brethren; schools that were to transform slaves into citizens. The remarks of one former slave exemplify this notion when he proudly declared that building a "school-house would be the first proof of *our* independence" (emphasis added).[84] Embedded in this declaration was the drive, initiative, and determination that not only provided the first schools for African Americans in Mississippi, but also "the grassroots foundation for the educational activities of Northern missionary societies and the Freedmen's Bureau" upon their arrival in Mississippi in 1863.[85] Intrinsic in this proclamation was the deep-seated and collective determination of formerly enslaved African Americans to use literacy and schooling as a means to obtain liberty and citizenship.

2 · EDUCATED LABOR

No sooner had Northern armies touched Southern
soil than this old question, newly guised, sprang from
the earth, — What shall be done with the Negroes?
—W. E. B. DU BOIS, *The Souls of Black Folk*, 1903

. . .

Give them the opportunity to purchase the land, equal rights in courts
of justice, the jury-room and at the ballot-box, and furnish them in their
transition state with Christian teachers and schools and they will speedily
give a satisfactory reply to the question: What shall we do with the Negro?
—S. G. WRIGHT, American Missionary Association, 1864

. . .

Dere isn't money enough in all old Massysippi to buy
what larning my chile got from you all.
—MISSISSIPPI FREEDMAN, 1869

Similarly to the self-supporting schools established by formerly enslaved
African Americans throughout Mississippi, grassroots schools for freedpeople established by teachers from the North had auspicious beginnings.
The schools arose and flourished for two primary reasons: first, the initiative
of formerly enslaved African Americans to seek out freedom in Union lines,
and second, the developments of the war. As the war entered Mississippi,
preachers and teachers from the North accompanied the Union army, arm-
ing themselves not with guns, but with Bibles, clothes, food, and knowledge.
These teachers did not have to venture from the protection of the military
to find their first pupils; in mass, enslaved African Americans came to them.
Such was the earliest development of the grassroots schools established by
northerners for African Americans in Mississippi, and given the incredible

needs of an entire race, these schools quickly became an undertaking most northerners, even the most dedicated, would soon balk at.

All the same, educating former slaves in Union garrisons was not the intention of President Lincoln, Congress, or the Union army. For the first two years of the war, the principle aim of the Union army was to defeat the secessionists, not to disrupt slavery or uplift and educate enslaved African Americans. By late 1862 this aim changed, however. Few knew better of these inevitable changes than John Eaton Jr., the Union army chaplain of the Twenty-Seventh Ohio Infantry Volunteers. In autumn 1862, the army had just fought and won battles in Iuka and Corinth, established temporary headquarters in Holly Springs, and was preparing to lead an intense assault on Vicksburg. It was then when Eaton received correspondence from Union army General Ulysses S. Grant that would dramatically change not only his future, but the future pursuits and opportunities of African Americans in Mississippi. Grant ordered Eaton to take charge of the contraband—fugitive or freedom-seeking enslaved African Americans—that daily entered his military outposts in Holly Springs and Corinth. He commanded that they be "properly cared for" and set to work for the U.S. government "picking, ginning and baling all cotton now out and ungathered."[1] Eaton was taken aback by the request. He was a month shy of his thirty-third birthday, and, in his mind, incapable of accomplishing the task before him. He professed, "No language can describe the effect of this order upon me."[2]

Nevertheless, Eaton would fulfill Grant's request. He chose Grand Junction, Tennessee, for the camp's location, a town north of where Grant wanted to send his army. According to Eaton, Grant was frustrated with the fact that Congress had done very little to "provide adequate escape from the military complications arising out of the conditions of slavery in the midst of which" Union soldiers were moving. Fugitive African Americans compromised Grant's position, staggered his movement, and brought a host of logistic and sanitary problems that Grant felt his army should not have to deal with. It was hoped that the establishment of a camp for freedom-seeking blacks would relieve his army of these complications.[3] Freedom-seeking blacks saw these developments differently. To them, as historian Ira Berlin concluded, "the official sanction of such camps signaled that the Union army would welcome and protect all fugitive slaves, not just men capable of military labor."[4]

The establishment of a camp for fleeing or freedom-seeking African

Americans in and around Mississippi set in motion the beginnings of another type of grassroots school for freedpeople, schools taught by northern-
born teachers, and this chapter chronicles its history. Between 1863 and
1870, representatives and teachers from various northern benevolent and
freedmen aid societies, such as the American Missionary Association (AMA),
the Freedmen's Aid Commission, Society of Friends, United Brethren, the
Friends' Association of Philadelphia, and others, established a network of
grassroots schools for freedpeople. By autumn 1865, many of these educational initiatives would consolidate under the auspices of the Freedmen's Bureau. As historians Henry Swint and, later, Jacqueline Jones explained, each
northern-based organization had various motives and resources for assisting
the South's newly freed masses.[5] All the same, the northerners that assisted
and educated Mississippi freedpeople shared a common goal: assist formerly
enslaved African Americans in their transition from slavery to freedom and
give them the moral and academic training necessary to understand their
duties as citizens and laborers in a post–slave economy South. Included in
each instructional exercise were morality lessons, principally from a New
England-based ideology, which devalued the cultural attributes and convictions of freedpeople. Also included was the blatant disregard of the aspirations of freedpeople to attain a greater degree of control over their freedom
and future schooling opportunities. In many ways, northern-born schoolteachers expected to teach former slaves how to live and labor as free men
and women. From their teachings, they expected freedpeople to learn the
fundamentals of what it took to become "educated laborers" in a new South.
This intention was arguably best stated by Reverend Edward N. Kirk, in his
address before congregants of the AMA in Homer, New York, in October
1867. "It is our task," Kirk opined, "to educate efficiently and sufficiently, the
African race now entered into the rank of citizenship. Educate them for the
country's sake. . . . Educate them for the sake of the States of which they are
citizens; for the laborer is productive and valuable just in proportion to his
intelligence."[6]

Whatever the motives of northerners, countless freedpeople remembered their first schooling opportunities, when and where they came about,
and who taught them when freedom finally came to Mississippi. Most were
extremely grateful for the tireless and often selfless acts of the northerners,
who sacrificed their time and livelihoods to teach among them. The epi-
graph from an unnamed freedman perhaps best sums up this sentiment:

"Dere isn't money enough in all old Massysippi to buy what larning my chile got from you all."[7] When they were interviewed by the Works Progress Administration during the 1930s, numerous formerly enslaved African Americans reminisced about their first schooling experiences and the fact that they were taught by teachers from the North. Though he only went to school two times in his entire life, Jim Archer remembered being taught by a "white person from the North" after the war ended in Vicksburg.[8] The same was true of Anna Baker of Aberdeen. "I went to school . . . and larnt to read and write. We had white Yankee teachers," stated Baker. She continued, "I larnt to read de Bible well enuf and den I quit."[9] "Atter freedom," stated Annie Coley, "I went to school in Camden and learned outn de ole Blue Back Speller. . . . The teacher was a white lady from the North."[10] Claiborne Bullen remembered getting his first teaching lessons in a barn "taught by a Miss Day, a white woman, during Reconstruction Days."[11] In his lifetime, Bullen would attend Rust College in Holly Spring, obtain an M.A. from the University of Chicago, teach English at Alcorn College, and become the principal of Fayette Negro High School in his hometown. Bullen's outcome, while exceptional in comparison to the outcomes for most ex-slaves, epitomized the expectations freedpeople and northerners alike had of schools and their transformative potential. Bullen, in his own lifetime, went from an illiterate slave child to an educated and successful man.

. . .

Still, the grassroots schools established by northerners for African Americans during and after the Civil War were not without complication. During this period, a host of factors—the vices of slavery, destitution, the war, limited resources and support, ideological disputes, and intense local opposition—shaped and reshaped the earliest grassroots educational opportunities northerners provided for freedpeople. To understand this development is to understand just how challenging it was to live amid these conditions, let alone to offer or attend school. Before the steady implementation of schools staffed by migrant northern teachers, both freedpeople and the northerners assisting them had to reckon with the "collateral damage" war brought to Mississippi and the vestiges of slavery that ruined the bodies and minds of black and white Mississippians alike. As John Eaton Jr. reported, "The situation confronting those of us who had the ordering of the early camps was really the clashing of the two antagonistic conditions,—liberty and bondage."[12] Even if they were as aware as Eaton was of the situation in the South, most northern teachers and volunteers were not prepared for the daunting realities that awaited them in the state known before the war as King Cotton. The repeated scenes of abandoned or destroyed plantation homes, ruined cotton gins and presses, proclaimed, in the words of one migrant observer, that "cotton was no longer king" in Mississippi.[13] As the Union army stead-fastly marched toward Vicksburg and through the heart of the state, ob-servers soon saw death and disease to go along with the ruined plantations. Death, disease, and hardship served as a reminder of the difficulty of mere survival for most of the state's inhabitants, but in particular for the freedom-seeking blacks, who, amid the confusion of war, abandoned their stations to flee to Union-occupied areas in the hopes of finding freedom and a safe haven.

As soon as they knew that the Union army occupied a nearby city or area, countless enslaved blacks fled their domiciles of bondage for the makeshift garrisons of the army. Vernon Lane Wharton and Noralee Frankel estimate that well over 100,000 enslaved Mississippians "tasted freedom before the end of the war."[14] If their estimate is accurate, that would mean that more than one-fourth of all enslaved African Americans in Mississippi fled slavery for asylum within the Union army or elsewhere. The massive rush of flee-ing blacks toward the Union army (and the poor conditions they arrived in) continually caught Union officials off guard. "As the Union armies progress further into the slave State," Phillip C. Garrett, a missionary for the Friends' Association of Philadelphia noted, "hundreds of the blacks leave their old homes and come into the lines. This is perhaps an every day occurrence; and as they are mostly without comforts when they arrive, their condition is often exceedingly deplorable."[15] Unprepared for the mass arrival of fugitive slaves, Union officials—whether they wanted to aid African Americans or not—hardly knew what to do with the tremendous influx. Provisions and housing were already limited to military usage, and Grant—thus far in his military campaign across the state—survived mostly on appropriated local provisions, minuscule tokens of his victories. Advance or surplus provisions were never calculated to meet a sudden influx of people such as the fleeing black Mississippians. The idea of a camp designated to meet the needs of flee-ing blacks did not become important until their encroachment upon Union-occupied territories. "There were no freedmen camps," Samuel Shipley, another missionary of the Friends' Association of Philadelphia, readily ex-plained, "until they were forced upon us by the arrival of black fugitives."[16]

The mass arrival of fleeing blacks prompted Grant's request that Eaton gather all freedom-seeking blacks in one central location away from his army. Despite the fact that Eaton set up a camp in and around Holly Springs, a host of new problems arose because freedom-seeking blacks repeatedly arrived in greater and greater numbers and in conditions far worse than Union or missionary officials could anticipate. Because of their often hasty and clandestine departures, fleeing enslaved blacks usually left behind most of the provisions needed to journey across Mississippi's countryside in search of freedom. The majority carried little more than their hopes of acquiring asylum among an army they believed were fighting a war to free them. Consequently, most arrived poorly clothed, malnourished, physically and mentally fatigued, and in serious need of medical attention. Their dreadful physical conditions shocked the very souls of most northerners accompanying the Union army. It gave them a better understanding of the detrimental impact of slavery and war, and the undertaking before them.

In the mind of A. D. Mayo, future commissioner of education for the United States, the responsibility of addressing the needs of these ex-slaves was "a task for a national sanitary commission rather than a young chaplain of volunteers."[17] Nevertheless, volunteers were all that were available in Mississippi, and a good many would write to their loved ones or superiors to express their disbelief at what they experienced. Few summed up their astonishment better than Major George W. Young, an assistant to John Eaton Jr., who, while laboring in Natchez for the benefit of the city's former slaves, fell ill from consumption and died before the end of the war. "I hope I may never be called on again," wrote Young in the spring of 1864, "to witness the horrible scenes I saw in those first days of the history of the freedmen in the Mississippi Valley."[18] Another volunteer wrote, "There were men, women, and children in every stage of disease or decrepitude, often naked, with flesh torn by the terrible experiences of their escapes."[19] A member of the Friends' Association of Philadelphia who came to Mississippi to teach former slave children exclusively was equally candid. "The pressing demand for the physical necessities of the freedmen," he wrote home to his mother, "must be met first, and their intellectual and social improvement must now be mainly neglected, unless increased means are forthcoming."[20]

By October 1863, four months after Grant captured Vicksburg, freedom-seeking blacks gathered in Union-occupied areas by the thousands, and nearly all "left food, clothing and other goods" behind.[21] Many, especially the women, were "poorly clad" or "half-naked" upon their arrival. So many came at once that John Eaton Jr., who was still attempting to direct fleeing blacks toward Grand Junction, decided that at least seven additional camps were needed throughout the state. So many freedom-seeking blacks came to the Union army between 1863 and 1864 that Eaton compared their arrival to the mass exodus of the Hebrews from Egypt. "They came," Eaton reported, "in rags of silks; feet shod and bleeding. There was no Moses to lead, nor plan in their exodus. The decision of their instinct or unlettered reason brought them to us."[22]

Fleeing or freedom-seeking Mississippi blacks, however, did subscribe to a definite "plan in their exodus." Their goal was to remove themselves from slavery or die in the process. Nothing short of death prevented these blacks from escaping the confines and tribulations of slavery and heading toward the occupied areas of the Union army. Their persistent flight gave a clear indication of their blatant disapproval of enslavement and their desire to live as free men and women. Moreover, given the fact that this "mass exodus" began shortly after Lincoln's Emancipation Proclamation and escalated after the Union army secured Vicksburg, African Americans probably paid attention to how the war was progressing. Still, in the process of fleeing Mississippi's "peculiar institution" thousands of blacks lost their lives. "Along the river bank," one Natchez woman recalled, "eleven thousand lie buried to whom freedom brought indeed a rest for their labors."[23] While this recollection was probably an exaggeration (Natchez had a black population before the war of 9,900), it nonetheless illustrates the mass movement of enslaved Mississippi blacks during the war and the devastating impact war and slavery had on a people in anxious pursuit of freedom.

Some blacks, however, had little choice in abandoning the plantation or small farm in which they regarded—by force or choice—as home. The onslaught and collateral damage brought about by the Union army in various parts of the state required many enslaved blacks to seek shelter elsewhere. In his military campaigns across the state in the winter of 1863–64, General William Tecumseh Sherman reported seizing "some 500 prisoners, a good many refugee families, and about 10 *miles of Negroes*" (emphasis added).[24] These blacks came to the camps to avoid homelessness, starvation, disease, and death. As one freedwoman recalled, "The soldiers came through . . . and I came away with them. I did not know one regiment from another; all I knew was that they were Yankee soldiers."[25] Reverend R. W. Fiske, a member of the New England Freedmen Aid Society, witnessed the tumultuous and vulnerable existence so many blacks experienced as war decimated the land that sanctioned their bondage. "These people came from plantations [from] which everything had been stripped," the Reverend wrote.

> Our armies during the summer had subsisted on the country, and so swept vast regions of all forms of supply. The blacks could not remain behind. Their only chance was to come to the river with the army, or flee further into the interior. They chose the former, of course, and so came in by long marches, without transportation for anything, in utter destitution. . . . Three-fourths of them had no change of raiment; probably one-fourth of the women had but one garment between themselves and utter nakedness. Many children were kept night and day rolled in the poor blanket of a family — its sole apparel. They had multitudes of these — no beds. There were no floors in their leaky tents, and no chance for fires. The wonder is, not that so many died, but that so many lived.[26]

Blacks who successfully ventured into the camps, by choice or out of necessity, were not necessarily any better off. "The scenes were appalling," wrote Eaton, because the "refugees were crowded together, sickly, disheartened, and dying in the streets."[27] Over 25,000 Mississippi blacks were accounted for in the state's eight camps by the end of 1863. When the Corinth camp in the northernmost part of the state was disbanded in December 1863, most of its black inhabitants dispersed to Memphis, Grand Junction, or other nearby camps in Alabama or Tennessee. By mid-January 1864, approximately a year after the Emancipation Proclamation, the camps were overflowing with freedom-seeking blacks, whose numbers soared to over 40,000, or one-tenth of the state's black population.[28] At best, eighty-five northern volunteers — mostly preachers and teachers — were sparsely scattered in these Union-occupied areas.[29] Most of the camps' black inhabitants were women, children, and infirmed or disabled men; the majority was unable to work.[30] Able-bodied men avoided the deleterious effects of the camps by joining the Union army or working as woodcutters, blacksmiths, and carpenters just outside the camps for the construction of additional shelters for their families and Union troops. Healthy freedwomen earned some of their first wages as cooks, seamstresses, and nursemaids for Union soldiers and the sick and elderly.

Nevertheless, death seemed as rampant in the camps as it was outside them. During the winter of 1863, at both the Young's Point and Natchez camps, as many as seventy-five African Americans died in a single day. This unfortunate scenario, however, when studied more closely, was not surprising. The Young's Point camp was directly adjacent to a recently excavated mass grave for soldiers slain in the war. Samuel Shipley, upon visiting Young's Point, recalled observing "dead horses and mules" lying among the camp's black inhabitants. He continued, "Large numbers of hawks and buzzards" circled the air and "occasionally alighted near an open grave when the bodies of Union soldiers had been removed for re-interment."[31] The Natchez camp fared little better. Within four months death and desertion had reduced its numbers from 4,000 to 2,100. "There was not one house at Natchez," one missionary regrettably confirmed, "where death had not entered, and the number of deaths in families ranged from one to eleven."[32] Friends of the Northwestern Freedmen's Association confirmed these stark realities. "We can easily account for the fact that sickness and death prevail to a fearful extent here. . . . No language can describe the suffering, destitution and neglect which prevails in some of their [freedmen's] camps."[33]

According to James Yeatman of the Western Sanitation Commission, the conditions in the camps were so unhealthy and unbearable that some Mississippi blacks chose to "return to their masters on account of their sufferings" in them.[34] Still, the majority chose to stay amid the filth and destitution, determined to obtain the fruits of freedom regardless of the costs. They choose to face uncertainty, even death, rather than return to the places and people that had enslaved them. Accordingly, these newly freed blacks were found everywhere "sleeping in the streets, lanes, alleys, and in hovels of all sizes" to obtain the minutest of rations, provisions, and medical attention, and equally important, to retain their newfound freedom.[35] Because of the overcrowded conditions of the camps or other Union-occupied areas, a significant number of ex-slaves camped in woods just outside those areas. During the winter of 1863–64, heavy rains combined with the filth, lack of clothing, and overcrowded conditions, produced outbreaks of cholera, smallpox, yellow fever, typhoid, and tuberculosis. At the same time, malnutrition, lockjaw, whooping cough, diarrhea, and hookworm — from inadequate personal hygiene — further contributed to the death toll. It was estimated that blacks who ventured toward or into the camps during this trying period died at the rate of *30 percent* per month.[36] Friends' emissary Samuel Shipley, upon witnessing this desolation in every camp he visited, spoke as if he saw the soul and anguish of these black men and women so desirous of freedom, but so disappointed with its spoils. "Everywhere I went," Shipley recalled, "they all ha[d] the same dejected look of a people who have found freedom thus far a sorry boon."[37]

Freedom had come at last to African Americans, but for most enduring its early beginnings in the camps, it was far from joyous. There simply were not enough persons or supplies to assist the overwhelming medical, physical, and emotional needs of fleeing blacks. On abandoned or confiscated plantations, infirmary farms were established to cater to the immediate medical needs of the old, the infirm, the young, and the helpless.[38] However, even these institutions initially seemed futile without the necessary governmental supplies, rations, or physicians to sustain them.[39] Governmental aid and volunteers were often unavoidably delayed because of wartime activity and continual bad weather. Likewise, the fact that the Union army destroyed much of the state's railways and established blockades along the Mississippi River ruined any chance that the needed provisions would get to the camps in a timely fashion. Local authorities were induced to help. Some whites, loyal to the Union and sympathetic to the aspirations of freedpeople, opened an orphan asylum or a hospital. However, as northerners soon discovered, these acts of benevolence were infrequent given the fragile and oppositional relationship whites maintained toward newly freed blacks or those sympathetic to their uplift.[40]

· · ·

Nevertheless, as common as death and suffering were to African Americans in these camps, so too were schools. Bell Wiley observed, "With the opening up of the country along the Mississippi from Cairo to Natchez the services of benevolent societies were offered for the education of the blacks."[41] "Teachers who first assumed their duties in this territory," according to Wiley, "were representatives of the American Missionary Association (AMA), the Western Freedmen's Aid Commission, the Western Sanitary Commission and the Society of Friends."[42] In late 1863, after the capture of Vicksburg, many more benevolent agencies, including the Northwestern Freedmen's Aid Commission, the National Freedmen's Relief Association, the Reformed Presbyterians, and the United Brethren of Christ, entered Mississippi to assist and educate African Americans in the camps established by John Eaton Jr.

These early grassroots schools in the camps served as the first schools provided by northerners to Mississippi freedpeople. Besides giving the first schooling to a previously enslaved and largely illiterate people, these schools ignited the hope and aspirations of freedmen and freedwomen who endured the difficulties commonly associated with the camps and the collateral damage of war and enslavement. What's more, the eagerness exhibited by freedpeople to attend school amid these hardships and conditions was a testament to the value African Americans placed on schools and learning. Schooling clearly represented one of the more positive attributes Mississippi freedpeople eagerly anticipated with freedom's arrival. An afterthought of Samuel Shipley's on the attitude freed children had toward school offers an excellent illustration. While Shipley recalled witnessing the look of dejection on the faces of many of the older freedpeople, he distinctly remembered "the want of life and spirit in the children" as they "joyfully entered" school.[43]

However, the establishment of a school or two in a camp for freedpeople did not guarantee that the masses of blacks that entered them would receive instruction. Few teachers in comparison to freedpeople ventured into the camps. Moreover, most teachers that labored in the camps found themselves maintaining multiple roles and responsibilities. Migrant northern-born teachers assumed the roles of medical attendants, ration distributors, house monitors, aids to the dependent, local judicial authorities, labor mediators—basically, whatever role was needed—before they served as teachers to former slaves and their children. Numerous AMA members recalled serving as teachers for only three to four hours a day and spending the remaining portion of the daylight hours as relief workers in nearby hospitals, infirmaries, or orphanages. Teachers from the Northwestern Freedmen's Aid Commission, along with the AMA, frequently made house visits to monitor the living conditions of newly freed blacks, and every teacher was expected to spend his or her evenings conducting prayer meetings and, if possible, a night school for adult freedpeople.[44] Even the ministers that migrated from the North to proselytize freedpeople into "proper Christians," assumed the duties of camp supervisor, teacher, and medic. During these early years most AMA ministers, for example, testified spending "most of their time in camps attending both schools and funerals."[45] As one AMA preacher recounted, "It is almost impossible to give you the amount of labor I have performed. . . . I have worked from early dawn till late at night administering to the wants of the needy."[46]

Lack of physical space to house a school also severely limited the earliest educational efforts on the part of northerners. The logistics and location of the camps themselves — being mostly in wooded or unincorporated areas — served as a major hindrance, but not as much as opposition from Mississippi whites. The war was still going on and Confederate guerillas roamed throughout the Mississippi countryside. But it was tacit opposition from whites (discussed in greater detail in chapter 3) during these initial years, and not violence, which served as the primary impediment to the establishment of grassroots schools for freedpeople by northerners. Many white Mississippians utterly refused to rent or sell property to anyone seeking to uplift former slaves. Subsequently, in the camps or nearby areas outside city limits, very few buildings could be obtained for the temporary or permanent establishment of schools. According to AMA Reverend S. G. Wright, space was so limited in some locales that some teachers were forced to rely almost exclusively on their own creativity in order to educate or assist Mississippi blacks. "In Aberdeen," Wright observed, teachers have "not been able to obtain a building for school purposes," so they instead held school outside and were seen going "shanty to shanty to ascertain the conditions and wants of the people."[47] Because of the tacit opposition of whites, there just were not enough schoolhouses or physical space to meet the educational needs of freedpeople. "No more schools could be established" in Jackson, explained Joseph Warren, "for want of rooms," as teachers and volunteers simply ran out of space.[48]

Tacit opposition was not the only impediment to finding suitable space to educate freedpeople. In Vicksburg, Meridian, and Natchez, medical needs many times took precedent over educational purposes. For example, a school of thirty Vicksburg scholars was discontinued because medical officials needed the space to attend to the infirm. Teaching was done "room by room irregularly" until a new location was secured.[49] In Meridian, a severe outbreak of smallpox closed a school taught by northern missionaries. The medical needs of the ailing in Natchez put an end to a school which had been temporarily established after being unavoidably relocated out of the city's orphanage a month earlier. The often unsettled conditions of the camps or in Union-occupied areas also forced a good number of teachers from the North to teach from house to house or to rely on their own creativity to figure out where a school could be established until more permanent spaces could be obtained.[50]

Suitable space to teach was not the only problem, however. Amid the confusion to find rooms and buildings for instruction, the shortage of teachers willing to work in Mississippi became quite apparent. By December 1863, only twenty-five teachers were employed from Holly Springs to Natchez.[51] Northern volunteers shunned Mississippi for being one of the most hostile states toward any person favoring emancipation or assisting blacks in their advancement. Others eschewed Mississippi for its distance, low pay, and inhospitable, and sometimes detrimental, summer climate. This latter observation seemed to be a particular issue. Various missionary societies forewarned would-be teachers and volunteers of the challenges that went along with their much needed services. Advertisements typically read, "Wanted Teachers: Male or female, having strength, courage, fortitude, and a heart for this work, willing to go for small salaries, and able to endure hardships as good soldiers of Christ."[52] Despite his desperate need for teachers, John Eaton Jr., now the superintendent of Freedmen Affairs, indicated to the chief secretary of the AMA, George Whipple, that he disfavored the recruitment of northern-born teachers unfamiliar with Mississippi's climate and inhospitality. "The dangers to health in coming into this climate," Eaton stated, "are such that *I would prefer not to take the responsibility of recommending strangers to come here*" (emphasis in original).[53] He further added, "Impractical romancing ideas have little place [in Mississippi] . . . good strength, sound common sense, a healthy Christian spirit and self sacrifice are essential."[54]

Historians Ronald E. Butchart, Clifford Ganus Jr., and Randy Sparks each indicate that few northerners ventured into Mississippi. While approximately 437,000 African Americans resided in Mississippi, the fourth largest total of blacks in any state, it had the fewest missionary teachers. Butchart calculated that between 1863 and 1870 the state averaged about 82 northern-born teachers. By comparison, the city of New Orleans alone averaged 60 teachers in these same years.[55] Clifford Ganus Jr. assessed that by the end of 1865, the entire state of Mississippi had only 67 teachers from the North. Again, by comparison, Tennessee, Maryland, Georgia, South Carolina, North Carolina, and Virginia each averaged more than 100 teachers.[56] Ganus, whose ascertainment stemmed solely from the reports of Freedmen's Bureau officials, attributed this reality to the beliefs northerners had of Mississippi, in that it was an unsafe environment to conduct their work.[57] Randy Sparks's study supports the findings of Butchart and Ganus. Utilizing the monthly

TABLE 2. Schools for Freedpeople Taught by Northerners, Early 1865

| | JANUARY | | |
SCHOOL LOCATION	Number of Schools	Number of Teachers	Average Attendance
Vicksburg	7	15	600
Camps by Vicksburg	2	7	325
Davis Bend	3	10	500
Natchez	11	22	600
Total	23	54	2,025

Source: Adapted from Joseph Warren, *Reports Relating to Colored Schools in Mississippi, Arkansas, and Western Tennessee, April 1865* (Memphis: Freedmen's Printing Office, 1865), 18.

reports of bureau and AMA officials, Sparks demonstrated that Mississippi, between 1866 and 1870, had on average 80 teachers a year, with the number of missionary teachers peaking in July 1868 at 128.[58]

Despite the limited number of teachers between 1863 and 1865, the schools established in the camps or in nearby towns served as the initial grassroots model for schools for African Americans throughout Mississippi. This was particularly true as more schools were established outside of the camps and in nearby areas or bordering towns protected by the Union army. By June 1865, Chaplain Hawley, the AMA superintendent of schools established for freedpeople in Vicksburg, reported that there were over thirty schools for African Americans in the state with an estimated enrollment of almost 3,000 pupils (see table 2).[59] This would have been an increase of nearly twenty schools in two years. And, despite the low number of northern-born teachers willing to labor in Mississippi, freedpeople, early on, readily welcomed the presence and services of those committed to assisting them. As AMA Reverend S. G. Wright observed, "Everywhere we have gone in the state the freedmen are anxious that a missionary should come and establish a school."[60]

When possible both freed children and adults attended school in between work hours and used any spare moments to advance their learning. Joseph Warren, the first of three superintendents for the Freedmen's Bureau in Mis-

FEBRUARY			MARCH		
Number of Schools	Number of Teachers	Average Attendance	Number of Schools	Number of Teachers	Average Attendance
7	15	616	11	22	1,089
3	8	335	4	9	440
3	10	532	4	9	531
11	22	600	11	20	750
24	55	2,083	30	60	2,810

sissippi, noted this upon his arrival in 1865. "One of the most gratifying facts developed by the recent revolution in their [the freedpeople's] condition is that they very generally desire instruction; and many of them seize every opportunity in intervals of labor to obtain it."[61] Warren's comment was not an isolated observation. He also reported finding blacks, both in the camps and in Union-occupied locales, "who, while at work or in-between, in many cases study desultorily" through their own private efforts.[62] An AMA agent working closely with Warren added that "even those who could not attend school, such as the workeman [sic] and soldiers, have picked up much and many of them can read."[63] Given the conditions of the camps and the freedpeople, Warren emphatically concluded, "Only an enthusiastic desire for improvement could lead any people to put forth the efforts which the freed people are making to procure instruction."[64] This latter assumption best explained John Eaton Jr.'s respect for Mississippi freedpeople in general, but particularly freedpeople in Vicksburg. He was so impressed by their enthusiasm for education that he was confident that within the first three months of his arrival in Vicksburg three AMA teachers, with the assistance of their more advanced pupils, had given over 2,000 African Americans a rudimentary education.[65] He was convinced that countless more could be schooled if he and others endeavoring on behalf of freedpeople were afforded additional personnel and resources. To Eaton, and so many other northerners laboring in wartime Mississippi, they saw the enthusiasm freedpeople exhibited toward learning as direct evidence of both their capacity and willingness to use schools as a means to achieve freedom, equality, and citizenship for themselves, families, and friends.

. . .

When the war ended, schools for Mississippi freedpeople progressed out of the camps and into areas that yielded greater stability, space, and opportunities. By April 1865, northerners were conducting their educational activities in towns and cities and within churches or the confines of property confiscated by the Union army during the war. Between June 1865 and June 1867, the number of schools for freedpeople grew from 26 schools with 53 teachers and 3,000 pupils, to 42 schools with 67 teachers and a reported 5,000 pupils.[66] Four types of schools were provided, each serving a specific need or population. Day schools were established for children between the ages of four and sixteen. Night schools were established for adults. Regiment schools were established to provide instruction to soldiers in the Union army, and Sabbath schools were open to anyone willing to attend.

Day schools served as the primary and immediate educational opportunity for freed children. Created in the image of the New England common school, day schools introduced freed youth to the rudiments of learning. Teachers concentrated on the basics—reading and spelling—early on; however, as their pupils progressed, teachers incorporated arithmetic, writing, and occasionally geography into their lessons. Many of the lessons were done orally or through rote memorization because of limited supplies and apparatuses such as writing utensils, paper, drafting boards, or desks.[67]

A concentrated sketch of the Rose Hill church day school in Natchez illustrates the curricular and pedagogical considerations of teachers in these schools. In addition, it informs one of the activities within the school, of the materials available, the educational preparedness of students, and how teachers adjusted their lesson plans to most efficiently and effectively teach their students. What occurred at Rose Hill typified the earliest school experiences of African American children in Mississippi. It was established in this city's principal "colored Baptist Church" on February 10, 1864. In June 1864, two northern-born teachers held two four-hour teaching sessions a day for about 180 students. The teachers taught primarily spelling, reading, and morality lessons and relied almost exclusively on the Bible to teach their pupils. The Bible was selected for very practical pedagogical reasons. Most freedpeople already possessed a copy of the Bible, and if they didn't, missionaries would gladly give them one. The fact that every freed child would have a copy of the Bible at home gave teachers a uniform text to teach from and students a uniform text to learn from. Unlike spellers or readers that had to be shipped to these newly established schools in Mississippi and would incur an additional expense, Bibles were already available and free. The Bible was, therefore, the preferred text, even over spellers and readers, because it allowed students to learn the rudiments of literacy and important moral lessons, without delay, from a uniform text.

Still, early in the history of this school, progress was slow. Spelling, principally through singing and memorization, and reading the Bible were the only reported instructional lessons for the month of June 1864, and despite the fact that 180 students regularly attended school, only about 40 could spell or read.[68] The differing needs, ages, receptivity, and educational preparedness of students, alongside limited resources, space, and support had to be a daunting task for even the most trained teacher. Nevertheless, by June 1865 — approximately one year later — reading and spelling was now coupled with mental arithmetic and writing; 135 out of 152 children (almost 90 percent) could spell and read; 24 were studying mental arithmetic, and 18 could write.[69] By September 1865, as the cotton harvest season progressed, enrollment dramatically dropped to seventy-eight students; forty-three males and thirty-five females. However, all were reported as being able to read, 24 were studying mental arithmetic, 26 were studying geography, and 54 could write.[70] By April 1866 — two years after the founding of the school — reading, spelling, mental and written arithmetic, geography, and writing were all integral parts of daily instruction and it would remain so until the school was incorporated into the state's first comprehensive tax-supported public school system in the fall 1870.[71]

Night schools, unlike day schools, were critical to teaching adult African Americans how to read and write. After a strenuous day's work, adult freed blacks — mostly women — congregated at church or at one of the homes of a more established member of the community. Night school attendance was considerably lower than the day school. Average attendance for a night school was approximately fifteen to twenty learners, and the duration of each session was no more than two or three hours. Most freed adults were taught the basics — spelling, reading, and simple arithmetic. As in the day schools, night school teachers relied heavily on the Bible as the primary text in the classroom. Again, accessibility, uniformity, and the fact that it was the preferred text among freedpeople, were the primary reasons. Night school students who mastered the rudiments of learning were thereafter introduced to mental arithmetic, mental geography, and, depending upon the available resources, writing. Given the limited time and opportunities to learn, however, most freed adults who attended night school never advanced beyond the basics. Still, as St. Louis–based Western Sanitary Commissioner James Yeatman recalled, this did not stop freedpeople from sharing their newly gained literacy skills with their children or others adults unable to attend school. "I saw a colored man," stated Yeatman, "who, after his return from his work, was seated in his cabin, surrounded by his own children and a few others from the adjoining cabins, teaching them lessons for the morrow."[72]

Regiment schools instructed freedmen who enlisted as soldiers or day laborers in the Union army. Attendance was typically larger than the average night school, and most regiment schools were transient as they closely followed the Union army. Until the congressional dismissal of black Union troops in April 1866, there were on average eight to ten regimental schools—in various locales—for African American militiamen in Mississippi. Each school taught the basics in reading, writing, written and mental arithmetic, and written geography.[73]

While learning the rudimentary basics was significant, regiment schools provided a more important arena for African American males to demonstrate their desire for attaining and testing their learning and citizenship status. Both Vernon Lane Wharton and Eric Foner speculate that many of Mississippi's black legislators acquired their first lessons in literacy and politics while serving in the Union army.[74] Heather Williams agrees. She surmises, "African American soldiers were indeed anxious to become literate, as they stood to become leaders in their communities after the war."[75] Regiment schools, however, provided more than an avenue for future community or legislative leadership. They provided a safe, visible, and immediate platform for adult African American males to demonstrate their capacity for learning and effective civic responsibility, a demonstration they would make to not only local freedmen and freedwomen, but also skeptical southern and northern whites.

Almost instantaneously, regiment schools—perhaps more than any other educational institution established for Mississippi freedpeople—directly challenged the prevalent theories about the societal inferiority of blacks. When repeatedly asked in her monthly school report whether her "colored scholars" demonstrated "an equal capacity for learning" as her white pupils, AMA teacher Anna Somers unequivocally and repeatedly replied, "without question."[76] Somers, like many other northern-born teachers who on a daily basis interacted, assisted, and taught freedpeople in Mississippi, soon after her arrival disregarded many of her preconceived notions about the inherent ineptitude of black people. These notions became especially specious after she witnessed how enslavement dramatically degraded African Americans. As Somers and others quickly recognized, black inferiority was a condition brought about by generations of enslavement, mistreatment, and denied opportunities, and not an inherent or cultural shortcoming of African Americans.

Sabbath schools served as additional places of instruction for all freedpeople. They were not only a place of learning, but also a place of worship, and they offered an easy way for teachers to coordinate and offer instruction to a mass of people at one time. "Every Sunday," explained AMA Reverend A. D. Olds, "we sat in our crowded chapel containing at least 250 to 300 [freedmen] . . . earnestly influenced to the Christian life that I have seldom seen."[77] Hundreds of freedpeople attended these Sabbath schools, where, as Randy Sparks pointed out, "religious instruction was supplemented with singing, reading exercises, and patriotic lessons."[78] Mississippi blacks learning the rudiments of literacy in a missionary-sponsored day, night, or regiment school, or in a relatively independent private black school, could expand and demonstrate their newfound skills by reading and reciting the Bible during Sabbath processions. Reading, explaining, and understanding scripture in Sabbath school allowed black Mississippians to coalesce two of their most personal ambitions: becoming literate and versed in the Bible at the same time.[79]

Between late 1865 and mid-1870, all of these grassroots schooling opportunities for freedpeople quickly became an ingrained feature in the state's postbellum political economy. A number of factors contributed to this reality, but two in particular were of overwhelming significance. The first and foremost—as already alluded to—was the end of the war. The Union's defeat of the Confederacy brought both stability and emancipation to Mississippi. Northern-born teachers were finally able to concentrate primarily on teaching and instruction rather than relief work among Mississippi blacks. River blockades ceased and this increased supplies for the construction and maintenance of schools. While they were still limited, these increased supplies nonetheless aided teachers in their schooling efforts. Still, the end of the war brought about more than societal stability; it also upended slavery and legally freed over 99 percent of all African Americans in Mississippi.[80] Black Mississippians were no longer slaves, or transitional figures such as contrabands, runaways, or fugitives; they were now legally free men and women.

Conversely, the end of the war also brought an unexpected hindrance to the educational expectations and opportunities of freedpeople. Presidential restoration policy dismantled some of the collaborative gains missionary officials and freed blacks established prior to the war's end. The most damaging effect of this policy was the restoration of confiscated or abandoned property to local whites. President Johnson's amnesty oath ordered the restitution of all confiscated or abandoned property to southern whites avowing the Confederacy's defeat and their unconditional allegiance to the Union. Thus, restoration forced the relocation or closing of a number of schools for freedpeople taught by northerners in Mississippi. At least two such schools closed in Vicksburg for this reason. Concurrently, schools for freedpeople started by northerners in Natchez, Jackson, Oxford, Hernando, Columbus, Holly Springs, Canton, Aberdeen, and Yazoo City also closed in the immediate aftermath of President Johnson's restoration policy. The provision, however, did more than close or consolidate a number of schools operating throughout Mississippi. It systematically displaced the little leverage Mississippi freedpeople and the northerners assisting them had gained during the war years. Moreover, it virtually eliminated the possibility of acquiring from disapproving whites the space, support, or resources needed to perpetuate and progress schooling opportunities for Mississippi freedpeople.[81]

The arrival of the Freedmen's Bureau in May 1865 was the second important factor. While the agency never instructed a single freed person, its presence assisted in consolidating and progressing some of the earliest postbellum educational opportunities for Mississippi freedpeople.[82] The bureau gave the educational opportunities by and for African Americans in Mississippi a greater degree of organization by consolidating—to the best of its ability—the school initiatives of the various benevolent associations, freedpeople, and assenting local whites. "The Bureau," according to Clifford Ganus Jr., attempted "to systematize, facilitate, and enforce conformity" among the multiple groups associated with black schooling not just in Mississippi, but throughout the South.[83] In early postbellum Mississippi, the bureau provided transportation for schoolteachers, salaries, books, and other learning aids, and secured additional teaching space by buying or renting property from assenting whites. The bureau also provided financial incentives. This was essential to expanding the number of schools that could be established in areas that were protected by the Union and in areas that were more rural and not protected by either the bureau or the military.

The combined efforts on the part of the bureau established a consolidated system of tuition-free grassroots schooling opportunities for African Americans. As an agency, the Freedmen's Bureau became the central organization that the overwhelming majority of freedmen aid and benevolent associations would solicit assistance from during their brief duration in Mississippi. Subsequently, schooling opportunities for Mississippi freedpeople expanded outside of the immediate camp areas and military zones and into locales previously unaffected by missionary and freedmen aid associations. State superintendent of education for the Freedmen's Bureau, Joseph Warren, broadened the range of educational opportunities for blacks to all parts of Mississippi. As a result, almost every city in the state saw an outgrowth of schooling initiatives for blacks.[84]

The arrival of the bureau increased the total number of schools available for African Americans in Mississippi. From March 1865 to May 1867, schooling opportunities for African Americans in Mississippi under the auspices of the Freedmen's Bureau increased by approximately 42 percent. In April 1868, the congressional extension of the Freedmen's Bureau Act further increased schooling opportunities. With the increase in funding the bureau was able to entice additional teachers to Mississippi, as well as hire the more advanced day and night school pupils to serve as teachers in the more rural sections of the state. As early as May 1868 (as table 3 indicates), schools for African Americans under the auspices of the bureau peaked at 115, with over 120 teachers, 45 of whom were black.[85]

However, table 3 also indirectly indicates how the environment, the state's cotton economy, and northern-based resources affected the educational opportunities of African Americans. For example, March, April, and May served as the peak months of black schooling during these early postbellum years. These months, between 1866 and 1870, boasted the highest number of teachers for freedpeople as well as the highest number of pupils. While Mississippi's cotton economy was a year-round cycle, these months, as economic historians Ransom and Sutch illustrated, demanded less labor because they were devoted more to seeding and planting the cotton crop

TABLE 3. Schools Consolidated by the Freedmen's Bureau for
Freedpeople, January 1867–May 1870

Date	Number of Schools	Number of Teachers	Number of Pupils
January 1867	43	57	3,183
May 1867	75	124	4,553
September 1867	30	30	1,449
January 1868	59	72	3,684
May 1868	115	128	6,238
September 1868	73	77	3,096
January 1869	63	91	3,841
May 1869	81	105	4,343
September 1869	46	47	1,770
January 1870	59	91	3,768
May 1870	63	96	3,918

Source: Adapted from Clifford Ganus Jr., "The Freedmen's Bureau in Mississippi"
(Ph.D. diss., Tulane University, 1953), 392–93.

than to its plowing, chopping, and harvesting.[86] Fewer labor expectations
gave freedpeople and their children more time to attend school. June, July,
August, and September were off months for most missionary teachers. Consequently, between 1866 and 1868, in these months schools for freedpeople
could hardly be found despite appeals by African Americans for teachers to
stay.[87] The sultry climate, as hitherto stated, and limited resources in these
months kept most teachers from remaining in Mississippi. Most teachers did
not return until after the cotton harvest, because enrollment would have
been too low as most able-bodied African Americans—male and female,
young and old—were expected to be in the fields harvesting the cotton
crop.

During the summer months most blacks did not want their teachers to
leave. The personal correspondence of teachers illustrates that freedpeople
repeatedly requested teachers to stay and that they raised funds and pro-

vided food and housing to meet their teachers' expenses during these summer months. The principal fear was that schools would be difficult to reopen after the departure of teachers because of the determination of local whites to either control or destroy these new schools. Prior experience also reminded freedpeople that many teachers simply did not return because of a loss of interest, general frustrations, other opportunities, or the continued fear of laboring in an extremely hostile state. School statistics from the summer of 1865 to the time the bureau departed Mississippi in 1870 illustrated that a few bureau-sponsored schools for freedpeople remained opened during the summer months. They were not, however, primarily taught by white teachers from the North. They were overwhelmingly taught by northern and native-born black teachers. For example, in Natchez during the summer of 1865, observed Joseph Warren, "two Negro women from the American Missionary Association taught about 275 pupils."[88] The two women, Lily Grandison and Clara Freeman, were both former slaves and natives of the city. "In Corinth," Warren continued, "a colored man taught 70 pupils." Similarly, "In Jackson, a black woman taught 50 pupils; and in Vicksburg, a colored woman taught 50."[89] The Vicksburg teacher was Blanche V. Harris, a former Oberlin student and AMA teacher who stayed in Mississippi during the summer months to teach freedpeople, despite her family's repeated requests for her to come home.

October and November ushered the return of most teachers willing to labor another year in Mississippi. Like September, these months were also the cotton economy's most labor intensive months when all available hands were expected to be in the fields picking cotton. Accordingly, enrollment during these months was always lower as labor demands kept both young and old blacks away from school. AMA Reverend J. P. Bardwell noted this while visiting a school for freedpeople in Natchez. He wrote, "The schools in this city are now small, because many children are in the country picking cotton, but this will be over soon and I am sure the schools will fill up again."[90]

For freedpeople associated with the bureau's grassroots educational efforts, December, January, and February provided the most invaluable time for them to take advantage of school. However, the cold and rainy weather often deterred students from attending school in a poorly constructed or makeshift structure with open windows, poor ventilation and insulation, and no stove or fireplace to keep them warm. In January 1867, strong winter storms forced many teachers in Natchez and Vicksburg to close their schools for lack of proper building insulation.[91] Moreover, inadequate or unsuitable clothing barely protected freed children from the cold rains and light frosts during these winter months. Lack of shoes was a common and unresolved problem, especially for black children who did not live in close proximity to school. Many black children, irrespective of the month, frequently worked and attended school barefoot despite numerous charitable attempts on the part of northerners to provide adequate footwear to former slaves and their children. Not surprisingly, black children's lack of adequate clothing and footwear, more than any other reason, dramatically decreased enrollment during the winter months.

Another determinant, irrespective of the month, was the accessibility of schools for the vast majority of African Americans in Mississippi. The scarcity and proximity of schools posed a great problem to African Americans wanting, but unable, to attend. The overwhelming majority of schooling opportunities for freedpeople were established in or around Union-occupied areas or along accessible river routes. Schools were rarely established in interior parts of the state where most Mississippi blacks resided. It was no wonder then that river cities like Vicksburg and Natchez boasted the largest number of schools given their accessibility to efficient means of transportation and perpetual military contact. However, it was also no wonder why so few northern-born teachers were willing to teach in the state's interior. Mississippi's interior, despite the end of the war, still showed signs of warfare. Opposed to the war's outcome, emancipation, and the activities of Mississippi blacks, postwar Confederate guerrillas, disgruntled whites, and disreputable and newly founded terrorist groups such as the Ku Klux Klan, often assaulted anyone favoring these developments.

Intrinsically, as one AMA representative was certain, most northern-born teachers "flatly refused to venture into interior counties where the protective arm of the military was not well established."[92] Their superiors wholeheartedly supported the reservations of these teachers. AMA Reverend Palmer Litts, superintendent of education in Natchez, believed it was utterly impractical to send teachers to places with no military protection considering the repeated acts of violence and intimidation missionary teachers and freedpeople faced in military-protected areas. After sending two AMA teachers to Fayette, an unprotected town, to establish a school for the city's freedpeople, Litts was notified that the "white citizens of the town became enraged and threatened to burn the building" that housed the school as well as take the lives of the teachers assisting the area's blacks.[93] Litts thereafter forewarned his superiors, "that teachers should not be sent unless troops were sent to protect them."[94] General E. O. C. Ord, the military commander in Arkansas and northern Mississippi, reiterated Litts's contention, believing that without the protection of troops, efforts made by the bureau and northern-born teachers were "worse than useless" in many parts of Mississippi, because of the pervasive opposition of Mississippi whites.[95]

In spite of Vernon Lane Wharton's assessment that most blacks who received some type of instruction during this period acquired it in a school taught by a northerner, the majority of African Americans in Mississippi never received a day of instruction until the state instituted its tax-supported public school system in 1870. In 1867, H. R. Pease, the bureau's third state superintendent of freedmen education, best expressed this reality when he reported that out of sixty counties, only twenty-seven had schools.[96] Most scholars who have devoted any attention to this subject agree that out of the 168,000 black children in Mississippi, 11,000 at best acquired a rudimentary education in one of the grassroots schools established by northerners.[97]

Nevertheless, the limited access African Americans in Mississippi had to a school should not discredit the efforts and progress made by freedpeople, assenting local whites, the Union army, northern benevolent societies and their teachers, or the Freedmen's Bureau. As historian Randy Sparks correctly asserts, "Northern missionary schools provided the nucleus of the state's budding public education system."[98] Additionally, these schools provided the needed human and material resources for blacks to extend and apply their own notions of freedom, education, and citizenship. As Sparks further says, "Leaders of the black community—from local preachers to men of state and national prominence like John R. Lynch—received an education and often inspiration from AMA teachers" and others associated with the state's grassroots schooling efforts.[99] Hence, the schooling opportunities that were established because of the hard work and sacrifice of freedpeople and the northerners laboring in Mississippi on their behalf should be more appropriately viewed as A. D. Mayo, field agent of the Bureau of Education, suggested in his report to his superiors. Mayo viewed these earliest schooling opportunities for Mississippi freedpeople as a precursor or a "sort of rehearsal for grand reformation of the church, school and society among Negroes, in the general improvement of their condition and development of the professional class of teachers, clergymen, physicians and leaders in their new industrial life."[100] The initial gains produced thus far, Mayo suggested, should not have been deduced as an end result. Rather, they should have been viewed as the beginning of a process that would shape and reshape the overall lives and opportunities of freedpeople as they continued to strive toward full citizenship and equality under the law.

. . .

Schools established by northerners were to assist freedpeople in their daily pursuits of acquiring greater rights and opportunities as citizens. Nevertheless, these schools had a definite social agenda. Of all the initiatives that the Freedmen's Bureau and various northern missionary associations established in Mississippi, schools were expected to be the only permanent institutions to remain upon their inevitable departure. Schools were to prepare African Americans to become self-sufficient and intelligent free wage laborers. Most northerners working with freedpeople used these schools to inform blacks of their rights and privileges as citizens. In many ways missionary teachers and bureau officials were more than schoolteachers and advocates for freedpeople. Besides teaching the rudiments of literacy, they continually assisted freedpeople in negotiating their labor contracts; they advocated for freedpeople the removal of legal barriers that hindered equality and personal and professional advancement; they supervised marital and religious ceremonies; they assisted freedpeople in independent business ventures; and after black males gained the franchise in late 1867, they aided them in participating in the electoral process.

Other developments occurred as well. Teaching and missionary work often went hand in hand as northerners sought to instill in ex-slaves their own New England or Midwestern Protestant values of thrift, hard work, prudence, sobriety, self-reliance, self-control, and fidelity. An embedded expectation in these teachings was to demonstrate to northern and southern skeptics that African Americans were capable of learning and laboring as free men and women. Consequently, schools taught by northerners was seen as both a local and practical attempt at addressing the nation's most perplexing postbellum question since Lincoln issued the Emancipation Proclamation: "What shall we do with the Negro?" Similar to the Lincoln and Johnson administrations and, later, Congress, which instituted national Reconstruction policies to transition slaves into freedmen and freedwomen; similar to state legislators, who implemented black codes to regulate the newfound liberties of Mississippi blacks; similar to freedpeople, who created and used various strategies to promote their own self-improvement, were northerners, who used their grassroots schooling initiatives as a platform to facilitate an answer to this unresolved question.

Implicit, however, in the pedagogical policies and practices of missionary and bureau officials, "were elements of racism, cultural imperialism and paternalism" that Mississippi freedpeople readily recognized and resisted as they gained greater autonomy over their personal and professional lives in the immediate postwar years.[101] Northerners sought to establish schools for the advancement and uplift of a downtrodden and previously enslaved people without much consideration of a freedperson's ability or desire to maintain control over his or her own life, time, labor and educational future. More distressing to Mississippi freedpeople than this blatant oversight was the societal expectation that accompanied the disregard northerners had of their overall aspirations. Schools established by northerners were to be the catalyst for local whites—most of whom abhorred schools for African Americans—to adopt and perpetuate upon their inevitable return North. This expectation not only severely limited, and perhaps removed, the possibility of freedpeople controlling their own educational futures, but it also highlighted the general skepticism many northerners maintained toward African Americans' ability to effectively establish, control, and perpetuate their own lives and educational futures.

This social expectation, however, was not solely a culturally imperialistic belief of the inherent inability of freedpeople to effectively manage themselves. The multiple educational initiatives of freedpeople witnessed by numerous northern-born officials directly contradicted this conviction. This contemplation had as much to do with local hostility over emancipation, the educational opportunities of freedpeople, black enfranchisement, and the overall vulnerability of blacks, as it did with racist or culturally chauvinistic northern ideologies of black inferiority. No spokesperson expressed the sentiment of why local whites should control the educational affairs of freedpeople upon the departure of northerners clearer than the Freedmen's Bureau chief commissioner General Oliver Otis Howard. In 1865, Howard, concluded that "the educational and moral condition of these people will not be forgotten. The utmost facility will be afforded to benevolent and religious organizations and State authorities in the maintenance of good schools (for refugees and freedmen) until a system of free schools can be supported by the recognized local governments."[102] Howard, like so many northerners laboring in Mississippi, anticipated that white, not black, Mississippians would inevitably control the state's overall affairs. This foregone conclusion was coupled with Howard's conviction that if whites did not acknowledge the need for schools for blacks prior to the bureau's departure, then all schooling efforts established by and for blacks in these early postbellum years would dissipate soon after local sovereignty was reinstated.

Thus upon this proclamation, Howard informed his state agents to work closely with local planters and legislators to assist blacks in obtaining work and schools. Bureau agents quickly became negotiators, exchanging whenever possible the labor of freedpeople for local support or the establishment of a plantation or rural school.[103] The goal was to demonstrate that schooling and work were not oppositional ideas. Blacks could be an educated labor force, educated to know what was best for them and white landowners in Mississippi. When Joseph Warren resigned, his successor, Colonel Thomas Wood, continued this initiative and sought even greater assistance than Warren from Mississippi whites. Wood's message was more poignant and straightforward than Howard's, and it summarized the expectations of the various missionary and freedmen aid societies in Mississippi. Wood was "thoroughly convinced that the great work of educating the freedpeople can only be accomplished by the hearty, vigorous, general efforts of the entire white population which inhabit[ed] the same soil with the Negroes."[104] Wood assumed, like so many other northerners who labored in Mississippi, that without the support of Mississippi whites, schools for African Americans would wholeheartedly fail upon their inevitable departure.

These educational expectations varied little from John Eaton Jr.'s and the Freedmen's Bureau's early economic attempts at developing a plantation-lease system for freedom-seeking blacks on the Davis Bend plantation. Blacks were to "learn the discipline of self-sufficiency, thrift and hard work" through independent farming ventures.[105] Schooling, like the Davis Bend experiment, served as the model not just for ex-slaves' academic instruction and advancement "out of their cold, lifeless depravity," but for whites, who would eventually recognize the value of maintaining a free-market economy and having a literate and more knowledgeable labor force. "Our greatest effort," declared Eaton, "should be not only to show that free labor can be made *profitable to the employer, but also to the laborer*" (emphasis in original).[106] Hence, northerners shared a general goal with freedpeople. They believed that former slaves should become self-sufficient free wage laborers, but their anticipation of freedpeople remaining the primary labor force, and whites controlling their educational futures, greatly differed from the expectations freedpeople had of themselves, their schools, and their futures. Northerners expected schools to make freedpeople an educated labor force; freedpeople expected schools to make them citizens.

Underlying these motives was the bureau's expectation to lay the foundation of a free labor ideology that would forever replace slavery as the state's economy. For this ideology to take firm root, however, bureau officials anticipated both planters and freedpeople to renegotiate their overall postbellum expectations, especially regarding labor. Labor renegotiating, "to an extent," explained historian Eric Foner, "meant putting freedmen back to work on plantations" but under contractual labor; a policy that Mississippi's planters indifferently approved, but independent-minded freedpeople wholeheartedly objected.[107] However, if freedpeople were expected to continue as the state's primary plantation laborers — under contractual agreement — bureau officials expected planters to assist blacks in their overall pursuits of obtaining greater opportunities and privileges as citizens. Planters were expected to offer freedpeople a livable wage and subsistence if they lived on their land, to assist and protect them from coercive antebellum slave labor practices, to promote education for them and their children, to protect African Americans against violence, and use their influence to advocate the removal of any legal or economic barrier to full equality and citizenship.

While wedded to the idea of free labor in postwar Mississippi, the dozen or so bureau officials to assist Mississippi blacks in the five years following slavery differed among themselves about its social implications. Some directly aligned their expectations with Mississippi's planters and sought to make certain that freedpeople remained the state's permanent and subjugated plantation labor force. Some positioned themselves closely with freedpeople, asserting that African Americans were entitled the "same opportunities to make their way up the social ladder of independent proprietorship as Northern workers."[108] While others, understanding the vulnerable and emaciated beginnings of Mississippi freed blacks, felt that the government should provide African Americans with some assistance or support to become independent farmers or landowners. However, until such provisions occurred, they expected freedpeople to seek labor on the nearest plantation or find immediate employment.

In many ways, the various activities of northerners who assisted Mississippi freedpeople were the vicarious examples of the value of practicing and maintaining a free labor ideology. The schools, bureaucratic efforts, and plantation-lease system they established demonstrated that a free labor ideology was a workable model and the best economic system for both white and black Mississippians in slavery's aftermath. In a series of circulars, the Freedmen's Bureau attempted to illustrate how a free labor ideology effectively served the self-interests of both black and white Mississippians and how the Freedmen's Bureau could serve as a mediator in this economic transition. "For the colored people," clarified Colonel Samuel Thomas, "the Bureau of Freedmen has been established and its officials placed throughout the district to offer protection to the colored people who are now free."[109] For white landowners, the circulars claimed, the bureau was organized to illustrate the validity of the free labor market over slavery.[110] The circulars, however, had very little impact on those whites that were convince African Americans would not work without compulsion. Bureau agent John E. Bryant recognized this upon his immediate placement in Mississippi. Offering some explanation of why a person, in general, "worked," Bryant attempted to make clear to whites disapproving of emancipation and free labor that "no man loves work naturally. Interest or necessity induces him to labor. Why does the *white man* labor? That he may acquire property and the means of purchasing the comforts and luxuries of life. The *colored man* will labor for the same reason."[111]

Upon his arrival in Mississippi, Thomas closely aligned his agenda to the aspirations of Mississippi freedpeople and attempted to convince landowning whites to adhere to the free labor model suggested by Bryant and others. Thomas recognized that most blacks needed some form of legal and physical protection from contentious whites and concluded that the most efficient method to guarantee this outcome was for whites to "accept their society's new developments" and assist freedpeople in their transition from slavery to freedom. He firmly believed that if whites learned to accept and support emancipation and schools for freedpeople, northerners' efforts in Mississippi and the life pursuits of all Mississippians would progress without serious complication upon their departure. He emphatically pleaded, "The Freed people must have schools. . . . if they are not educated they will be at a constant disadvantage with white men. Where they have had schools it has been proven that the colored children can learn easily."[112]

Accompanying this plea, Thomas reiterated the bureau's commitment to assisting Mississippi planters in securing the necessary laborers for the forthcoming harvest. While doing so, he once again attempted to instill in them the benefit of having an "educated laborer," one understanding of the need to work hard for a livable wage through contracts and negotiation, than a laborer whose work was obtained through coercion, force, or physical abuse. "Contracts," Thomas stated, "are of great importance to all parties concerned. . . . [They] are not only useful to educate the Freedmen to secure to them justice, and to teach them how to deal with men; they also promote the Planters by holding the people to steady work."[113] Appealing to the economic self-interests of Mississippi planters, Thomas concluded that it was "evident to all that intelligent labor is more valuable than that of the ignorant and degraded. The Planters will therefore serve their own interests, if they aid us [the Freedmen's Bureau] to elevate the Freedmen and contribute to support their schools and encourage all improvements."[114]

Yet Thomas's plea also came with a warning to blacks still hesitant to sign into yearlong or long-term labor agreements. The collective resistance on the part of freedpeople to contractual plantation labor undermined the bureau's attempt to placidly implement a free labor system in Mississippi. In the years immediately following the war, many freed blacks were under the strong impression that they were to receive some form of land compensation for their years of forced enslavement. "A large number of Freedmen," stated Natchez bureau agent George D. Reynolds, "have received the idea that it was at one time the intention of the Government to divide the lands of the former owners among them, giving each family a small farm."[115] "This idea," concluded Reynolds, "is all wrong [because] the United States Government never had any such intention."[116] Whether there was an intention or not, the belief that freedpeople would receive "forty acres and a mule" combined with the antagonistic practices of landowning whites toward the newfound rights of blacks turned many freedpeople away from the plantations and toward the Union army and the Freedmen's Bureau. The migration of freedpeople out of the country and toward these northern agents in late 1866 was so persistent that bureau officials issued the strictest warning to blacks thus far with regard to their sporadic postbellum labor practices. "The Government does not intend to issue any rations for the next year," one bureau circular staunchly read, "work or starve will be the position of all."[117]

The bureau, however, overlooked an important aspect in the agency of freedpeople. Most blacks did not want to remain in a subservient position reminiscent of slavery, nor did they want contentious whites, southern-born or northern-born, controlling their opportunities. The immediate disapproval over signing an extended contract indicated freedpeople's dissatisfaction with the overall expectations northerners had of them. As Thomas observed, freedpeople were quick to note that "idle white men" were not bound to signing any contracts for hire, nor were they threatened or punished if they did not adhere to the expectations of the bureau.[118] Moreover, many blacks felt they should have been treated and compensated better for their years of forced enslavement, some to the point of demanding reparations in the form of land redistribution. "Land enough existed," wrote former slave Merrimon Howard, "for every man and woman to have as much as they could work."[119] What blacks got after the war, he continued, was "no land, no house, not so much as a place to lay our head. . . . Despised by the world, hated by the country that gives us birth, denied of all our writs as a people, we were friends on the march . . . brothers on the battlefield, but in peaceful pursuits of life it seems that we are strangers."[120] If reparations were not an option, then perhaps common courtesy, respect, and acknowledgement of all that African Americans had done for their state and nation could be recognized. This dissatisfaction with persistently being underrecognized epitomized the repeated frustrations freedpeople had with the bureaucratic policies and expectations of all associated with their transition from slavery to freedom.

Such frustrations over being devalued or disrespected may explain the outgrowth of the virtually independent schools established by freedpeople in Mississippi. Few teachers from the North could rationalize why some Mississippi blacks insisted on their children attending a school virtually independent of northern support. That being the case, they frequently insulted the judgment of freedpeople for preferring to attend a school established and "conducted by incompetent colored teachers . . . rather than a bureau school where instructors were qualified" and tuition was cheaper, if not free.[121] For much of their duration in Mississippi, northerners repeatedly criticized the educational credentials of teachers in these virtually independent schools because they had not attended any formal schooling and because some could barely read and write.[122] Moreover, they criticized the judgment of black parents who would continually send their children to these schools. These remarks questioned the competency of freedpeople and their ability to teach and make good judgments regarding what was best for their children. They also revealed the displeasure and culturally chauvinistic assumptions northerners had of freedpeople. But most important, they revealed that some ex-slaves were as selective about choosing a school conducive to their child's educational needs and social expectations as they were about choosing an employer. The choice to send their children to a private school conducted by a perceived "incompetent colored teacher" rather than a school taught by a northerner implies a number of scenarios. First and foremost, it suggests that some freedpeople recognized little benefit in attending or sending their child to a school taught by northerners—even if the quality was better—if the school did not offer instruction deemed relevant by blacks. Second, given the denigrating sentiment in the aforementioned remarks, it was feasible that freedpeople would have preferred "an incompetent colored teacher" more receptive to their child's educational development, background, difficulties, and needs than a "qualified" northern-born teacher replete with negative preconceptions about the educational potential, ability, and societal place for blacks in slavery's aftermath.

But there could have been other, more benign, reasons. Black teachers, as Eric Foner correctly asserts, "played a number of roles apart from education, assisting freedpeople in contract disputes, engaging in church work, and drafting petitions to the Freedmen's Bureau, state officials, and Congress" that would convince some freedpeople to prefer them over white northern teachers.[123] These actions lead to a greater sense of trust between black Mississippians and their native- or northern-born black teachers assisting them. Last, but not least, freedpeople might have preferred paying a higher monthly tuition at a black private school to ensure greater autonomy or some degree of control over their child's educational development than paying a lower tuition—or none at all—and relinquishing control over their child's schooling opportunities. In any case, it was evident that a number of freedpeople—for perhaps these reasons or others—did not indiscriminately accept whatever schooling opportunities were presented to them, but pursued their schooling options based on how these institutions advanced their own definitions of freedom, education, and citizenship.

This reasoning also extended into the schools consolidated under the bureau and even as to the type of teacher freedpeople began to demand as their societal status improved. By 1868, a number of freedpeople working closely with missionary and bureau officials refused to allow these agencies to maintain absolute authority over their educational resources and opportunities, and most refused to relinquish their bureaucratic educational control to local whites. According to H. R. Pease, the third superintendent of education for the Freedmen's Bureau in Mississippi, local black ministers in Natchez and Vicksburg greatly opposed the establishment of any school that they could not maintain or control in some form.[124] This adamant proposition became such a source of contention that many black parents refused their children permission to attend a school under the auspices of the bureau until some compromise could be arranged. Mississippi freedpeople, however, were most adamant about having blacks — southern- or northern-born — as their teachers. As the aforementioned discussion alluded to, the lack of black teachers in these early grassroots schools for freedpeople perhaps led to the significant number of independent black schools in the state. Randy Sparks extended this contention when he demonstrated that "in order to compete with the existing black schools the AMA sent black teachers in response to freedmen's demands."[125] If Sparks is correct, it explains the increased number of black teachers in bureau schools. Moreover, it illustrated the ever present, but virtually unrecorded, influence these relatively independent private schools had on the direction of black education in early postbellum Mississippi. Black teachers in Mississippi went from 10 in January 1867 to 25 by January 1868 to 40 out of 100 in January 1869.[126] Accordingly, this, and the previously discussed adjustments, were due in large part to the proactive attitude of Mississippi freedpeople concerned about their educational opportunities and who would ultimately control them.

In conclusion, it is evident that the educational opportunities for freedpeople progressed in postbellum Mississippi despite the numerous obstacles and hindrances in their path. For approximately seven years numerous northern missionary and freedmen aid associations, with the assistance of freedpeople, the Union army, and, later, the Freedmen's Bureau, established and maintained a significant number of educational opportunities for African Americans in Mississippi. One chief indicator of the permanence of these grassroots schooling efforts was the fact that many of these schools were directly incorporated into the state's tax-supported public school system upon its formal establishment in autumn 1870. A second indicator was the number of Mississippi blacks that received their first instructional lessons in slavery's aftermath. African Americans, as never before, had acquired the rudiments of learning and soon after obtaining these skills began utilizing them in their daily life opportunities. Moreover, within this short seven-year period, grassroots schooling opportunities for freedpeople became such an ingrained feature in Mississippi's postbellum landscape, that "the very creation of the state's public school system is scarcely imaginable" without the groundwork that freedpeople, teachers, emissaries, and bureaucrats from the North helped lay.[127] Without question, these schools provided the overall framework the Mississippi legislature would need to draft and implement the state's first comprehensive public school system.

3 · EDUCATION FOR SERVITUDE

It is astonishing how little the slaveholders of the South, despite their supposed
knowledge of the negro, really knew of what was in him. . . . The difficulty
was that slavery was a perpetual barrier to an intimate acquaintance with the
negro; it regarded him as a *thing*, and was never concerned to know what was in
the sodden and concealed mind of a creature that represented only so much of
productive force, and was estimated, body and soul, in dollars and cents.
—EDWARD A. POLLARD, "The Romance of the Negro," 1871

. . .

There does not appear in any class [of whites] a very general confidence in
the capability of the Negro to attain a high degree of civilization. The whites are
willing to accord to him that justice and aid which may be of use in his sphere, or
which may be granted by a superior to an inferior race, but do not seem to recognize
his claims as due from man to man. They regard the colored race as inferiors
by nature, and believe that no legislation or philanthropy can elevate
them from the state in which they consider nature has placed them.
—JOHN ALVORD, *Fifth Semi-Annual Report*, 1868

. . .

It is an undeniable truth that the best slaves were the educated. The most
useful were the well informed. A servant who could read, write, and cypher,
with good manners and morals, was at a high premium above the man
of bones, and thews, and brawn. The same facts still hold good.
—EDITORIAL, *De Bow's Review*, 1867

The self-improving and educational measures taken by freedpeople and the
northerners that assisted them produced mixed reactions among whites in
Mississippi. Reactions ranged from a gradual acceptance of the inevitable
changes to befall the state's postwar political economy, to political and legal
measures implemented to challenge the overall initiatives of freedpeople, to

tacit disapproval, to violence and outright hostility. Overall, whites in Mississippi detested emancipation and the proactive demeanor of formerly enslaved African Americans. Ira Berlin correctly asserts, "Former masters did not accept the new circumstances easily, interpreting the freedpeople's actions as ingratitude or insolence."[1] Landowning whites in Mississippi in particular expected black men and women to continue laboring for them, and poor whites expected former slaves—in every manner possible—to remain subservient and accepting of this societal expectation. The war may have abolished slavery, but it did not do away with these deep-rooted beliefs. Still, nothing spoke more loudly of the aspirations of freedpeople than the schools that appeared "like mushrooms after a storm" in Mississippi.[2] The schools that freedpeople and northerners established in slavery's aftermath posed a direct challenge to the expectations that whites had. The very existence of these schools illustrated that emancipation prevailed over slavery and that life in Mississippi would never be the same.

How whites responded to emancipation and the budding schooling opportunities for African Americans is the focus of this chapter. As already alluded to, most whites opposed the establishment of schools for African Americans, but a small number of whites recognized the necessity of creating schooling opportunities for freed blacks. From their perspective, the labor force of Mississippi was demanding schools for themselves and their children, and if landowning whites did not oblige their request, someone else, such as northern whites, would. Consequently, the support offered by most whites in Mississippi coincided with their own self-interest of first securing a stable labor force in slavery's aftermath, and second displacing the role northerners played in the transition of slaves into freedmen and freedwomen. Whites who supported the education of freedpeople attempted to use schools to entice blacks to remain working on their cotton plantations. They invariably saw African Americans as *freed* laborers, not *freed* citizens; and, if schools for freed blacks were to exist, whites envisioned these schools as training African Americans for a life of servitude. Still, to best understand the various responses of whites toward emancipation and schools for freedpeople, a brief look at postbellum Mississippi and how whites understood the changes to befall the state is necessary. To understand how whites came to grips with emancipation and attempted to impose their expectations on former slaves following the Civil War, is to understand why they were collectively resistant to freedpeople attending school.

Before the Civil War, few states were as economically prosperous as Mississippi. Rich with fertile land, Mississippi maintained an extensive plantation economy with cotton as its primary cash crop and black slaves as its primary labor force. The northernmost county of Marshall gives an excellent indication of how prosperous cotton had become in antebellum Mississippi. On the eve of the Civil War, Marshall County yielded almost 50,000 bales of cotton; the largest number according to acreage produced by any county in the country.[3] Michael Wayne's analysis of the lower Mississippi River valley, in particular the Natchez district, offered an equally impressive case history. "Planting," explained Wayne, "was of course, the *ne plus ultra* of every [southern] man's ambition."[4] Some of the wealthiest men in the South lived in this Mississippi region, and their landholdings and property extended "far beyond the locality," well into the North and Europe.[5] It was the business transactions of these gentry that made Mississippi King Cotton.

However with the outbreak of civil war, wartime operations and regional devastation halted Mississippi's economy. Industrial nations overseas looked toward Egypt and India as their new cotton distributors as federal embargoes and blockades restrained the export of southern cotton. The economy changed very little after the war, and the state's overall adjustment was, at best, distressing. The state went from being King Cotton to an economic nonentity in the years immediately following the war, and practically every county suffered from what white Mississippians deemed the "Federal invasion of 1863."[6] Consider for a moment Marshall County, which had boasted the highest cotton yield for a county a half decade earlier. By war's end it was impoverished and destitute. "Fences were down, barns were burned, seed and stock were scarce," as one county native sorely admitted, "and the lands were badly worn by neglect."[7] The 1870 census reported that the cotton output for this county was little more than one-third of that produced a decade earlier.[8] Other counties experienced similar outcomes. Pontotoc, Newton, Lawrence, and Jefferson were in deplorable conditions and the war's casualties were most felt in these areas. In Pontotoc, for example, of the 3,500 white men—mostly poor landless white men—enlisted in the Confederate army, many never returned, and of those that did, many were badly wounded or disabled. The county's white population decreased from 22,113 in 1860 to 12,525 a decade later.[9] Lawrence County lost approximately 1,500 white men for the "southern cause," and nearly 700 enslaved blacks fled the county during the war.[10] Proudly, Newton County sent "every man of military age" to the frontline of the "War of Secession" only to see a handful return unscathed.[11]

The planter class, in particular, sustained a major setback from the war. Many abandoned their homes for residency elsewhere during the armed conflict. As demonstrated in chapter 2, many of their bondsmen also abandoned their stations to seek shelter, freedom — or both — in Union camps or on nearby dwellings. Accordingly, the planter's property suffered heavily from neglect and larceny as local raiders or federal troops stripped small farms and plantations of much of their personal belongings, livestock, horses, cotton and seed surpluses, and other possessions. As Whitelaw Reid, who toured the South during the war, retrospectively remarked, "Respect for the rights of absent property owners was nowhere . . . a very marked characteristic of the movements of Northern armies."[12] Even those who stayed witnessed comparable assaults. For example, after Union officials promised to respect the property of Joshua James, a Vicksburg planter, troops still usurped his "cows, hogs, poultry, grain, and garden crops, and burned down his gin-house, barn, stables, carriage, and slave quarters."[13]

From a landowning perspective, however, these outcomes were acknowledged by-products of military defeat. And while the loss of life was not redeemable, land and its personal or agricultural furnishings were. Totally unacceptable, however, was the loss of wealth Mississippi's slave-owning gentry had accumulated in slave property as well as the loss of unrestrained authority they once maintained over African Americans. The South's defeat not only brought an end to the war, but it abolished chattel slavery and emancipated approximately 437,000 African Americans in Mississippi. As slave-property blacks in Mississippi maintained a valuation of over $218 million, and this loss in wealth was virtually unrecoverable.[14] This lost wealth and unrestrained authority, as historian Eric Foner says, combined with the conflicting ambitions black and white Mississippians had about emancipation, quickly progressed into a postbellum "battleground between former master and former slave."[15]

For formerly enslaved African Americans, emancipation was auspicious and insecure, especially regarding work. It granted blacks a newfound freedom to seek work conditions that best suited their personal and professional interests. Not surprisingly, Mississippi freedpeople were no different than freedpeople elsewhere. They aspired to live and work independently on land purchased for themselves and their families and created strategies or solicited outside assistance to realize these ambitions. As Sir Frederick Bruce, the British ambassador to the United States, observed, "The Negro here seems to object to labour for hire, and desires to become proprietor of his own patch of land."[16] In many cases this was accurate. Yet, Bruce's observation was not inclusive of the extensive contractual arrangements agreed upon between Mississippi freedpeople and landowners which demonstrated that freedpeople did not resist "laboring for hire," but resisted labor that resembled slavery or that steadfastly denied them the possibility of landownership.[17] To freed black men and women, land that they owned was more than a piece of property. Like schooling, it symbolized freedom, and it meant autonomy, privacy, and unconditional control over their time, lives, families, and labor.

However, only a small percentage of Mississippi blacks—about 5 percent—purchased abandoned, confiscated, or personal real estate from 1865 to 1890.[18] Unlike early twentieth-century studies that ascribed low black landownership to some genetic deficiency or cultural ineptitude, historian Michael Wayne claimed racial discrimination, social coercion, and slow or insufficient capital of freedpeople were the primary reasons for the low percentage of black landowners in the state.[19] Some blacks were rarely able to acquire or purchase land, in large quantities nonetheless, in the early years after the war. For instance, as a group, freedpeople in Coldwater Creek—northeast of Holly Springs—purchased more than 2,000 acres of land from a white resident of Marshall County.[20] Joseph Davis, brother of Confederate President Jefferson Davis, sold his two estates at Davis Bend to Benjamin Montgomery, a former servant slave.[21]

However, for the masses of freedpeople unable to acquire real or personal property, finding employment compatible to their self-interests was of the utmost concern. This liberty, perhaps more than any other, caused the most conflict between landowners and freed blacks. The right to choose an employer somewhat accordant with their overall concerns and newfound rights was a privilege few black Mississippians possessed in the antebellum era.[22] In itself, emancipation brought forth a new agency in freedpeople. It allowed them to use their understanding of plantation economics to initially establish a middle ground with would-be employers. If freed African Americans controlled little else, they knew that their familiarity with plantation labor and cotton was an asset and that rebounding planters were in desperate need of laborers with this invaluable knowledge.

As a result, freedom of choice and the newly gained mobility of freed-people became the arsenal used in negotiating compatible employment with labor-starved planters in Mississippi's immediate postwar economy. "One ob de rights ob bein free," explained ex-slave James Lucas decades later, "wuz dat we could move around en change bosses."[23] The commentary by George D. Reynolds, acting assistant commissioner of the Freedmen's Bureau in southern Mississippi, on employment practices of freed blacks explicitly illustrated this detail. It further illustrated freed black Mississippians' attempt to define and exercise their newly gained independence. "They will remain this year on their old places," summed up Reynolds, "for support and such remuneration as the crop raised can give them, but say next year they will leave and make arrangements. They say that they have tried their old masters, know what they require, and how they will be treated, and that as they are now free, they will try some other place and some other way of working. They take this view not because they are tired of working, or because they want to be idle, but because they are now free."[24] One unnamed freedman was even more direct, however. As a freed man, he simply refused to accommodate to the expectations of whites and work for the person who had enslaved him for more than twenty years. "If the old massa want to grow cotton, let him plant it himself," he steadfastly remarked, "I'se work for him dese twenty years, and done got nothin' but food and clothes, and dem mighty mean. Now I'se freedman, and I tell him I ain't going to work cotton nohow."[25]

Not surprisingly, the economic aspirations of freedpeople and their views on enslavement directly conflicted with the control and workload expected by planters. In the minds of whites, according to historian David M. Oshinsky, "bondage had been good for the Negro . . . because the system kept his primitive instincts in check."[26] For most planters, therefore, the idea of negotiating with their former bondsmen over employer-employee obligations denigrated the social foundation generations of slaveholders had established in Mississippi. From their outlook, planters found it unforgiveable for freed blacks to disavow their obligations as obedient and subservient toilers. The fact that military and northern-born personalities arduously assisted and protected freed African Americans in Mississippi in negotiating compatible labor contracts, and that freedpeople pursued interests in direct conflict with the expectations of planters, only heightened the antagonism whites in Mississippi had of emancipation, black advancement, and northerners. Emancipation and the responses of freed blacks proved to be very real threats to the perpetuation of an antebellum racial status quo. The words of the wife of a Natchez planter epitomized this concern when she crooned, "Everything seemed sadly out of time" with the loss of much of the planter class's property, labor, antebellum social status, and of course, expeditious means of reestablishing them.[27]

. . .

Regardless of the war's outcome, planters in Mississippi still sought to immediately regain their prestige and statewide authority by enforcing strict and sometimes extraordinary economic measures—immigration, black codes, and violence, among others—to halt the changes of their Mississippi society. Assured that slavery was the best system of labor and that freed blacks would only work under compulsion and not within the parameters of a free labor ideology, many planters following the war sought to replicate an economic system reminiscent of antebellum slavery. Freedpeople's initial refusal to sign into a labor contract, in fear that it might jeopardize their opportunities to own land, or that it meant reenslavement, reinforced the contentions of many dissatisfied landowners that blacks would only work under compulsion. In 1866, the London-based National Freedmen's Aid Union noted this in their report entitled, *The Industry of the Freedmen.* "The Freedmen have been known to refuse entering into Contracts for labour until assured by their teachers that the Form of the Contract was not a written instrument designed to re-enslave them."[28]

Nevertheless, some Mississippi planters resorted to immigrant labor to contest the marketplace aspirations of freedpeople and force them to work under conditions reminiscent of the old regime. However, as Eric Foner correctly asserted, "Immigration was not intended to undermine the plantation system, but to preserve it."[29] Planters wanted to maintain the antebellum status quo, and it was supposed that transplanting a new labor force would induce this outcome. Consequently, Chinese, German, Danish, Irish, Swedish, and Swiss immigrants were contracted in various parts of the state in an effort to challenge the leverage freed African Americans initially maintained following slavery. Planters in Adams County, for example, transported Irish laborers. Whites in DeSoto County established the "Free Land and Colonization Company," also intended to induce European immigrant labor.[30] Swedes and Norwegians were brought to Monroe County to be used as servants.[31] As early as 1865, and as late as 1872, some Mississippi planters requested the delivery of a number of "Chinese coolies" from Cuba and California to work under five- to seven-year contracts. About 700 Chinese immigrants were brought to Meridian to do railroad work at a cheaper wage than what was paid to freed blacks, and by 1871, an unspecified number of Chinese labored the cotton plantations of the Yazoo-Delta region.[32] One Adams County landowner, Ayres P. Merrill, was so convinced of the practicality of choosing "Oriental" labor over European or black labor that he voiced his enthusiasm in the then-cosmopolitan southern periodical *De Bow's Review*. "Having no attachment for other countries than his own," stated Merrill, "he [the Chinese] is not likely to covet ownership of the soil, and being content with any government which protects him in the fruits of his labor, he is not likely to become a politician."[33] The latter comment about the presumed disinterest in landownership and politics on the part of Chinese immigrants spoke volumes about the expectations African Americans had after the war and the frustrations whites felt who did not wish for African Americans to gain these prospects.

Immigration, however, was nothing more than a short-lived experiment. Difficulties in enticing import laborers on "plantation wages" were recurring problems, and immigrants that eventually came deserted the plantation for self-employment or better opportunities in nearby towns.[34] Moreover, many were unprepared for the demands of plantation work, the unbearable conditions of a Mississippi summer, or the overall expectations of their southern employers. Cultural, linguistic, and social discrepancies served as major predicaments in the postbellum immigration experiments of planters. Planters wanted an obedient, controllable, and hard-working labor force; while newcomers wanted what freedpeople were demanding: good pay, favorable work conditions, and the opportunity of acquiring some land. As Whitelaw Reid pointed out, European immigrants in particular demanded more provisions and personal time than freedpeople, and they worked considerably fewer hours than blacks. Reid was convinced that the majority of these immigrants came to Mississippi with the sole purpose of quickly obtaining some land.[35] If Reid's observations were correct, these demands—along with the aforementioned hindrances—destroyed the hopes of planters securing an obedient migrant labor force to displace the aspirations and economic leverage of freed blacks in slavery's aftermath.

Immigration was a measure used by few Mississippi planters. It simply was not feasible according to one planter, who, in 1871, penned his discontent of it under the pseudonym "southerner" in *The Galaxy*. "The southern planter at the present time is compelled by force of circumstances to depend almost entirely on labor upon the freedmen. They are the only class of laborers there in large numbers; they understand the labor required of them; they are habituated to the climate; and are accustomed to the exactions of plantation life."[36] More prominent and successful were initiatives such as short-term labor contracts with freedpeople and the creation of legislation that restricted the overall opportunities of freed blacks. At the legislative sessions of 1865–66, the new state legislature—which President Johnson endorsed under his Reconstruction Plan—passed a series of laws regulating the life and labor of blacks. The outcome was a series of black codes that outlined the legal rights of freed and free Mississippi blacks. To paraphrase the early twentieth-century Reconstruction traditionalist Walter Lynn Fleming, no laws existed for the incorporation of ex-slaves into Mississippi society. "Those on the statute books," stated Fleming, "applied only to whites or to free Negroes under a slavery regime."[37] To Fleming, the purpose of Mississippi's black codes was to assist the "now free, ignorant, helpless, brutal, demoralized and dangerous" freedpeople in their transition from slavery to freedom.[38]

Historians David Sansing and Donald Nieman in their respected publications agreed with Fleming's critique of Mississippi's black codes, as far as the codes provided some legal statutes to help African Americans achieve full citizenship. They noted that the codes granted freedpeople the rights to acquire property, marry, file legal suits, sue and be sued, testify in court decisions involving members of their own race, and establish contractual arrangements with fellow state citizens.[39] However, they also confirmed that the primary purpose of the codes was to reinforce and perpetuate the landowning gentry's authority over the economic, political, and social opportunities of African Americans. The codes made blacks a permanent and subservient underclass.

Many components of the codes, for example, compelled blacks to move away from towns or incorporated areas—where a significant number migrated during the war—and back into the countryside to work in some form of supervised plantation labor. Still, blacks were not allowed to own land in rural Mississippi. Section one of the codes mandated that the renting or leasing of land to blacks outside incorporated towns, or in other words rural Mississippi, was illegal. This, Donald Nieman explained, "would not only prevent 'Negro colonies' from springing up . . . but it would ensure that

Mississippi blacks did not become semi-independent farmers."[40] Similarly, a statute for apprenticing orphaned black children—boys until the age of twenty-one, girls to the age of eighteen—to "some competent or suitable person" was established under the guise of benevolence to ensure these children's safety and well being.[41] However, preference was not given to a near relative, but to the child's former owner. As historian William Leon Woods illustrated, many white planters "went through the country forcefully abducting the children needed regardless of the parent's ability to provide for their young."[42] "This practice," reported Lieutenant Stuart Eldridge, was "generally being carried into effect with one idea," and that was "to secure the labor of all minors possible."[43] Black parents repeatedly complained and petitioned to bureau officials about these outrages and abuses. Almost on a daily basis fathers and mothers were obligated to give monetary or contractual bonds to show proof of their children's support and care, but these acts did not deter white landowners from taking their children. Mississippi's apprenticeship law indiscriminately broke up the black family and provided labor-starved planters with a cheap and long-term source of labor. As bureau agent John J. Knox summarized, "It is nothing but a system of slavery as I am not aware of any minors apprenticed under the state laws who are not able to support themselves."[44]

In addition to the apprenticeship law, over half of the amendments in the black codes pertained to the economic "rights" of freed blacks. These "rights," however, read more as requirements rather than entitlements to prospective citizens. Blacks were required to show written proof each year of a "lawful home or employment," a work permit from a county official to move from one employment opportunity to the next, or a signed labor contract on the nearest plantation in order to maintain good "citizenship standing." Any violation of these provisions constituted African Americans as "vagrants"; moreover, it subjected them to a minimum fine of $50 and up to ten days in jail. Those unable to pay their fines would be hired out to any person—typically their former owner or another white landowner—willing to pay the accrued cost and fees. They were required to work for this person until the costs and fees were reimbursed.

Additional sections of the black codes were equally stringent in its attempt to govern the overall livelihoods of African Americans in Mississippi. Bear in mind the black codes applied to all *persons of African ancestry*. Consequently, many of the antebellum privileges Mississippi's few free blacks procured before slavery's demise were systematically lost, because the black codes grouped together both free and freed blacks. Still unanswered is what effect these codes had on the opportunities of free blacks and their postbellum relationships with freedpeople.[45] The black codes stated that blacks, regardless of antebellum status, could not possess or own a firearm—which most free and freed blacks used for hunting and protection—without a registered license, nor could they act or live as free people unreservedly in most public settings without harsh repercussions. County officials, for instance, repeatedly arrested blacks for insignificant transgressions, such as disturbing the peace, trespassing, or for using seditious or abusive language, and these fines ranged from $10 to an exorbitant $100. Disturbing the peace could literally mean an African American not tipping his hat to a passing white. Trespassing could literally mean entering any space—public or private accommodations or even the municipal sidewalk—that whites assumed was for whites only. The tensions were extremely high in these years immediately following emancipation, as illustrated by the codes and the responses of many whites to emancipation. Every word and action of African Americans were closely watched. "The infernal sassy niggers," one white angrily sneered, "had better look out, or they'll get their throat cut." "Let a nigger come into *my* office," another white decried, "without tipping his hat, and he'll get a club over it" (emphasis in original).[46]

The following passage from one of the amendments of the codes illustrates their restrictiveness and the constant surveillance and scrutiny that African Americans would be under. Section 1 of the Vagrancy Act stated,

> Be it enacted that all rogues and vagabonds, idle and dissipated
> persons, beggars, jugglers, or persons practicing unlawful games
> or plays, runaways, common drunkards, common night-walkers,
> pilferers, lewd, wanton, or lascivious persons who neglect their calling
> or employment, misspend what they earn, or do not provide for the
> support of themselves or their families, or dependents, and all other
> idle or disorderly persons, including all who neglect all lawful business,
> habitually misspend their time frequenting houses of ill-fame, gaming
> houses, or tippling shops, shall be deemed and considered *vagrants*.
> [emphasis added][47]

As David Oshinsky illustrates, the codes were vigorously enforced. "Hundreds of blacks were arrested and auctioned off to local planters. Others were

made to scrub horses, sweep sidewalks, and haul trash."[48] The definitive goal
was to deter emancipation and put black people to work in a manner that
met the expectations and demands of whites. Black codes were repealed in
late 1866. While short-lived, they nonetheless were the best indication of
the expectations whites had of blacks following slavery and the prevailing
antagonistic attitudes landowners and legislators had toward emancipation,
the initiatives of freedpeople, and the idea of free labor.

The ultimate resolution to Mississippi's labor problem was the peonage
system of sharecropping. Freedpeople would work the lands of whites for a
share of the crop at the end of the year. In the initial years of emancipation
this labor system seemed to be the best arrangement for most blacks who
had few resources to migrate elsewhere and purchase their own lands, and
whose only source of residence and employment was with their former masters. Historian Ronald K. Davis suggested that sharecropping in the initial
years of emancipation was a negotiation process, and "not a compromise
between planters and freedpeople and Yankees." Still, he concluded, "Of all
the actors involved in the system's birth, only the freedmen wanted it."[49]

While this conclusion perhaps exaggerates each group's endorsement—
and rejection—of sharecropping, it does reinforce an important perspective.
Freedpeople were not interested in partaking in any economic initiative that
resembled the conditions and experiences of enslavement. Freed blacks did
not what to be physically abused, did not want someone to have unconditional control over their time, families, and labor, and did not want to be
bound to someone for an indefinite time. In many ways freedpeople probably saw sharecropping as a viable economic system. First and foremost, it
was more conducive to their professional and personal ambitions than any
economic measure Mississippi's landed elite entertained at the time, and second, it somewhat fit within their pursuit of greater personal and economic
freedom. To work for a wage or a share of the crop was far better than working for the profit of solely another. In the minds of freedpeople, earning a
share of the crop was a step away from slavery and toward freedom. The per-
chance overstatement of one white Mississippi farmer gives some indication
of the labor preferences of freedpeople: "A share in the crop is the universal
plan, Negroes prefer it . . . and I am forced to adopt it. Can't choose your system. Have to do what Negroes want. They control this matter entirely."[50]

The words of this farmer in many ways illustrates the ebb and flow of a
Mississippi society in transition and the continual conflict and negotiation

between former masters and former slaves in the initial years of emancipation. Freedpeople expected to live as citizens and have duties and opportunities as citizens; white landowners expected things to continue as they were prior to the war. Yet the quote does not accurately assess the leverage freedpeople had to negotiate labor contracts. Freedpeople were illiterate, homeless, at the mercy of a hostile society, and most were clueless with regard to labor negotiations; planters, irrespective of their stature, understood this. Accordingly, in an effort to conform or reshape Mississippi's postbellum economy into a recognizable antebellum composition, planters imposed their authority over freed blacks to disenchant them from exercising their newly gained liberties. Where freed blacks, for example, seeking wage or share compensation, would no longer work for free or according to the conditions expected of a slave, former slaveowners would no longer provide medical care, housing, food, clothing, or any other provision once required under plantation law. If ex-slaves' "paternalistic sense of duty," as Eugene Genovese conjectured, did not convince them to keep laboring for their former masters in these trying postwar years, then perhaps starvation and homelessness would.[51]

Still, even this approach was not wholly reliable, and when it failed to secure the anticipated response from former slaves, intimidation and violence quickly became the preferred tactic. Violence and intimidation, however, denigrated planters' hopes of reviving a stable, antebellum-like agricultural system. Planters anticipated that hiring white vigilantes would intimidate blacks into signing long-term labor agreements or at least force them into complying with the agreements they signed. In Magnolia, the area's local white militia as an example publicly murdered one black that refused to uphold the agreements in his labor contract. The freedman felt he had been misled and tricked, but the white landowner felt otherwise. According to bureau agent James H. Matthews, *"The Negro was murdered, beheaded, skinned and his skin was nailed to the side of a barn"* (emphasis in original) as a warning to other freedpeople thinking of challenging the conditions specified in their contracts.[52] Violence of this sort attempted to send another message as well: whites were still masters and blacks were still slaves.

Yet such actions did more harm than good. Instead of freed blacks feeling coerced to sign yearlong or long-term contracts, many refused to sign any contract and migrated away from the threats of violence toward Union-occupied areas. "I don't know of one instance in which the militia has assisted in the restoration of law and order," espoused Colonel Samuel Thomas, assistant commissioner of the Freedmen's Bureau.[53] "Instead," he continued, "they have assisted in paralyzing the restoration of law and order . . . in paralyzing labor and adding difficulties under which this state has labored."[54] Thomas was well aware of the destructive forces that awaited blacks in search of freedom and greater opportunities. Prior to the murdering and beheading of the freedmen in Magnolia, he summarized the prevailing sentiment whites had of emancipation and black advancement:

> The Negro has no chance for justice at the hands of Mississippians. . . . I everywhere hear the people talk in a way that indicates that public sentiment has not come to the attitude in which it can conceive of the Negro having any rights at all. Men who are honorable in their dealings with their white neighbors will cheat a Negro without feeling a single twinge of their honor; to kill a Negro, they do not deem murder; to debauch a Negro woman they do not think fornication; to take property away from a Negro, they do not consider robbery. The reason for this is simple and manifest; they esteem the Negro the property of the white man by natural right and however much they may confess that the Presidents' proclamation broke up the relation of the individual slaves to their owners, they still have the ingrained feeling that the black people at large belong to the whites at large and when a black person is found loose, and opportunity serves, the white people cannot as yet feel that he has any rights that should prevent them from treating him just as their profit, caprice, and passion may dictate.[55]

These attitudes and practices, in many ways, were white Mississippians' final efforts of resisting emancipation and invigorating in postwar Mississippi a society and labor system reminiscent of slavery. Collectively, planters candidly believed sharecropping did not ensure the requisite degree of control over its black labor force.[56] Indeed, it did and could not. As economists Roger Ransom and Richard Sutch indicated in their book, *One Kind of Freedom*, numerous freedpeople in Mississippi did not return to the cotton fields in the aftermath of slavery.[57] Emancipation disrupted and dramatically altered the cotton system Mississippi planters grew to expect. New political, social, economic, and educational opportunities dramatically changed the "average work day" of black agricultural workers, which included men, women, and children.

Freed adult males, seeking both professional and personal self-improvement with their new free time, worked considerably fewer hours than required under slavery, or sought work in another capacity or region. Some black males joined the Union army, some moved off the farms into more urban areas, and some simply refused to sign a labor contract. Freed women in general viewed work on a plantation or in a field as "unladylike"; consequently, they sought employment in other areas or simply stayed at home. Schooling and church services, clubs and leisure activities, occupied the time of young children, adolescents, and elderly freed persons, who once worked the cotton fields or maintained the odds and ends of the manor during enslavement. Ransom and Sutch estimated that black labor throughout the South decreased by almost 40 percent.[58] This decrease in labor explains why many planters regularly complained about the lack of workers, the unmanageable idleness of newly freed blacks, or the fact that they now had to negotiate work arrangements with their former slaves.

. . .

Overall, the actions of whites in Mississippi demonstrated that they did not want African Americans to advance even to the status of a freed laborer, let alone a citizen. Their intentional belittling of postwar Reconstruction efforts reinforced in the minds of freedpeople, northerners, and southern Unionists alike that Mississippi whites were not ready to fairly deal with African Americans. If left to legislate itself, the state would probably attempt to forcefully reenslave every African American that stepped foot in Mississippi, it was assumed. Many Unionists vigorously opposed the state's actions toward its freedpeople, but they were not alone. Mississippi freedpeople directly challenged this white resistance. In 1866, in response to their ill-treatment and the state's adoption of black codes, blacks in both Vicksburg and Natchez drafted a petition demanding that African Americans, nationwide, be granted the franchise so that they might protect themselves against these injustices. To the surprise of many, Massachusetts Senator Charles Sumner read this petition before Congress.[59]

On March 2, 1867, African Americans throughout the nation fortuitously became the recipients of this request. A Republican Congress had halted President Johnson's prosouthern Reconstruction policies and instituted a number of national requirements — the Thirteenth and Fourteenth Amendments — that Congress obligated seceded states to have ratified in their constitutions before readmission into the Union.[60] In addition, Congress temporarily disfranchised former Confederate officers, and even more significant, enfranchised African American males, which in Mississippi, roughly constituted more than half of the state's voting population. Giving African American males the right to vote, as historian Vernon Lane Wharton asserted, was not an act of benevolence on the part of a Republican Congress. Rather, it was "a reluctant political and economic impetus to consolidate Republicanism and industrialism in a purely agricultural and embittered Democrat South" during the postwar years.[61] In short, Republicans anticipated that the black vote would solidify a perpetual Republican voice in a deeply entrenched Democratic South. As recorded by the *Congressional Globe*, debates raged among northern senators over black suffrage. From these debates it is clear that benevolence was not the primary motivation.[62]

Regardless of Congress's motive, however, the entrance of freed blacks into politics was revolutionary to say the least. The possibility of freedpeople exercising their political—and majority—votes to voice their concerns and elect persons supportive of their aspirations further worsened the already great apprehensions whites had of emancipation. Rumors of "black rule" exacerbated the trepidation with which whites viewed both their evolving society and the future of blacks within it. "Negro suffrage was an unmitigating evil," surmised the ardent secessionist Judge J. W. Robb of Natchez, "without the slightest alloy of good."[63] In an attempt to beseech a collective backlash from the state's white residents, Robb sensationally professed that black suffrage would invoke a race war, "leading eventually either to the extinction of his [the black] race upon this continent, or, through civil convulsions, the final overthrow of the Republic and the total extinguishment of liberty in the Western Hemisphere."[64] An editorial in the *Natchez Democrat* was equally forthright in its cynicism about black suffrage. Rather than suggesting a race war, it predicated its argument on a white supremacist platform, and appealed to the apathy of disgruntled whites to oppose any Republican policy that attempted to disfranchise white male citizens. "The question is not whether the Negro shall vote," clarified the editorial, "for that is a foregone conclusion and will come to pass as sure as the sun rises on the day of the election, but the great question is shall our white population vote at all!"[65]

As whites accepted that black suffrage was inevitable, many became, in the words of Vernon Lane Wharton, "much more concerned with the freedmen as a political actor than as a worker."[66] There were at least three reasons for this new acceptance of black suffrage. First, whites did not want to live under military rule any longer. Second, they felt that if they did not cooperate with Congress, it was believed that political measures more radical than enfranchisement might be forced upon them. Lastly, many felt that "if they did not accept the black vote, they would be in no position to control it."[67] Few printed it more plainly than the editor of the *Natchez Democrat*: "If we fail to teach them [freedpeople] these lessons [of politics], we shall fail in a plain duty, and place ourselves completely at the mercy of radical intruders; and we will regret our present in-action when it shall be too late to avoid its certain iniquitous results."[68]

The newfound "acceptance" of black suffrage on the part of whites was based on the collective voting power blacks took to the polls. Local and state Democrats understood the significance of the black vote in future elections and accordingly attempted to solicit them away from a burgeoning Republican Party. However, freedpeople viewed their evolving political opportunities differently. They optimistically inferred them as an indication of progress, and an additional stride toward acquiring full citizenship. Almost immediately blacks used their newly gained voting power to elect state and county officials who were considerate of their economic, social, and political interests. In small groups or with their families, freedpeople attended both Republican and Democrat conventions to best ascertain which candidate would better serve their needs and interests as state citizens. They formed Loyal Leagues to discuss party ideals and educated would-be voters in electoral procedures. However, freed blacks decidedly voted Republican because, unlike the Democratic Party in Mississippi, the party was not premised upon a white supremacist platform and was not responsible for the injustices African Americans endured during and after enslavement.

Some Mississippi blacks became active participants in politics. In the 1868 Constitutional Convention at least sixteen blacks were members of the one hundred-person assembly.[69] They promoted civil rights, suffrage, education, protecting blacks' properties and families, and greater civic opportunities for all Mississippians. During the convention, it was delegate T. W. Stringer, an African American from Warren County, who introduced a resolution for universal suffrage in the state.

> Suffrage shall be made universal and all male citizens of any race and color without regard to any previous condition, excepting such as have

been disfranchised for participating in the late rebellion or war against the United States or for a felony committed against the laws of any state of the U.S., whereof parties have been convicted in any court having jurisdiction thereof, who have attained the age of 21 years and have been residents of the state for the last twelve months and of the county six months preceding the day of election and are citizens of the U.S., shall have the right to vote at all elections held in this state; and the legislature shall provide by law for the faithful execution of this article.[70]

On the same day, Henry P. Jacobs, a free black from Natchez, called, in essence, for a system of integrated public schooling in the state. "None of the public money of this state," suggested Jacobs, "should ever be used in supporting any sectional school whatever."[71] Following Jacobs's proposition, Stringer suggested that "the legislature shall provide for the education of all children between the ages of 6 and 18, by maintaining a system of free public education, by taxation or otherwise, and that said children *be required* to attend school" (emphasis added).[72] It was clear from their recommendations that these two black delegates were seeking a mandatory and integrated public education system to be established in Mississippi. While Mississippi in 1870 did establish a system of free public schools based on the initiatives of the convention's black delegates, as William Leon Woods illustrated, the issue of mandatory and integrated schooling was never a serious consideration. "At the time," Woods concluded, "mandatory attendance would have altered the labor supply" and the idea of integrated schooling only contributed to disapproving whites' mounting paranoia of blacks obtaining social equality in the state.[73]

When the proposed constitution went before voters in June 1868 it was rejected, largely because it would have ratified the disfranchisement of ex-Confederates. It also failed because the first chance to vote for black Mississippians—who strongly supported this constitution—was met with intimidation, violence, and strong economic pressure. One delegate of the Constitutional Convention informed Congressman Thaddeus Stevens from Pennsylvania of the violence and intimidation waged by whites determined to defeat the proposed constitution. "Previous to and during the elections," stated U. Ozanne of Claiborne County, "gangs of white men, opposed to Reconstruction prowled around the night hunting up the leading Freedmen who took an active part in the canvas, perpetuating on them gross outrages and by doing so, frightening hundreds and thousands."[74] While in Forest, bureau agent George Corliss noted that local authorities were collecting special taxes from anyone, black or white, known to be a Republican, in an effort to keep "special watch of their activities" prior to the election.[75]

The prospect of losing one's means of survival also hindered freedpeople from voting. "Many freedmen," exhorted the editor of the *Hinds County Gazette*, voted Democrat, alongside their employers, "through necessity, which they would not have been compelled to do at any other season of the year, for many Freedmen are dependent upon their Rebel employers for rations to finish their crops."[76] Thus, when the tallies were counted, the proposed constitution of 1868 was defeated and Mississippi did not reenter the Union. Yet, within a year and a half, the same constitution—short of the disfranchisement clause—was voted in by both the state's black and white residents, and the state of Mississippi reentered the Union. All the same, the antagonistic actions taken by the most outspoken Mississippi whites to black enfranchisement established a clear precedent of the extent many were willing to go to to maintain a society built upon slavery's racial caste system.

. . .

During these transitional years, schools for freedpeople progressed in postbellum Mississippi. Schooling, like the postbellum economic, social, and political pursuits of blacks, represented a definite challenge to the expectations of whites, especially landowning whites, that blacks would remain a subjugated and permanent labor force. Just as many local whites opposed the initiatives freedpeople and the northerners assisting them took to affirm the citizenship status of African Americans, so too did they oppose the educational initiatives of these groups. From the onset, most whites recognized the push by freedpeople to acquire an education as a viable means to better themselves and their conditions. Such an outcome would disintegrate any possibility of reproducing the antebellum status quo with blacks as the primary labor force. To most whites, schools for freedpeople represented both the perceived and real loss of the economic, political, social, and psychological control they had maintained over African Americans—in one form or another—before the war.

Mississippi whites in general—regardless of societal status—opposed the educational initiatives by and for blacks. In a society determined to maintain and perpetuate its agricultural and antebellum practices, most whites were adamant about keeping African Americans as they were prior to emancipation: as the state's subjugated labor force with few, if any, rights. Without a doubt, the burgeoning number of schools for freedpeople made this more unlikely. Yet, as was the case with suffrage, as it became more apparent that universal schooling for freedpeople was going to happen, a significant number of whites quickly turned to the idea that educational opportunities established for African Americans should be maintained and controlled by them. This recognition varied, however, and was not collectively accepted. In a number of instances, some whites assented to the idea of schools for freedpeople without consideration of controlling their educational affairs. From their perspective, schooling represented an excellent opportunity for newly freed blacks to improve their conditions. Superintendent of education for the Freedmen's Bureau, Joseph Warren, readily welcomed the benevolence of these whites. "There is no doubt," Warren noted, that some citizens of the state "see the propriety and necessity of educating the colored people."[77] "But," he quickly added, "they are greatly in the minority."[78]

Between 1865 and 1870, a handful of whites throughout the state assisted freedpeople, northern religious and freedmen aid associations, and the Freedmen's Bureau in establishing schools for African Americans. In his 1865 inaugural address, provisional military governor and Mississippi native, Benjamin G. Humphreys led the call and urged whites to support the establishment of schools for freedpeople. Humphreys empathetically surmised that "the highest degree of elevation in the scale of civilization to which they [freedmen] are capable, morally and intellectually must be secured to them by their education and religious training."[79] His request fell on deaf ears. This was most noticeable as his own legislature altogether ignored the question of schooling for African Americans. Nonetheless, two years later, Humphreys personally responded to his proposition and established a school on his cotton plantation.[80]

Aside from Humphreys, less-recognized whites founded or supported schools or willingly served as teachers in schools established by and for freedpeople. In Holly Springs, for example, whites founded a Sunday school for blacks. Reconstruction traditionalist Thomas Battle Carroll identified at least seven whites in Oktibbeha County who "willingly" taught freedpeople; one being a former Confederate general.[81] In Port Gibson, whites defended the endeavors and school activities of freedpeople and their teachers.[82] Similar respect for schools of freedpeople was found among a number of whites in Rodney.[83] In addition to teaching at or establishing a school, historian

Henry Swint demonstrated that some whites contributed money and materials on behalf of schools for African Americans. A wealthy and highly influential white citizen of Meridian donated buildings for school and church purposes. A white Baptist minister in Canton organized a private school for the city's blacks, and in the years immediately after the war leading officials in Columbus denounced local antagonism toward northern teachers and the city's schools for freedpeople.[84] Similarly, the mayor of Aberdeen cooperated with freedpeople and northern officials in the establishment of a couple of schools for African Americans.[85] A bureau agent in Tupelo informed his superior, H. R. Pease, that he "found no opposition from any citizen towards the organization of schools for freedmen."[86] He added that many of the city's white residents, including its planters, favored the enterprise and considered "it an important step towards securing the confidence and contentment of the freedmen."[87] Even the *Panola Star*, a local, extremely prosouthern newspaper, reported that an ex-Confederate officer opened a school for the benefit of its black residents.[88]

However, acceptance of schools for freedpeople was not universal. Another segment of Mississippi whites quickly recognized the need to educate freedpeople, but this concern had more to do with maintaining local bureaucratic control and authority over the educational affairs of freedpeople rather than any benevolence toward them. The editor of the Democratic newspaper *The Oxford Falcon* best summarized this contention. "If blacks were to become good law-abiding citizens," stated the editor, "then the proper training must be made available to them . . . then they [the freedmen] will identify with us in promoting all other interests."[89] As black suffrage and questions pertaining to the civil rights of African Americans became an increasingly foreseeable outcome throughout the nation, other Mississippi counties catered similar arguments. James J. Shannon, editor of Jackson's *Daily Clarion*, printed an editorial entitled: "Who Shall Educate the Negro?" Seeing black education, and definitely black suffrage, as inevitable, he urged white men and women in Mississippi to do their duty and teach African Americans and not let northerners control this development. "The Negro educated by the Yankee," Shannon proffered, "will be more dangerous than the Yankee himself. . . . [However,] the Negro educated by ourselves will double our strength. Let us encourage Southern men to teach the Negro; who we rely on after all as *our laborers*" (emphasis in original).[90] Prior to this editorial, the *Daily Clarion* reprinted an editorial from the *Selma Times* which asked southern whites to quickly develop an interest in the education of African Americans or suffer the consequences. "The Negroes are among us, for good or evil," the editorial asserted, "therefore they must be taught to support themselves and contribute to the commonwealth."[91]

Similarly, the *Hinds County Gazette* reported that whites in "Raymond proposed to establish a day and Sunday school for the Freedmen with white loyal Southern teachers in an effort to stifle what they called the fanaticism of Plymouth Rock Adventures and Cape Cod schoolmarms and masters."[92] The newspaper also noted that similar "educational initiatives" took root in Holly Springs, where "J. W. C. Watson, late Confederate State Senator was superintendent of a black school" and two other Confederate officers each taught a school for freedpeople "to offer the best instruction to their black laborers."[93] In a succeeding editorial, white readers still disapproving of blacks acquiring an education and the vote were reminded to begin accepting these "inevitable changes," because if they did not teach Mississippi blacks, then someone else would, and "whoever thus benefits them [freedpeople]," concluded the *Gazette* editorial, "would win an influence over them and would control their votes."[94]

Many of the state's planters who requested teachers for their plantation had a similar agenda. Between 1865 and 1870, about two dozen planters cooperated with bureau and missionary officials and established a school on their property. With a sense of accomplishment, Joseph Warren informed one of his colleagues in November 1865, that "a very few planters have expressed a desire to have schools which the children of their laborers may attend."[95] He was confident that many of these planters were beginning to adjust and accept the postwar changes and was sure that they believed schools would be "an inducement for laborers to engage with them."[96] Thus, American Missionary Association (AMA) and bureau officials were encouraged to take the middle ground when they became involved in planter-freedpeople labor negotiations. They were expected to solicit the support of planters in establishing schools on their plantations or to expand schooling for freedpeople in the more remote and less-trafficked areas of Mississippi. Concomitant to this initiative, they were advised to encourage laboring freedpeople to negotiate, when possible, a plantation school or some schooling opportunity in their labor contracts. These combined practices, accordingly, induced some planters to request a bureau-sponsored teacher or to create a school for African Americans on their plantation.

For example, a planter on the Yazoo River proposed paying a teacher $15 a month to teach the laborers on his plantation.[97] John Lynch, a northern migrant and, as noted by AMA Reverend J. P. Bardwell, "an old Oberlin student," leased a parcel of land at the Goodrich's Landing plantation.[98] He too was in search of a teacher and was prepared to board a teacher and pay her or him up to $10 a month to teach the laborers on his land. Despite being new to Mississippi and its plantation economy, Lynch, like most of the planters requesting teachers from the bureau, was convinced that the addition of a school would be a good inducement for African Americans to labor for them. Similarly, in Aberdeen, Panola, and Williamsburg an unspecified number of landowning whites accepted schools "as necessary to keep their laborers in good humor, . . . [and] many of the planters," according to the bureau superintendent, H. R. Pease, "are seeing the necessity of educating the Negroes for their own protection and benefit."[99]

AMA Reverend S. G. Wright also illustrated that some planters who sought to establish a plantation school for their laborers usually requested a certain type of teacher. While these requests were minimal in comparison, Wright nonetheless illustrated that many planters requested current or former students of schools established by northerners as teachers. Wright himself was very encouraged by this prospect, declaring that "a large number of [his] pupils had secured schools on plantations, as planters are frequently asking our Supt. to furnish them teachers . . . colored teachers it seems to be their preference."[100] The AMA and Freedmen's Bureau endorsed this development for two reasons. First, it allowed them to establish a teaching force in the state's interior, a region most northern white teachers refused to enter. Second, these schools, because of their relative isolation, would be largely self-supporting and accordingly would induce a greater degree of black participation and self-sufficiency. It was assumed that this reality would foster greater black and white cooperation without the intervention of outside assistance.[101] The planter's rationale for preferring native-born blacks as teachers rather than northerners also suggests a number of possible expectations. A sense of moral persuasion was, perhaps, an underlying factor. More likely, however, it was the understanding Mississippi blacks had of southern culture. They were familiar with the day-to-day activities and schedule of plantation life and the cotton economy. They better understood antebellum culture and the social expectations of the two racial groups. They understood local black-white behaviors and power relationships; and as significant, they best understood how to effectively negotiate the wants and desires of both the planter and the laborer. Finally, a native-born teacher—black or white—posed less of an obstacle to the authority and control planters were determined to reestablish in slavery's aftermath. Hence, this logic extends the assertion of historian Robert C. Morris that native black teachers were considered more acceptable than "the hated Yankee missionary teachers."[102] Northerners were viewed with suspicion and were often despised by Mississippi's landed elite for their presence and perpetual interference in the local and everyday disagreements between freedpeople and whites.

The latter assumption conceivably explained why so few whites, not just planters, were willing to appease the educational needs or requests of freedpeople. "Even the efforts by General Thomas J. Wood to interest the white citizens of the state in the establishment of schools for freedmen," explained one historian, "failed almost completely."[103] Between 1865 and 1870, "very few planters," to reiterate Joseph Warren, were willing to establish a school on their plantation despite the collective refusal of freedpeople to sign any labor contract that did not specify this request. White Mississippians' staunch disapproval of black advancement had as much to do with their discontent with emancipation and its aftereffects and their ingrained beliefs in the inherent inferiority and incapacity of African Americans to learn, as it did in their unwavering hopes of reviving or reinventing a society premised upon the antebellum status quo.

In the minds of most whites, African Americans were not scholars, pupils, or newly freed citizens; they were labor, and the necessary component to a quick economic restoration. Consequently, the often-repeated expression "schooling ruined Niggers," quickly became the catchphrase most disapproving white landowners used when they were approached by a bureau or missionary official about establishing a school or supporting the educational ambitions of freedpeople.[104] Despite the *Oxford Falcon's* one-time appeal to its citizens, the collective resistance of Oxford's middling and well-to-do planters was so pervasive that the bureau agent sent to establish schools in the area was "not able to ascertain upon what plantations freed[men] schools [could] be established . . . from the fact that the landholders are almost universally opposed" to blacks being schooled.[105] When this bureau agent finally established a plantation school in the city after about a year of negotiation, it was burned to the ground a month later by disgruntled whites.[106]

Disapproval and resistance extended to the legislature as well. The 1865 legislature that introduced the black codes was also vehemently opposed to the idea of schools for African Americans. After witnessing the actions of the state assembly with regard to emancipation, Joseph Warren did not seem surprised to report that "the members now in session in public speeches have declared that no appropriation shall be made by the state for school purposes."[107] This sentiment was further witnessed when Warren listened to the chancellor of the University of Mississippi, William Waddell, deliver his address on the subjects of black education and suffrage before the members of the 1865 state assembly. According to Warren, "He uttered not one word respecting the education of the Freedmen."[108] Moreover, Warren continued, "In the course of his remarks, he expressed a sentiment which may be justly styled as a narrow minded sectionalist. The sentiment to which he alluded was expressed as follows—'It has been said that this must be a white man's country and that is not enough. I go further and say *that this must be a Southern white man's country.*' This sentiment was loudly applauded."[109]

White opposition to schools for freedpeople took multiple forms. It ranged from the individual to the collective, from moderately tacit to extremely violent, and while freedpeople were the primary victims, teachers from the North and assenting Mississippi whites were also casualties. Much of the opposition found throughout Mississippi directly challenges historian Henry Swint's insistence that the greater-South did not oppose black education, but that it opposed northerners "indoctrinating" freedpeople with "New England propaganda."[110] The violence directed toward the educational initiatives by and for African Americans also challenges the Reconstruction traditionalists who maintained that little opposition existed toward African Americans or their schools in the years immediately following the war.[111] The brief, but contemporary summary of Carl Schurz of the War Department gave every indication that these historical interpretations were mistaken or that they intentionally neglected the plight of Mississippi blacks and their schools. When Schurz toured Mississippi he reported that "due to the prejudice prevailing in the state, colored schools could be established and carried on safely only under the protection of our military forces and where the latter are withdrawn, the former have to go with it."[112] His assessment was no exaggeration. Wherever northern teachers, bureau agents, or freedpeople sought to establish a school, they were immediately met with opposition. "No help can be expected from the [white] citizens," explained a bureau agent in Woodville, "as very little interest is manifested by them in regard to the welfare of the Freedmen. Planters here refuse to aid them [freedmen] as their contracts all expire this year and none of them wish to employ the same freedmen a second year."[113] Bureau agents elsewhere made similar observations. H. R. Pease was informed by one of his subordinates that Columbus "planters seem deaf to augment the educational interests of freedmen . . . a prejudice exists against educating the freedmen, which at present, is difficult to overcome."[114] Opposition was so collective in Philadelphia, that bureau agents who attempted to establish a school stated that "there was little or no inducement to establish schools in this district" on the part of whites.[115] In Hernando, bureau intermediaries noted that the resistance of whites stifled much of the educational enthusiasm and activities of freedpeople. "The Freedmen are generally very anxious to have opportunities offered them to become educated," explained bureau agent T. Wiseman, "however, little assistance can be expected because of disapproving whites."[116]

Most whites, landowning or not, opposed schools for African Americans and their expected outcome. Many northern teachers, like freedpeople, wanted African Americans to have the opportunity to pursue their personal and professional interests as citizens. In general, whites, especially the planter class, directly opposed this result and saw such sentiment as advocating the social equality of blacks and whites, Republicanism, and an antisouthern way of life. However, in reviewing the correspondence, school reports, and available lesson plans of teachers of freedpeople, not one incident could be found to support the argument that northern teachers attempted to instill Mississippi blacks with antisouthern or anti-Democrat propaganda. In his unpublished dissertation, Ross Moore also challenged this postulate and presumed that "the real foundation of the Southerners' hatred" of northerners was firmly rooted in their continual presence in local and state affairs. "Planters," Ross concluded, "did not want any interference from anyone in handling their laborers. . . . [They] were opposed to any organization of the Negroes, and did not want the black man's interest looked after by the Bureau."[117] In the opinions of whites, the mere presence of northerners gave freedpeople alternatives. It gave them greater opportunities to express and remedy their discontent, and more important, it was perceived by many whites as the fundamental reason their ability to maintain absolute control over African Americans was virtually lost.

Tacit resistance to schools for African Americans was the most prevalent tactic used by whites. For example, teachers and bureau agents throughout the state could not find suitable housing or buildings in which to live or conduct their educational efforts. Most often, whites refused the patronage of northerners or refused to sell land or rent property to freedpeople or those endeavoring on their behalf. When whites did sell their property, commercial goods, or materials, they typically charged higher prices. Resistance was so staunch that many teachers were forced to take up residence with African Americans, and in some cases with their pupils, in order to stay in Mississippi and teach. Finding land or physical plants for schools was equally vexing. This was one of the principal reasons why teachers from the North instructed their pupils from "house to house" or conducted their schools in local black churches. Some whites were willing to sell or rent their property, but most, as historian Clifford Ganus Jr. pointed out, did so with a lingering fear of being ostracized or other repercussions. "White opposition to Negro education often caused property owners to think twice," Ganus stated, "before selling or renting property for educational purposes."[118]

In addition to tacit resistance, Mississippi whites commonly harassed schoolteachers or spoke contemptuously of freedpeople's inability to learn. The Aberdeen *Sunny South*, according to Joseph Warren, repeatedly called northern teachers "imported trash," "nigger teachers," and other derogatory epithets and time and again referred to their pupils as "uneducable plowmen."[119] Some teachers were even accused of having inappropriate sexual relations with their students. Joseph Warren recalled how many of his teachers were called "unchaste miscegenationists," "promoters of social equality," and "encouragers of idleness" for their activities and close relationships with freedpeople.[120] The most verbally contentious threatened the lives of teachers, because in their mind teachers from the North continually disregarded southern traditions and established black-white social relationships.

Comparing the concerted opposition in Mississippi to that in other southern states, John Alvord deduced "that such attitudes existed in other states," but "not to such a degree as in Mississippi."[121] In some locales it was virtually impossible to establish or maintain a school for freedpeople without military supervision. In Columbus, the withdrawal of troops resulted in "increased hostility and personal abuses" to many of the city's black residents, and two schoolhouses established by the AMA were burned to the ground in early spring of 1867.[122] In Summit, whites in the midnight hour threatened to take the life of a northern teacher if he did not collect his belongings and leave the following morning.[123] In Fayette, enraged whites "threatened to burn the home of anyone who boarded teachers and to take the lives of those who taught" a school for freedpeople.[124] In the summer of 1866 as the final troops withdrew from Meridian, AMA teacher Addie Warren, her sister, and friends were verbally harassed in the midnight hour by local whites for teaching freed blacks. She frantically recalled how "the powers of darkness let loose upon this God forsaken, distracted, demoralized, half-civilized country" as night-riding vandals harassed and attacked them.[125] Their crime was teaching freedpeople.

Even when troops were present or restationed, opposition sometimes escalated into violence. On November 4, 1865, at a town meeting on education held by Natchez's leading blacks, "drunken rowdies" mocked and abused the meeting's speaker for some time before finally breaking up the engagement.[126] In Okolana, a white teacher from the North was physically accosted and had several warning shots fired toward him for being what his assailant called "a nigger teacher."[127] Four white residents in Adams County "tarred and feathered" an AMA teacher.[128] Likewise, disapproving whites in Liberty continually broke up the town's night school.[129] One of the more severe incidents occurred in Grenada, as AMA Reverend J. P. Bardwell was nearly beaten to death for his educational activities among Mississippi blacks.[130] When Grenada's bureau agent, Lieutenant Blanding, filed a formal complaint against Bardwell's attacker, Blanding was attacked for his "interference in the affair" and shot in the chest three times.[131] He died two days later. In similar fashion, two Corinth teachers in March of 1866, as reported by one bureau official, "were either murdered and secretly buried or were driven from town by a mob"; either way they never returned.[132]

Freedpeople received the most abuse. In Coffeeville, a local black preacher and teacher, who was reported missing by his students, was later found brutally beaten and shot to death in a nearby wooded area.[133] This incident occurred approximately five months after Blanding's killing. Between 1864 and 1868, one black teacher, Helen M. Jones taught in at least five different Mississippi counties. She moved constantly because of the opposition and violence whites posed to schools for freedpeople. In each locale she recalled her "black scholars were verbally and physically harassed to and from school" by whites.[134] While in Brookhaven she offered some rationale for their antagonistic behavior. "The persecution arose," she stated, "from a feeling of jealousy as many of the white people express their astonishment that the 'little niggers' learn so fast while their own children attend school month after month without getting beyond the primer."[135] Such antagonism was also evident in Jackson as white children would throw stones through the windows of schools in operation for black children.[136] In Meridian, white youths continually attacked black schoolchildren and pelted them with stones as they walked to and from school.[137] In Holly Springs, AMA teacher M. E. Gill informed another teacher that despite her repeated appeals to local authorities, a number of men continued to harass her and her female students by pulling them "down in the gullies to prevent them from going to school."[138]

The introduction of the Ku Klux Klan and other white militia organizations in the northern and eastern counties of Mississippi exacerbated white on black violence and further hindered the hopes of freedpeople living normal lives and peacefully attending school. Militia organizations such as the Klan served as a discreet agency for whites unable to accept the dramatic changes transforming their lives and society. Undoubtedly racial hatred combined with a strong abhorrence of the aftereffects of the Civil War compelled a number of whites—young and old, male and female, landed or not—to join such organizations or, at the very least, tolerate their existence. Between 1868 and 1872, the Ku Klux Klan was a highly active organization in Mississippi. It first peaked during the state's 1868 election as members guarded the roads leading to and from the designated registration areas by day, and by night, terrorized ambitious freedpeople from going to the polls on election day.[139] The Klan was also used by planters, who hired them to intimidate freedpeople into signing or accepting their labor contract. Such intimidation was also directed toward black schools and their teachers, as these grassroots initiatives became more prevalent in Mississippi. As historian Allen Trelease surmised, "One of the greatest offenses to the Klan was to teach a Negro school."[140]

That many whites used violence or accepted violence was a very disheartening problem for freedpeople, the primary victims of these vicious assaults. The possibility of being murdered was a daily reality for Mississippi blacks in this era. At the same time, the possibility of a white murdering a black without punishment or reverberation was also a reality African Americans were required to tolerate. "The danger was everywhere," espoused historian David Oshinsky. "Northern senators charged that 'two or three black men' were being lynched in Mississippi everyday. The true numbers will never be known, because local authorities did not bother to investigate 'nigger killings' and the newspapers carefully played them down."[141] Some numbers have been tallied. In a much later report on lynching in the South, it was estimated that between 1868 and 1872, 260 blacks were lynched in Mississippi.[142] If accurate, this means that freedpeople in Mississippi were lynched at an appalling rate of *five per week*. Lynching was just one of many forms of murder blacks feared on a daily basis. No one expressed better the likelihood of this heinous daily reality for freedpeople than ex-Confederate General Richard Taylor in his autobiographical memoir, *Destruction and Reconstruction*. "From 1865 on," Taylor proudly wrote, "the white race of the South devoted itself to the killing of Negroes. It appeared to be an inherent tendency in a slave driver to murder a Negro. It was a law of his being as of the monkey's to steal nuts, and could not be resisted. Thousands upon thousands were slain. Favorite Generals kept lists in their pockets, proving time, place and numbers, even to the smallest Piccaninny."[143]

. . .

Taylor's recollection summarized the absolute control that whites strove to have over freedpeople in slavery's aftermath and their freedom to murder blacks without fear of any repercussion. It also demonstrated the vulnerability of blacks and the inability of northerners to require civil authorities to address and prevent these atrocities. "The pervasiveness of violence," according to Eric Foner, "reflected whites' determination to define in their own way the meaning of freedom and their determined resistance to blacks' efforts to establish autonomy, whether in matters of family, church, labor, or personal demeanor."[144]

Still, such opposition or violence did not destroy the gains and strides made by freedpeople. Despite the tacit opposition and violent atrocities, freedpeople made major strides since enslavement and left an indelible imprint on Mississippi's postbellum landscape. Blacks proved to all around them their determination to become citizens, in spite of the insistence on the part of many whites to treat and keep them as slaves. Their refusal to sign labor agreements that they deemed unacceptable dramatically altered the postbellum economy that many Mississippi planters anticipated in slavery's aftermath. This allowed freedpeople the opportunity to find employment that suited their personal and professional interests. Suffrage rights for African Americans were constitutionally guaranteed and immediately proved to be a critical consideration among Democratic and Republican politickers seeking to align their platforms to the needs and concerns of the state's new voting majority. These combined developments, alongside the educational initiatives of freedpeople, northerners, and assenting whites, paved the way for the establishment of the state's first comprehensive tax-supported public school system for all children in Mississippi.

PART TWO

. . .

1870–1875

4 · UNIVERSAL SCHOOLING

As the stability of a Republican form of government depending
mainly upon the intelligence and virtue of the people, it shall be the duty
of the Legislature to encourage, by all suitable means, the promotion
of intellectual, scientific, moral, and agricultural improvements,
by establishing a uniform system of free public schools, by taxation or
otherwise, for all children between the ages of five and twenty-one. . . .
—ARTICLE VIII, Mississippi Constitution, 1868

. . .

None of the public money of this state should ever be used
in supporting sectional schooling whatever.
—HENRY P. JACOBS, native of Natchez, 1868

. . .

How the freedman yearned to learn and know, and with the guiding hand
of the Freedmen's Bureau and the Northern schoolmarm, helped establish
the Public School in the South and taught his own teachers in the New
England College transplanted to the black South. . . .
—W. E. B. DU BOIS, *Black Reconstruction*, 1935

Grassroots activities by freedpeople, northerners, and assenting whites were
not the only educational initiatives occurring in postwar Mississippi. Schooling initiatives were also being debated and hammered out on the legislative
floor as well. The state constitution, which was approved in 1869, authorized
the establishment of a uniform system of tax-supported public schools for
all children between the ages of five and twenty-one.[1] While some members
of the Constitutional Convention wanted compulsory schooling and integration initiatives, these resolutions never received serious consideration.
What was instituted was a de facto system of segregated public and private

schools for Mississippi's white and "colored" children, a system that would exist almost undisturbed for nearly a century.[2] Still, what transpired at the Constitutional Convention of 1868 were revisions in the state's school law that would ensure that a comprehensive tax-supported public school system, inclusive of all educable children, would forever be a permanent institution in Mississippi. What's more, unlike the sporadic, decentralized, and highly privatized antebellum public school initiatives, this new public school system was very bureaucratic, highly centralized, and principally funded through local property taxes.

In many ways Mississippi's postbellum school system closely imitated the Protestant common school model implemented throughout the antebellum Northeast and upper Midwest.[3] This should not come as a complete surprise considering that the first elected superintendent of education in Mississippi was a Connecticut native and former common school teacher and administrator, Henry R. Pease. Pease was no stranger to Mississippi, however. Between 1869 and 1873, Pease supervised the state's entire education system and infused the highly centralized and bureaucrat New England education model into Mississippi's past and present educational initiatives. Just a year earlier, he served as superintendent of education in Mississippi for the Freedmen's Bureau, and before that as a teacher among freedpeople. He had extensive knowledge of Mississippi, its inhabitants, and the new legislature. Still, Pease planned to bring the common school model and its bureaucracy to Mississippi. As superintendent, he worked conjointly with state officials, appointed a state board of education, and appointed county superintendents to handle local affairs and to monitor and distribute school funds. In all, these transplanted initiatives ensured the unprecedented establishment of schools in every Mississippi county; they provided consolidation and a centralized means to distribute school funds and maintain schooling operations; and they saw that the state's majority and newly freed population was not overlooked.[4]

As a result, public schooling—like many of the other opportunities freedpeople obtained in slavery's immediate aftermath—expanded with the adoption and implementation of these educational provisions. This chapter's opening passage, as suggested by two black delegates at the Constitutional Convention of 1868, virtually guaranteed freedpeople's legal inclusion in Mississippi public schools. Schools were to be free and accessible to every child, irrespective of their race, gender, class, or previous societal standing.

Unlike their postwar economic and political prospects, which improved, but not as significantly during the first half decade of the 1870s, the educational opportunities of blacks substantially increased. In the first year alone, the number of black children in school increased almost tenfold.

A closer examination of public schooling in Mississippi prior to the Civil War better illustrates this point. In 1860, as noted by Warren County Representative Cassius D. Landon, there were 1,216 public schools in Mississippi with 1,215 teachers, 30,970 white male and female pupils, and *"two free colored females"* (emphasis in original).[5] Landon's numbers regarding the number of African Americans schooled prior to 1860 were correct, but his estimate regarding the number of public schools in 1860 were slightly off. There were 1,116 public schools and they were sporadically scattered throughout the state. W. E. B. Du Bois reasoned that "Mississippi did lip service to the idea of public education in her earlier constitutions, but little tangible was accomplished."[6] Du Bois was correct in his assertions. As historian William D. McCain noted, public education developed originally in Mississippi in 1803 when it was still a territory, but nothing of substance developed before the late 1850s.

Despite the fact that Mississippi, early on, attempted to adhere to the spirit and requirements of the Northwest Ordinance of 1787 for its white children—the ordinance required all new territories west of the original colonies to incorporate a system of schools for its inhabitants—not much was established in the name of public schooling. In 1840, for example, the state had a total of 382 public schools which served 8,000 white students. Nearly all the schools were ungraded and most only taught reading, writing, and arithmetic. By 1850, however, public schooling nearly doubled. There were a total of 762 public schools educating 19,000 white students. By 1860, the schools almost doubled again. Notwithstanding the gains, private education still seemed to be the preferred system in Mississippi prior to the Civil War. Wealthier white Mississippians had their children tutored at home, or sent them abroad to obtain an education commensurate with their presumed future station in life.[7]

Between the state's founding, in 1817, and 1860, countless laws were passed in support of public education, but provisions within these laws gave a clear indication that the political leadership in Mississippi was not really interested in establishing a system of public schools. The truth was, McCain wrote, the legislation "satisfied no one, for it went too far for those who opposed public education and failed to establish a decent school system for those who advocated it."[8] As a result, on the eve of the Civil War, Mississippi had a "bewildering maze of school systems," as one historian described it, and not a centralized and accessible school system for its white youth.

Public schooling for whites came to a halt with the advent of war. According to Reconstruction traditionalist Elise Timberlake, whites "were too busy fighting to have time or thought for schools."[9] "Who could blame the small boys for running away from school to see the soldiers drill," espoused one white women in Natchez, "or for deserting their text books to listen to the more exciting political speeches" discussing secession and Mississippi's role in the forthcoming conflict.[10] Ironically, it was children of former slaves, not white children, that would be the beneficiary of schools as war ravaged Mississippi. By 1865, few white children attended school. Conversely, more than 3,000 African Americans were in school, thanks to the grassroots efforts from various religious and freedmen aid societies, the Union army, and the freedpeople themselves. By 1868, these grassroots efforts, combined with the initiatives of the Freedmen's Bureau, reached their peak with a reported 6,200 students schooled, and between 1867 and 1869, these schools averaged 4,500 students.[11] While impressive to say the least, these efforts did not compare to the number of African American children educated in public schools. By the end of the first year, over 45,000 black children attended school, and by the close of 1875, over 90,000 black children would be enrolled in a public school.

The dramatic growth in black student enrollment is somewhat misleading, however, and should be approached with caution. This development is only an indication of the increased educational opportunities of black Mississippians following the state's readmission into the Union. The dramatic increase in enrollment offers very little information regarding the type or quality of schooling black children received during these formative years. The type of education freed children acquired depended highly upon how freedpeople and northern and Mississippi whites controlling this burgeoning public school system perceived the future roles and opportunities of blacks in the state's postbellum political economy. Resistance on the part of the average Mississippi white without question carried over into the decade. Whites simply did not think that "cotton-picking slaves" needed to be schooled, and throughout this period there was a strong disapproval of the idea of a tax-supported public school system principally controlled by freedpeople, northerners, and Mississippi whites loyal to the Republican Party. Most, according to historian William Charles Sallis, "saw no need to adulterate the unskilled labor supply with schooling which would demoralize Negroes and make them discontent with their humble station."[12] There was an equal, if not greater, apprehension to the fact that white landowning taxpayers would fund this new public school system. Whites would once again resort to violence and intimidation toward freedpeople to express their frustrations toward these new developments, the war's outcome, emancipation, black enfranchisement, and the other initiatives by and for blacks. All of these factors shaped and reshaped the rise of universal schooling for African Americans in postbellum Mississippi, and this chapter details this history.

. . .

When the delegates gathered for the Constitutional Convention of 1868 and discussed creating an educational provision for all children, there were many issues to consider regarding the establishment of a comprehensive tax-supported public school system. Economics, race relations, and bureaucratic control were clearly three factors that contributed to the legislation's hesitancy to establish schools at the public's expense. Postwar Mississippi was virtually bankrupt, black-white relationships and expectations were more volatile than ever before, and the legislative direction of the state was in political turmoil. With regard to resolving the state's postwar fiscal inability to finance a statewide public school initiative, convention members proposed funding the new school system in multiple ways. The following provisions were taken from the state's antebellum school statutes as one means of providing a fiscal basis for the proposed school system:

> (1) Funds derived from swamp lands granted to the state for school purposes (with certain exceptions); (2) funds derived from the lands vested in the state by escheat, purchase, or forfeiture for taxes; (3) fines collected for the breach of penal laws, and all moneys received for licenses granted for the sale of intoxicating liquors; (4) all moneys paid as an equivalent for exemption from military duty, funds arising from the consolidation of the township funds, and moneys donated for the state for school purposes.[13]

In addition, the convention's delegates agreed that a poll tax, not to exceed $2 annually per person, would be collected to aid in the financing of public schools. The poll tax ensured that landless blacks and whites contributed to the public school fund and that the burden of taxation would not wholly rest on Mississippi property owners.

The poll tax contribution should not be underestimated. In some counties, especially the state's majority-black counties, this portion of the school fund constituted the majority of the money collected and used for school purposes. Still, a two-dollar poll tax alone could not efficiently establish and perpetuate a virtually nonexistent school system. Convention members agreed that if a proposed comprehensive public school system was to be chartered and financed, it had to be established and maintained through the systemic taxation of property owners. This proposition caused a major uproar among Mississippi's landed and ex-slaveholding class still attempting to quickly recover their losses from the war, emancipation, and two years of bad cotton crops. Many felt that the "burden" of taxation for the proposed public schools indiscriminately fell upon them, because most whites were landless tenant farmers and few freedpeople owned or possessed property significant enough to be taxed for school related purposes. Overlooked, however, was the fact that despite repeated attempts on the part of freedpeople to own or purchase personal property, local antagonism toward black landownership stunted this initiative and correspondingly created the conditions white property owners readily objected.[14]

Historian Allen Trelease offers an excellent synopsis of how white landowners approached the idea of property taxation to support public school initiatives, especially those for freedpeople. "It was a matter of debate," surmised Trelease, "whether hard-pressed white farmers should have to pay taxes to send their own and their white neighbors' children to school." But it was deemed "outrageous" Trelease continued, for these farmers "to pay school taxes for black cottonpickers."[15] In 1869, while the debate over the future of universal schooling evolved in Mississippi, John W. Alvord personally witnessed this attitude. "The sentiments of former masters as to education," Alvord deduced, "are by no means elevated to the standard of public school systems at the North. General taxation for this purpose is questioned. Paying for 'educating other people's children' for the public welfare, is not well understood. Quite inferior schools are thought sufficient for the colored race. But with universal suffrage conceded, surely the freedmen's vote should be intelligent; as the colored man is to become a part of society, he must have substantially its privileges; taxation for schools implied the unquestioned right to have schools."[16] This sentiment foreshadowed the type and quality of education Mississippi blacks could expect among a people that unconditionally recognized them as inferior, subservient, and only worthy as slave property and not fellow citizens.

Still, no issue provoked more consternation in the minds of Mississippi whites than the perception that public schools would promote social equality and integration. When the committee on public education proposed at the Constitutional Convention that "a school should be maintained in each school district at least four months in the year" native-born white delegates—Republican and Democrat—uniformly opposed it and argued that the proviso suggested the establishment of an integrated public school system.[17] The following language was used to revise the amendment. It stated: "That *separate schools* for the white and colored children be maintained in each district. And provided further, that should there not be a sufficient number of either race to maintain a separate school, the minority race shall have the privilege of sending [their children] to school in an adjoining district" (emphasis in original).[18] This amendment—which clearly supported a de jure public school system—was tabled along with a third provision intended to maintain private schooling in sparsely settled districts for the benefit of the minority race.[19] This latter amendment was specifically aimed to appease whites that resided in predominantly black counties and to ensure that their children would be able to attend a school wholly separate from black children.

Traditionalist Stuart Grayson Noble contended that the tabling of these proposed amendments constituted a desire on the part of convention delegates to establish a system of "mixed" or integrated schools in every Mississippi county.[20] While little evidence supports this claim, it was evident that the majority of the 1868 convention delegates—for whatever reasons—did not want to constitutionally decree a dual system of education. Their hesitancy was perhaps due to the volatile reaction on the part of many whites to view the measure as a northern attempt to promote social equality and racial integration. For example, The Daily Clarion, a pro-Democrat newspaper, led the call following the tabling of the amendment. "As the measure now stands," stated the Clarion, "A fund will be raised by taxing the property of the people to build a gigantic system of 'Public Education,' under the control of imported amalgamationists. The white people, who, it is designated, shall pay the tax, will be admitted to the enjoyment of its benefits only on the condition that they will send their children to these mixed schools. This they can never do, without violating all the instincts of their nature, and degrading themselves and polluting their posterity."[21]

Even without the sensationalism of the local press, many Mississippi whites—landowning or not—were staunchly opposed to the idea of their tax dollars aiding schools for blacks or their children attending the same school as blacks and fraternizing with them. Such a prospect disturbingly "violated all of the instincts" of Mississippi whites' "natural" selves and systematically dismantle the racial caste system of privilege and subordination well established through generations of slavery. As the constitutional convention continued to amend the public school bill, *The Daily Clarion* once again led the call for whites to oppose this proposition if it lent any support to racial integration. It informed its readership that "no intelligent and true friend of the Negro, much less of the white race, can look upon this measure with any other feeling but of loathing and disgust."[22] The newspaper concluded that the proposed school law was "a heinous abomination of mongrelism" and that the intent of the constitution's drafters was "sacrilegious" and aimed to "set the indestructible laws of God at defiance and subvert the usage of the white race in both sections of the Union."[23]

Blacks, however, saw these debates and developments differently. While they were not indiscriminate, African Americans welcomed the introduction of a system of public schools because it perpetuated their initial efforts and expectations of using schools to obtain freedom and citizenship in slavery's aftermath. Stuart Grayson Noble was partially correct when he maintained that "Negroes generally seemed to favor mixed schools as the means of securing equal advantages with the whites."[24] But freedpeople, in general, were not too much concerned with the idea of black and white children attending school together as they were with having a system of available public schools. They were more concerned with having a school system that did not legally discriminate against them, granted them some control and autonomy, and provided their children with equal access and funding to a quality education. These were much greater concerns than having their children attend school with whites. Whether these objectives were achieved in de facto integrated or segregated public schools, blacks would welcome these developments.

The sixteen black delegates at the Constitutional Convention of 1868 were very outspoken on this issue. Unanimously they voted in favor of tabling every amendment that proposed the legal establishment of segregated schools. As the discussion over establishing a system of dual schooling ensued and gained support among the majority of the convention delegates, African American delegate Henry P. Jacobs of Natchez proposed that "none of the public money of this state should ever be used in supporting sectional schooling whatever."[25] Recognizing the future educational opportunities of African Americans under segregation by law, Jacobs sternly opposed this measure. His reasoning echoed the opinions and actions of freedpeople who wanted a written guarantee that the state legislation they elected with their new franchise would not codify a legal mandate that discriminated against them and authorize the permanent establishment of segregated public schools. Jacobs's push against "sectional schooling" and for integrated schools sought to secure equitable funding and schooling opportunities for newly freed black children. If black and white children attended the same school, Jacobs, like many of the other black delegates, assumed they would receive the same resources and advantages. This rationale was not based on a belief that blacks were equal to whites or a political stratagem to promote social equality, but was rooted within their understanding of the pursuits of freedpeople and their recognition of the antagonism of whites. Jacobs simply wanted to ensure that black children were afforded the same educational considerations as white children in Mississippi.

Almost seven years later, in 1875, Speaker of the House of Representatives, Natchez native, and ex-slave, John Roy Lynch best summarized blacks' collective sentiment to be granted equal access, consideration, and protection under the law when white fears of integrated schooling resurfaced in the school clause of the 1875 Civil Rights Bill. Lynch extended Jacobs's contention and argued that nationwide African Americans cared very little about the societal ramifications of integrated schooling or white fears of racial amalgamation. According to Lynch, blacks in Mississippi — and elsewhere — wanted to be acknowledged as the Fourteenth and Fifteenth Amendments decreed, as American citizens, irrespective of their race or previous condition of servitude. Moreover, they wanted to be able to choose their child's educational opportunities based on personal interest and not compulsory laws that promoted segregation. Lynch deduced, as Jacobs did before him, that blacks were more concerned with generating measures and practices that alleviated racial discrimination than with creating provisions that forced racial integration. "The colored people," Lynch deduced,

> in asking the passage of this bill . . . do not thereby admit that their children can be better educated in white than in colored schools; nor that white teachers because they are white are better qualified to teach than colored ones. But they recognize the fact that distinctions when made and tolerated by law is an unjust and odious proscription; that you make their color a ground of objection, and consequently a crime. This is what we most earnestly protest against. Let us confer upon all citizens, then, the rights to which they are entitled under the Constitution; and then if they choose to have their children educated in separate schools, as they do in my own State, then both races will be satisfied, because they will know that the separation is their own voluntary act and not legislative compulsion.[26]

In December 1869, when the constitution was put to a statewide vote and finally ratified, it appeared that the suggestions made by African American delegates at the convention were heeded. The final public school bill read:

> Be it enacted, that all children of the state between the ages of five and twenty-one shall have, in all respects, equal advantages in the public schools. And it shall be the duty of the school directors of any district to establish an additional school in any sub-district thereof, whenever parents or guardians of twenty-five children of legal school age, and who reside within the limits of the sub-districts, shall make written applications to said board for the establishment of the same.[27]

The public school bill did not authorize Mississippi to establish a dual system of public schools, and for a moment it left in the air the possibility of black and white children in Mississippi attending school together.

Such a possibility was short-lived, however, as the idea of an integrated school system perplexed whites no end. Since the school bill stated that the county superintendent determined the establishment and number of public schools in each county, integrated schooling was still a possibility. This concern lingered in the minds of whites staunchly opposed to schools for African Americans in general, but to racial integration in particular. What if county superintendents who were northern, or Republican, or insensitive, indifferent, or unknowing of the racial etiquette and expectations of Mississippi whites, authorized the "mixing" of black and white children in the more rural, sparse, or poverty-stricken areas of the state? What were whites to do then? Dissatisfied with the final school bill and the limited control white Mississippians seemed to have regarding this matter, Thomas S. Maxey, a leading Democrat from Rankin County, submitted a dissenting minority report to the committee on public education. He argued that the "taxpaying people" of not only his county but the state wanted a law that made the establishment of separate schools mandatory.[28] He also wanted some guarantee that Mississippi whites, and not "Negroes or Carpet-Baggers" would control all future considerations of public schools. The legislation never responded to Maxey's petition, but his request spoke volumes of the rigid color line Mississippi whites were seeking to establish as public schooling became increasingly inevitable.

Maxey's appeal aside, it was obvious that public schools would not be integrated, no matter the loose language of the public school bill or who was hired to supervise the schools. Popular consensus among landowning whites willed this decision as did the newly elected government. In his inaugural address, Republican governor and Mississippi native James Lusk Alcorn reassured white Mississippians that under his administration public schools would remain "absolutely separate."[29] Lieutenant-Governor R. C. Powers reaffirmed Alcorn's position on separate schooling and further argued that the current administration had no intention to force black and white children into the same schools without the consent of the people. Acknowledging the new school bill as an asset and not a liability, Powers added:

> The provisions of this bill are wise in this respect, for while it recognizes no class distinctions (which of itself should render any law odious in a republican government), it nevertheless consults the convenience and meets all the reasonable demands of the people, by providing for the establishment of an additional school or schools, in any sub-district where the parents or guardians of twenty-five or more children desire it. . . . This leaves the details of the law where they rightly belong— and where they can be readily arranged, and all conflicting interests harmonized—with the people. If the people desire to provide separate

schools for white and black, or for good and bad children, or for large or small, or for male and female, there is nothing in this law that prohibits it.[30]

Accordingly, what opened in the fall of 1870 was a de facto dual public school system, one for "colored" children and one for white children in Mississippi.

. . .

Mississippi's public schools went into operation in the fall of 1870. Heading the state's public school system was newly elected superintendent, former Connecticut native, and previous head of the Freedmen's Bureau schooling operations in Mississippi, Henry R. Pease. Few at the Constitutional Convention of 1868, and even fewer who headed the state government and educational affairs in 1870, doubted that the initial cost of establishing and maintaining a tax-supported public school system would be an extraordinary financial expenditure. The fact that it was a dual system—one for "colored" and one for white children—greatly enhanced the financial expenditures needed to successfully launch the initiative. Legislators and educational administrators accordingly approached this new school system as a formidable assignment. The system had to be built from the ground up. Buildings and schoolhouses had to be erected, a working bureaucracy and centralized administration had to be agreed upon and established, and numerous teachers had to be hired.[31]

The challenge "to erect the necessary school houses and to reconstruct and repair those already in existence," Stuart Grayson Noble contended, "was by no means an easy task."[32] While the 1860 census reported over 1,100 public schools for Mississippi white children, most were in private homes or taught in buildings severely damaged during the war. Some were salvageable. Pease's first superintendent report indicated that some of these institutions survived the war and accordingly were incorporated into the new school system. Pease noted that 381 schools for whites taught by an equal number of teachers were operational and ready to be incorporated into the new system.[33]

Black children in Mississippi were not so lucky. Salvaging or incorporating the grassroots schools established by or for freedpeople in the first half decade of freedom was nearly impossible. Most of the schoolhouses were on rented property or in poorly constructed makeshift buildings, and the freedpeople themselves owned very little land. Throughout these early years, the black church served as the temporary schoolhouse when white opposition refused to rent or sell property to blacks or the northerners assisting them. While the church proved to be the safeguard of these grassroots educational efforts, they were impractical spaces for public schools. Most had extremely limited space and could not accommodate equipment such as writing desks and blackboards. Nonetheless, the black church remained an integral educational institution in the black community. It continued to serve as a night school for freedmen and freedwomen too old to attend a public school, and it also became the venue for countless private schools established for African Americans in this period. At least 53 private schools for African Americans with 49 black teachers and over 1,400 pupils were noted by Pease in his first superintendent report, and the majority of these students were taught within the hallow confines of the black church.[34]

The establishment of a centralized educational bureaucracy was also a major undertaking, and it too had to be assembled from top to bottom. Its organizational structure was borrowed from the New England common school model. Heading the public school system was Pease. Below him, were county superintendents; their job was to establish and monitor schools, hire teachers, and report to Pease. The bureaucracy did not end there, however. County superintendents appointed school directors, supervisors, and local officers to assist them in establishing schools and assessing their progress.[35] These numerous appointments ensured the establishment of public schooling in every Mississippi county. Most Mississippi whites already opposed to the idea of universal public schooling saw these developments as needless extravagance. Many assumed it was simply another way on the part of the Republican Party to ensure that every county had a Republican appointee to monitor the local affairs of people. Who was appointed tells a different story, however. Approximately 80 percent of the individuals appointed by Pease were white and from Mississippi. But most, in the words of Stuart Grayson Noble, were self-proclaimed "Republican scalawags" and not "loyal Democrat."[36] This, according to Noble, gave "loyal" Mississippi white taxpayers little voice in determining school-related matters and "vested the power of raising local funds in the hands of men who had little appreciation of the difficulty the southern whites were having in trying to adjust themselves to the new economic situation."[37] Pease had a differing assessment of these first appointees. He relayed that the appointed superintendents and officers were well-respected men in their particular county and were deemed capable of judicially and expeditiously performing the tasks before them.[38]

Many landowning whites, from the well-to-do planter to the semi-independent farmer, were nevertheless skeptical of the conditions proposed to establish and sustain public schools. They felt that their taxable income was contributing to an endeavor that was much too costly, that minimized their control and representation over its affairs, and that benefited the wrong people. According to state historian William Henington Weathersby, "township control" determined the educational progression of the antebellum school system, and the county boards of police—and not the state super-intendency—previously appointed school commissioners and other school officials.[39] Under the circumstances, those who beforehand maintained some authority over the progression of antebellum schooling felt that the new school administration was unlawfully breaching the rights and responsibilities of Mississippi whites to handle their own affairs. What Mississippi whites neglected to take into consideration was the fact that they were no longer the only citizens in the state; blacks were also citizens, and Pease and his administration sought to ensure that individuals throughout the state were hired to advocate on their behalf as well.

This did not stop whites from protesting the new considerations and costs of public schools. Rally cries from state newspapers such as "improper taxation without representation" suggested Mississippi's public school system was an oppressive and discriminating institution against whites.[40] White Mississippian and future state superintendent Thomas S. Gathright expressed his discontent over the new school taxes, who administered the public schools, and who inevitably—in his mind—benefited the most from these new educational initiatives. "I consider the law not only a failure in accomplishing good," surmised Gathright, "but an unmitigating outrage upon the rights and liberties of the white people of this state."[41] He sharply continued, "In Noxubee County, for an example, the tax to build schoolhouses will be $40,000, and not twenty-five white children in the county can be benefited, while the colored population pays almost no part of this tax. I exhort the friends of our southern children to pay the tax, and then send their children to their own private schools."[42]

The cost of establishing a brand new public school system inclusive of all Mississippi children was expensive, but not to the degree contended by Gathright. The bulk of the initial expenses went toward the construction or refurbishment of schoolhouses and the hiring of teachers. In fact, the hiring of teachers proved to be most challenging. Finding teachers for schools for white children was not as critical a problem as securing teachers for schools for black children. Many schoolteachers who taught white children before the Civil War were rehired by Pease and his staff. The overwhelming majority chose to only teach in schools for white children. Finding teachers qualified and willing to teach in schools for black children proved to be a far more daunting challenge. Aside from the few northerners who remained in Mississippi after the Freedmen's Bureau departure in July 1870, and the freedpeople who acquired enough learning in grassroots schools established by northerners or from other freedpeople, schools for black children had few options. Virtually every county superintendent informed Pease of their extreme difficulty in securing teachers for these schools. Few whites, especially those qualified to be public schoolteachers, were willing to jeopardize their professional careers or lives to teach black children. Racial prejudice and fear of ostracism and violence deterred most from even considering teaching black children. Traditionalist historian M. G. Abney illustrated that even when white citizens agreed that they should be the ones to teach in schools for African Americans, the few that taught were harshly ostracized.[43] Fellow traditionalist Nannie Lacey offered a similar anecdote demonstrating that a number of local whites in Leake County "lost their popularity by teaching in colored schools," and one resident even lost his life.[44] Still, some did teach in the first public schools for black children; they did so because they had a sincere interest in teaching children, irrespective of race, and not as some Reconstruction traditionalists have argued, to "earn a living" and "avoid poverty."[45]

The shortage of teachers for schools for blacks left educational officials little choice other than to once again solicit the services of teachers from the North. Yet Mississippi's reputation as being the most hostile state toward northern migrants served as another impediment to securing a sufficient number of teachers for these public schools. To entice a strong pool of applicants, Pease offered a very competitive salary, $50 to $75 per month, depending on the teacher's grade. This pay induced some of the religious and freedmen aid teachers from the North to remain or return to Mississippi. Anne Harwood and Carrie Segur, two American Missionary Association (AMA) teachers, were prime examples. Each taught in public schools for blacks in Grenada well after the AMA discontinued their grassroots schools.[46]

Still, amid the fleeting scramble to secure qualified teachers for schools for black children, at least three institutions — Tougaloo College, McDonald Hall, and Shaw University — were positioning themselves to train the future teaching force for schools for African Americans in Mississippi. Unlike the majority of religious and freedmen aid associations that departed Mississippi with the Freedmen's Bureau in late 1870, the AMA remained an active organization well into the 1870s. Arguably, the lasting legacy of the AMA in Mississippi was its establishment of the first normal school for African Americans. Established in 1869, Tougaloo College became the state's first normal school and institution of higher education for the training of black teachers. It also served as an industrial and manual training center for many students.[47] McDonald Hall — later renamed Rust University — was the state's second normal school for African Americans. It was established in Holly Springs, was privately funded by Marshall County blacks, and was taught by three northerners: Rev. A. C. McDonald, his wife, and a man named Hooper. In 1870, the local Methodist Episcopal Church established Shaw University, also in Holly Springs. By 1871, Shaw's normal school department, according to traditionalist Ruth Watkins, had a total of sixty-five black students learning the art of teaching.[48]

While appreciative of the existence of these institutions of higher education and the opportunities they provided, Mississippi blacks were disturbed by the fact that they maintained no positions of authority within these establishments. More than anything, they wanted to have some say in the admission and training of the future teachers of their children. And as important, they wanted to have access to an institution of higher education that prepared them for more than the prospect of teaching. Mississippi blacks petitioned their local legislators, and in April 1870, black legislators — including John Roy Lynch and Senator Hiram Revels — responded by requesting to the governor that African Americans be granted admission into the University of Mississippi, or be granted a "university of their own." Alcorn was taken aback by the request and knew that whites would not allow the University of Mississippi to be integrated, so he contacted the field secretary of the AMA, Edward Smith, to see what measures could be taken to get African Americans greater representation at Tougaloo. Alcorn informed Smith, "a university of their own" meant just what it said and that there was "very little probability that they [blacks] would have the American Missionary Association or anyone to run the machine but themselves."[49] To appease their demands, Alcorn proposed placing Tougaloo in the hands of blacks. However, the AMA abhorred this idea, and Smith patronizingly informed Alcorn that the AMA would most likely sever its ties in Mississippi if "such power and money in connection with the institution would go for the aggrandizement of some Dinah or Sambo."[50] Understanding the ramifications of both the AMA removal and the collective resolve of blacks, Alcorn rejected this idea. Instead he established Alcorn College and appointed as its first president former senator Hiram Revels.[51] Nevertheless, the most important factor in the creation of the state's first institutions of higher education for blacks was their desired end result. Tougaloo, McDonald Hall, Shaw University, and Alcorn College are important for two reasons. The first is that it was through these institutions that the state would generate its future black teachers. The second is that they demonstrated the demand on the part of African Americans to have access to higher education on their own terms without delay.

. . .

With the construction and repair of schoolhouses, the hiring of teachers, and an intact working bureaucracy, public schools officially opened in Mississippi in October 1870. In his first annual report, Pease reported that in 75 districts, comprising 69 counties and 6 incorporated towns, 3,450 public schools opened and they employed approximately 3,200 teachers, 400 of whom were black. Roughly 111,000 out of 246,842 educable Mississippi children — or 45.2 percent — enrolled in a public school and the system's average attendance was 85,330 (see table 4).[52] Seventy county superintendents, 450 school directors, and 659 school officers ensured that every county had a school. Over 600 schoolhouses were built or purchased in the first year, and the total value of the public school property was estimated at $400,000.[53] "Considering the time and labor to organize the system," Pease said,

> and the unfavorable circumstances existing at the time of its
> inauguration—the State in transition from the old policy of
> government, under slavery, to the new, under freedom; and the
> school policy adopted as an experiment, being very crude in its own
> adaptation and necessarily imperfect in its workings . . . viewing these
> considerations in all their bearings, the forgoing summary of results
> presents a development of our educational scheme truly marvelous—

TABLE 4. School Population, Enrollment, and Average Attendance
of Educable Children, 1870–1871

Race	Educable Children (Ages 5–21)	Number of Children Enrolled in Schools	Percentage of Children Enrolled	Average Attendance of Enrolled Children	Average Attendance as a Percentage of Enrolled Children
Black	126,769	45,429	35.8	36,040	79.3
White	120,073	66,257	55.1	49,290	74.4
Total	246,842	111,686	45.2	85,330	76.4

Source: Adapted from *Annual Report of the Superintendent of Public Education of the State of Mississippi for the Year Ending December, 1871* (Jackson, Miss.: Kimball, Kaymond, State Printers, 1872), 124–31.

a success which must be highly gratifying to the friends of popular
education, and indeed, to all who earnestly desire the advancement of
the moral, intellectual and material interests of the people.[54]

Black and white children benefited. As table 4 shows, approximately
45,429 out of the 126,769 black children, or 35.8 percent, enrolled in public school. Almost 80 percent of these children attended school on a daily
basis. Comparably, 66,257 out of the 120,073 white children, or 55.1 percent,
enrolled in public school, and approximately 74.4 percent of these students
maintained a daily attendance. While black children constituted a majority
of the children in the state—roughly 51.3 percent—nearly 21,000 more white
children were enrolled in school. This result, however, had more to do with
the educational opportunities available to black children—smaller or fewer
schools or fewer teachers—than with the enthusiasm or attitudes they had
toward schooling. As table 4 indicates, black children who enrolled in a public school regularly attended when the opportunity to do so arose.

That black children attended school when they had the chance to do so
is more apparent when one looks at attendance by county. In majority-black
counties, Mississippi blacks took full advantage of the educational opportunities before them. Their majority representation, mounting economic
leverage, and growing political voice assisted them in their educational

pursuits. Moreover, the fact that so many African Americans could financially contribute to the burgeoning public school system greatly increased
their children's schooling opportunities. The two-dollar poll tax on all adult
males (including freed black males) was paid and collected in these counties,
but—as it will be seen—much of the monies raised from this tax went more
toward the establishment and perpetuation of white rather than black public
schools.

On average, as table 5 demonstrates, the enthusiasm blacks maintained
toward public schooling in these predominantly black counties, if again mea-
sured by average daily attendance, was slightly more pronounced than their
white counterpart.[55] On average, roughly 82 percent of black children who
enrolled and 76 percent of white children who enrolled attended school.
More evident, however, were statistics that suggest the seemingly apparent
disregard black children held for attending school. Only 21,327 out of the
counties' 72,873 black children, or 28 percent, enrolled in a public school. In
contrast, 18,584 out of the counties 37,920 white children, or approximately
48 percent, enrolled in a public school. These statistics, if studied alone,
offered a direct challenge to the contentions by contemporary historians
that southern blacks strongly favored the possibility of attending school.[56]

Then again, as table 6 reveals, these totals are misleading and do not reflect a disregard for learning or a change in attitude on the part of blacks
toward the idea of universal schooling. Rather, they reflect the limited or
poor schooling opportunities available to black children. Charles C. Walden,
superintendent of Adams County, spoke of this when he summarized the
shoddy conditions of the schools established for blacks in the inaugural year.
"Several of these schools are wretchedly poor," stated Walden, "and all are
wholly unfit for school purposes; consequently the schools do not show
the full attendance our large colored population would warrant."[57] What is
more, it was evident that blacks still rushed to attend school because each
public school averaged over forty pupils. Adding to the argument that limited schooling opportunities were the primary reason for low enrollment
of black children were the relatively high pupils per school ratios in these
counties. As table 6 displays, the average school for black children had an
enrollment of 53 students, whereas schools for white children maintained
an average enrollment of 38 pupils. Schools for African American children
in at least five counties—Claiborne, Hinds, Holmes, Lowndes, and Noxu-

TABLE 5. School Population, Enrollment, and Average Attendance of
Black and White Youth in Fifteen Majority-Black Counties, 1870–1871

	Educable Youth		Enrolled Youth		Average Attendance	
County	Black	White	Black	White	Black	White
Adams	6,680	4,579	1,084	494	911	423
Carroll	4,631	3,870	1,106	1,923	831	1,574
Claiborne	3,263	1,192	934	574	721	459
DeSoto	5,117	5,254	1,225	2,975	1,198	2,115
Hinds	8,020	2,211	1,840	1,701	1,710	1,300
Holmes	4,954	2,444	2,400	1,300	1,600	900
Lowndes	6,882	2,486	2,205	1,086	1,772	775
Marshall	5,445	3,677	2,277	2,327	1,596	1,754
Noxubee	5,641	1,918	1,482	909	1,399	890
Panola	5,140	3,402	750	1,225	473	842
Tallahatchie	1,512	1,012	822	741	633	551
Tunica	1,537	399	563	71	487	50
Warren	5,086	2,678	2,266	932	1,573	669
Wilkinson	4,395	1,016	1,671	820	1,431	369
Yazoo	4,570	1,782	702	1,506	534	1,102
Total	72,873	37,920	21,327	18,584	16,869	13,773

Source: Adapted from *Annual Report of the Superintendent of Public Education of the State of Mississippi for the Year Ending December, 1871* (Jackson, Miss.: Kimball, Kaymond, State Printers, 1872), 124–31.

TABLE 6. Enrollment, Number of Public Schools, and Number of Enrolled Pupils per School in Fifteen Majority-Black Counties, 1870–1871

County	Enrolled Youth		Number of Public Schools		Number of Enrolled Pupils per School	
	Black	White	Black	White	Black	White
Adams	1,084	494	26	17	42	29
Carroll	1,106	1,923	22	45	50	43
Claiborne	934	574	15	15	62	38
DeSoto	1,225	2,975	40	85	31	35
Hinds	1,840	1,701	30	39	61	42
Holmes	2,400	1,300	31	29	77	45
Lowndes	2,205	1,086	29	24	76	45
Marshall	2,277	2,327	39	76	58	31
Noxubee	1,482	909	21	26	70	35
Panola	750	1,225	18	31	42	40
Tallahatchie	822	741	23	24	34	32
Tunica	563	71	13	2	43	35
Warren	2,266	932	33	16	68	58
Wilkinson	1,671	820	43	32	39	26
Yazoo	702	1,506	19	27	55	41
Total	21,327	18,584	402	488	53	38

Source: Adapted from *Annual Report of the Superintendent of Public Education of the State of Mississippi for the Year Ending December, 1871* (Jackson, Miss.: Kimball, Kaymond, State Printers, 1872), 124–31.

bee—maintained an enrollment of more than 60 pupils, while only public schools for white children in Warren County maintained a pupil enrollment above 50.[58]

Only schools for black children in DeSoto County had a lower enrolled pupil per school ratio than their white counterparts. However, as tables 5, 6, and 7 demonstrate, this should not be surprising given the very low educable to enrolled black student ratios. Tables 6 and 7 show that in virtually every majority-black county analyzed, a significant number of public schools still needed to be constructed, purchased, or established to appease *just* the educational interest of the enrolled black children in these counties, not all black children in the county. Data demonstrate that all of the aforementioned counties fell far short of appeasing the educational interests of blacks if a school was to be established—as the state's common school law specified— for the parents of every twenty-five children who petitioned to have a school or local institution of instruction.[59]

Additionally, sharp differences in the type of public schools offered to black and white children in these black-majority counties were also apparent. As table 8 indicates, most of the public schools—approximately 77 percent—established for black children were primary or elementary schools. While not illustrated, most—approximately 66 percent—were taught by black teachers.[60] The chief aim of these schools was to teach the three basics—reading, writing, and arithmetic. Poorer areas within these school districts established "mixed grade schools," or schools that taught every grade level, to accommodate the multiple educational levels and needs of students. These schools best accommodated the adolescent and older student who had little or no educational training or those deemed too old to attend a primary school. Most blacks fit within these parameters because they were largely uninstructed former slaves. Consequently, primary and mixed grade schools combined for over 90 percent of schools established for blacks in these counties. School officials felt that these schools would best introduce blacks to the learning process and systematically tackle the high illiteracy rate among freedpeople.[61]

By comparison, table 8 also reveals that only 17 percent of schools for white children in these counties were classified as primary schools. While speculative, this low percentage may be due to a lower illiteracy rate among whites. Illiterate whites, according to Pease's first annual report, constituted only about 10 percent of the state's population; albeit, what constituted a

TABLE 7. School Population, Enrollment Percentage, and Average Attendance Percentage of Black and White Youth in Fifteen Majority-Black Counties, 1870–1871

County	Educable Youth		Percent of Enrolled Youth		Average Attendance as a Percentage of Enrolled Children	
	Black	White	Black	White	Black	White
Adams	6,680	4,579	16.2	10.7	84.4	85.6
Carroll	4,631	3,870	23.8	49.8	75.1	81.8
Claiborne	3,263	1,192	22.1	48.1	100	79.9
DeSoto	5,117	5,254	23.9	56.6	97.7	71
Hinds	8,020	2,211	22.9	77	92.9	55.9
Holmes	4,954	2,444	48.4	53.2	66.7	100
Lowndes	6,882	2,486	32	43.6	80.3	71.3
Marshall	5,445	3,677	41.8	63.2	70	75.3
Noxubee	5,641	1,918	26.2	47.3	94.3	97.9
Panola	5,140	3,402	14.5	36	63	68.7
Tallahatchie	1,512	1,012	54.3	73.2	77	74.3
Tunica	1,537	399	36.6	17.8	86.5	70
Warren	5,086	2,678	30.9	34.8	100	71.7
Wilkinson	4,395	1,016	38	80.7	85.6	45
Yazoo	4,570	1,782	15.3	84.5	76	73.1
Total	72,873	37,920	27.9	48	82	76

Source: Adapted from *Annual Report of the Superintendent of Public Education of the State of Mississippi for the Year Ending December, 1871* (Jackson, Miss.: Kimball, Kaymond, State Printers, 1872), 124–31.

TABLE 8. Number of Public Schools for Enrolled Black and White
Youth in Fifteen Majority-Black Counties, by Type, 1870–1871

	NUMBER OF SCHOOLS FOR ENROLLED BLACK YOUTH				
COUNTY	Primary Schools	Grammar Schools	High Schools	Mixed Grade Schools	Black Total
Adams	22	4	—	—	26
Carroll	15	2	—	5	22
Claiborne	1	2	—	12	15
DeSoto	30	5	—	5	40
Hinds	10	8	—	12	30
Holmes	7	—	—	24	31
Lowndes	22	—	1	6	29
Marshall	36	3	—	—	39
Noxubee	21	—	—	—	21
Panola	—	—	—	18	18
Tallahatchie	23	—	—	—	23
Tunica	13	—	—	—	13
Warren	27	6	—	—	33
Wilkinson	39	3	1	—	43
Yazoo	18	—	—	1	19
TOTAL	284	33	2	83	402

Source: Adapted from *Annual Report of the Superintendent of Public Education of the State of Mississippi for the Year Ending December, 1871* (Jackson, Miss.: Kimball, Kaymond, State Printers, 1872), 124–31.

Primary Schools	Grammar Schools	High Schools	Mixed Grade Schools	White Total
	NUMBER OF SCHOOLS			
	FOR ENROLLED WHITE YOUTH			
7	8	2	—	17
4	32	7	2	45
2	1	1	11	15
10	64	11	—	85
7	9	2	21	39
—	—	—	29	9
7	—	8	9	24
27	39	10	—	76
6	4	—	16	26
—	—	—	31	31
—	—	—	24	24
—	—	—	2	2
4	10	1	1	16
9	21	2	—	32
1	—	2	24	27
84	188	46	170	488

literate person was unclear. Only about 2 percent of this illiteracy rate—at best—stemmed from these counties. One explanation for the low illiteracy rates of whites in these majority-black counties was the fact that these counties were also the state's richest counties because of the wealth generated by its resident cotton and slave owning planters. During the antebellum era, these landowning whites provided their children with private tutelage or sent them to private schools abroad. These combined practices would have ensured a lower illiteracy rate among this sector of the white population.[62]

More striking, however, was the number of high schools for black and white youth. In the majority-black counties analyzed, only two high schools with a combined enrollment of 580 pupils existed for black adolescents. Two additional black high schools—with a total enrollment of sixty students—existed in the entire state, and they resided in Madison County; a county where African Americans were 51 percent of the population.[63] Only 4 high schools in the entire state left blacks very little opportunity to advance their educational training beyond the grammar school. By contrast, there were 46 white high schools established in the inaugural year in these analyzed counties and a total of 78 scattered throughout the state.[64]

According to Pease, the primary goal of the high school was to prepare students for future leadership. In the initial years of public schools in Mississippi, however, a more pressing expectation was to use high schools to produce the state's teaching force. Based on their sheer numbers, whites who attended high school would be in a far better position than African Americans to become the leadership and teaching force of the state. In the first year alone, 5,045 whites were enrolled in a high school, while only 260 African Americans were enrolled. The ratio of whites to blacks in high school was 19 to 1. If as Pease proposed, the high school was the "keystone in the arch" of education and provided the missing element for a "complete and unbroken connection from the primary school up to the University," then African Americans seriously lagged behind and were in no position to quickly catch up.[65] Without high schools, African Americans could not attend colleges or universities; without high schools they could not prepare themselves for future leadership positions in their cities, counties, state, or nation.

. . .

Major disparities existed in the public school opportunities of black and white children in the state's majority-white counties as well. However, unlike the state's majority-black counties, these counties were relatively poorer, vaster, and less populated. Not surprisingly, the educational opportunities of black and white Mississippi children reflected this reality. Semi-independent white farmers were the counties' principal landowners and the majority of the residents—black or white—were tenant farmers or sharecroppers. Blacks in these counties, unlike those in majority-black counties, had an even poorer chance of obtaining an education beyond the primary level. And because of their limited numbers, economic leverage, and political voice, they had little chance of challenging this seemingly inevitable outcome. Blacks living in majority-white counties were, therefore, extremely vulnerable to the overall expectations whites had of them and had little recourse—besides migrating to another county or state—if they did not accept their schooling opportunities.

The educational statistics associated with these counties illustrate this reality. On the whole, white children constituted 70 percent of all children eligible for schooling in these majority-white counties, and they outnumbered black children by almost 25,000. This fact directly affected the public schooling opportunities of black children. As table 9 demonstrates, only 5,326 black children—or approximately 27 percent—enrolled in a public school in these counties.[66] However, approximately 74 percent of the enrolled black children in these schools attended on a regular basis. The most ironic finding associated with these statistics was how the enrollment percentage of black children in these selected majority-white counties compared to the enrollment percentage in the selected majority-black counties. Enrollment for black children in selected majority-white counties was almost four times lower than in selected majority-black counties; however, their total enrollment percentage differed by less than 1 percent.

By contrast, table 9 and table 10 also show that 44,324 white children in these selected majority-white counties—roughly 47 percent—enrolled in a public school. Reflective in this statistic, when compared to enrolled whites in the selected majority-black counties, was that fewer white children—about 3,100 fewer—in these selected majority-white counties enrolled in a school than white children residing in the selected majority-black counties. However, the fact that whites in these counties were mostly poor tenant farmers and sharecroppers and had few resources to meet the educational needs of its citizens probably had more to do with this educational coincidence than any other factor.[67] Disinterest in schools and labor demand could have been other factors.

TABLE 9. School Population, Enrollment, and Average Attendance of Black and White Youth in Fifteen Majority-White Counties, 1870–1871

County	Educable Youth		Enrolled Youth		Average Attendance	
	Black	White	Black	White	Black	White
Alcorn	1,003	3,416	239	1,960	181	1,250
Choctaw	3,134	5,948	644	4,300	600	3,600
Coahoma	1,780	6,041	769	296	507	240
Covington	602	1,113	85	595	42	298
Itawamba	397	2,653	55	—	40	190
Jackson	539	1,320	165	454	120	225
Leake	917	1,992	650	1,784	328	1,070
Lee	1,599	3,494	395	2,321	238	1,441
Montgomery	2,740	3,802	1,305	1,657	1,189	1,329
Pontotoc	1,294	3,329	476	1,875	380	1,247
Scott	1,389	1,557	150	1,060	100	710
Smith	583	2,038	59	1,085	23	771
Tippah	824	2,938	—	—	—	—
Tishomingo	424	3,598	—	3,200	—	2,342
Wayne	695	1,085	334	344	174	332
Total	17,920	44,324	5,326	20,931	3,922	15,045

Source: Adapted from *Annual Report of the Superintendent of Public Education of the State of Mississippi for the Year Ending December, 1871* (Jackson, Miss.: Kimball, Raymond, State Printers, 1872), 124–31.

Indeed poverty and labor demands, alongside considerable resistance, most likely accounted for the lower enrollment and attendance percentages of black students in these white counties. As table 11 shows, blacks in these counties were very enthusiastic about their schooling opportunities. Approximately 74 percent of the black youth that enrolled in a public school

TABLE 10. School Population, Enrollment Percentage, and Average
Attendance Percentage of Black and White Youth in Fifteen
Majority-White Counties, 1870–1871

County	Educable Youth		Percent of Enrolled Youth		Average Attendance as a Percentage of Enrolled Children	
	Black	White	Black	White	Black	White
Alcorn	1,003	3,416	23.8	57.3	75.7	63.7
Choctaw	3,134	5,948	20.5	72.2	93.1	83.7
Coahoma	1,780	6,041	43.2	4.8	65.9	81
Covington	602	1,113	14.1	53.4	49.4	50
Itawamba	397	2,653	13.8	—	72.7	—
Jackson	539	1,320	30.6	34.3	72.7	49.5
Leake	917	1,992	70.8	89.5	50.4	59.9
Lee	1,599	3,494	24.7	66.4	60.2	62.1
Montgomery	2,740	3,802	47.6	43.5	91.1	80.2
Pontotoc	1,294	3,329	36.7	56.3	79.8	66.5
Scott	1,389	1,557	10.7	68	66.7	66.9
Smith	583	2,038	10.1	53.2	38.9	71
Tippah	824	2,938	—	—	—	—
Tishomingo	424	3,598	—	89	—	73.1
Wayne	695	1,085	48	31.7	52	96.5
Total	17,920	44,324	27.4	47.2	73.6	71.8

Source: Adapted from *Annual Report of the Superintendent of Public Education of the State of Mississippi for the Year Ending December, 1871* (Jackson, Miss.: Kimball, Kaymond, State Printers, 1872), 124–31.

TABLE 11. Enrollment, Number of Public Schools, and Number of Enrolled Pupils per School in Fifteen Majority-White Counties, 1870–1871

County	Enrolled Youth		Number of Public Schools		Number of Enrolled Pupils per School	
	Black	White	Black	White	Black	White
Alcorn	239	1,960	6	45	40	43
Choctaw	644	4,300	13	72	50	60
Coahoma	769	296	12	10	64	30
Covington	85	595	2	22	42	27
Itawamba	55	—	2	50	27	—
Jackson	165	454	5	13	33	35
Leake	650	1,784	10	35	65	51
Lee	395	2,321	6	50	66	46
Montgomery	1,305	1,657	22	27	59	61
Pontotoc	476	1,875	12	46	40	41
Scott	150	1,060	5	31	30	34
Smith	59	1,085	2	40	30	27
Tippah	—	—	9	43	—	—
Tishomingo	—	3,200	3	42	—	76
Wayne	334	344	4	28	84	12
Total	5,326	20,931	113	554	47	38

Source: Adapted from *Annual Report of the Superintendent of Public Education of the State of Mississippi for the Year Ending December, 1871* (Jackson, Miss.: Kimball, Kaymond, State Printers, 1872), 124–31.

attended on a regular basis, though very few schooling opportunities existed for them. Whites' refusal to contribute their taxes to schools for black children and the relative impoverishment of blacks were certainly two factors that limited the schooling options of black children in these counties. Blacks in these counties could rely only on themselves, and most of the school-houses for black children in these majority-white counties were financed and constructed at the private expense of blacks.[68]

Their meager resources had a significant impact on the number of pupils a school for black children could enroll. As table 11 further indicates, public schools for black children in these majority-white counties had a higher pupil per school ratio than public schools for white children. Schools for black children averaged forty-seven pupils per school; again, primarily because of the few public schools existing for black children in these counties. This rate was very comparable to the black pupil per school ratio in the analyzed majority-black counties. At least six out of the thirteen counties with complete data averaged more than fifty black children per public school, with Wayne County averaging the highest pupil per school ratio. Its four schools for black children averaged an astounding *eighty-four* students. Equally important, however, were the limited opportunities available to African American parents who might have wanted to enroll their child in a public school. If by some chance all of the educable black children in these counties wished to attend a public school, the schools for black children would have averaged 172 *students*, an utterly impossible number to accommodate.[69] As was the case in the majority-black counties analyzed, the initial efforts of school officials in these majority-white counties fell far short of appeasing the common school law and the educational ambitions of blacks.[70]

Comparably, public schools for white children averaged thirty-eight students, and given the discrepancies, it was quite apparent that most of the resources in these counties were aimed at appeasing the interests — educational and otherwise — of whites. Table 12 further extends the argument that most of the resources in these majority-white counties went toward the educational benefit of white children. The fact that the enrolled white students in these counties, while fewer, had almost seventy more public schools and nearly fifty more private schools than whites in the majority-black counties, and that the number of private schools for whites exceeded the number of public schools for blacks in these counties, illustrates this assertion. These educational developments occurred in spite of the impoverished economy

TABLE 12. Number of Public and Private Schools for Black and White
Educable Youth in the Black and White Counties Analyzed, 1870–1871

Counties	Black Schools			White Schools		
	Public	Private	Total	Public	Private	Total
Black counties	402	14	416	488	70	558
White counties	113	5	118	554	117	671
Total from analyzed counties	515	19	534	1,042	187	1,229
State total	862	53	915	1,739	381	2,120

Source: Adapted from *Annual Report of the Superintendent of Public Education of the State of Mississippi for the Year Ending December, 1871* (Jackson, Miss.: Kimball, Kaymond, State Printers, 1872), 124–31.

of many of these counties and the persistent objection on the part of whites
to the state's public school tax structure. It is arguable that almost 85 percent of these counties' common school fund, given the black to white public
school ratio, went primarily toward the establishment and maintenance of
schools for white children and there was little blacks could do to challenge
or redirect these discriminatory practices.

Another way to identify where resources were directed in these majority-
white counties is to examine the type of schooling that was offered. Similar
to the majority-black counties, the type of schooling opportunities available to black children in these majority-white counties reflected both their
educational level as well as the overall sentiment whites maintained toward
blacks and their educational advancement. As in the majority-black counties, schools for black children, as table 13 indicates, in these majority-white
counties were exclusively primary and mixed grade schools, and approximately 77 percent of the educable black youth, or 4,116 black children, in
these counties attended a primary school. The fact that schools for black
children were solely primary and mixed grade schools, and mostly taught
by native-born whites, were a cause of concern to Mississippi blacks. While
most Mississippi blacks were overwhelmingly illiterate and former slaves,
they were, as the state's grassroots missionary and bureau school officials
demonstrated in prior years, "quick and eager learners." Yet, as table 13

shows, no resemblance of an intermediate school—grammar school—or high school existed for black youth in these counties once they advanced beyond the primary level. Moreover, given the state's overall antagonistic attitudes toward integrated schooling, there was very little chance for even the most ambitious or accepted black child to attend a grammar school or high school established for whites. At best, blacks could only hope to acquire additional instruction in one of the mixed grade schools available, and if this was not possible, then to relocate to another county or state, or be satisfied with what learning they had acquired. These limited schooling options did little for the blacks aspiring to use their educational training to obtain employment outside of domestic work and sharecropping. And, it did very little to extend the aspirations black parents had for their children's future opportunities as citizens. Primary schools, at best, gave blacks the basics, but they would not advance many beyond the state's lowest occupations. In the end, the circumscribed schooling opportunities that blacks received in the initial year of public schooling invariably prepared them more for a life of servitude and second-class citizenship than for a life of meaningful opportunities and citizenship.

Schooling options for most white children in these majority-white counties were not too different than their black counterpart. They too attended mostly primary and mixed grade schools; however, there existed a number of grammar schools and some high schools scattered throughout these counties for white children to advance their learning if they so desired. Primary and mixed grade schools constituted 80 percent of the white public schools in these majority-white counties. The establishment of so many of these cost-efficient schools directly reflected attempts on the part of county officials to balance the educational opportunities of whites with their limited fiscal budget. Moreover, the creation of so many mixed grade schools also suggested that a number of adolescent or older whites had very little academic training prior to the Civil War and were more than likely illiterate.

Further supporting this argument was the relatively few high schools for white youth. Just over 1,000 white students attended a high school in these counties. By comparison, 2,465 whites in the previously analyzed majority-black counties attended a high school, and this number doubled by the end of the school system's second year.[71] Nonetheless, whites in these majority-white counties, as opposed to their black counterpart, had an ample number of options regarding their educational advancement. This reality not only

TABLE 13. Number of Public Schools for Enrolled Black and White Youth in Fifteen Majority-White Counties, by Type, 1870–1871

| | NUMBER OF SCHOOLS FOR ENROLLED BLACK YOUTH | | | | |
COUNTY	Primary Schools	Grammar Schools	High Schools	Mixed Grade Schools	Black Total
Alcorn	5	—	—	1	6
Choctaw	13	—	—	—	13
Coahoma	12	—	—	—	12
Covington	2	—	—	—	2
Itawamba	—	—	—	2	2
Jackson	5	—	—	—	5
Leake	9	—	—	1	10
Lee	—	—	—	6	6
Montgomery	16	—	—	6	22
Pontotoc	11	—	—	1	12
Scott	5	—	—	—	5
Smith	2	—	—	—	2
Tippah	—	—	—	9	9
Tishomingo	3	—	—	—	3
Wayne	4	—	—	—	4
Total	87	0	0	26	113

Source: Adapted from *Annual Report of the Superintendent of Public Education of the State of Mississippi for the Year Ending December, 1871* (Jackson, Miss.: Kimball, Raymond, State Printers, 1872) 124–31.

NUMBER OF SCHOOLS FOR ENROLLED WHITE YOUTH				
Primary Schools	Grammar Schools	High Schools	Mixed Grade Schools	White Total
26	—	—	19	45
15	57	—	—	72
5	—	—	5	10
19	—	—	3	22
—	—	—	50	50
—	—	—	13	13
9	1	—	25	35
—	—	—	50	50
10	10	1	6	27
1	—	3	42	46
24	4	3	—	31
15	—	—	25	40
—	—	—	43	43
17	22	3	—	42
11	6	—	11	28
152	100	10	292	554

guaranteed them the possibility of obtaining many more years of additional schooling than blacks, but it also guaranteed that they would be better educated and prepared to fulfill bureaucratic and political duties—locally and statewide—when such opportunities presented themselves, as well as seek employment beyond menial labor and sharecropping.

. . .

The delegates at the Constitutional Convention of 1868 sought to create a public school system inclusive of all Mississippi children, irrespective of their background. One of the primary goals of public schools was to use them to assist former slaves in their transition from slavery to freedom. What they did not envision, however, was that the very school system they proposed and established would systematically limit the educational opportunities of blacks. Blacks were attending school in record numbers, but the type of schooling they received and the resources afforded to their schools were severely circumscribed. Black youth were relegated to attending schools designed to teach them only the basics. Consequently, the most that black parents could expect their children to gain from these schools was an elementary education. Despite their apparent limitations, public schools served as a promising supplement to the aspirations of freedpeople who wanted to use schools to aid them in becoming citizens. They provided the first schooling opportunities for the majority of African Americans in the state, and in many ways introduced to freedpeople the necessary foundational knowledge needed to secure freedom and citizenship in slavery's aftermath. But as data illustrate, the knowledge and opportunities Mississippi blacks received in these public schools—if the pattern continued—would only prepare them for the most menial of opportunities and very little more.

5 · PUBLIC SCHOOLS, 1871–1875

In the babel of many voices arising in the South, it is difficult at
times to determine just what is the attitude of the southern white people
toward the education of the Negro. It is frequently asked: Do southern
people believe that the Negro can and should be educated?
—STUART GRAYSON NOBLE, *Forty Years*, 1918

. . .

The sentiments of former masters as to education are by no means elevated
to the standard of public school systems at the North. General taxation
for this purpose is questioned. Paying for "educating other people's children"
for the public welfare, is not well understood. Quite inferior schools are
thought sufficient for the colored race. But with universal suffrage conceded,
surely the freedmen's vote should be intelligent; as the colored man is to
become a part of society, he must have substantially its privileges; taxation
for schools implied the unquestioned right to have schools.
—JOHN W. ALVORD, 1869

. . .

The colored citizens would never be less citizens than they are today.
—GOVERNOR-ELECT ADELBERT AMES, 1873

Mississippi's dual public school system, despite its limitations, was a promising start for African Americans. On the whole, blacks were very receptive
to their initial public school opportunities. While they promptly recognized
that their opportunities were not equal to whites or reflective of their total
need, they nonetheless viewed public schools as a progressive beginning.
They maintained this attitude because public schools gave them an additional and virtually permanent prospect to improve their personal and professional lives and to demonstrate to all naysayers that African Americans

were capable and deserving of equal consideration under the law. They held this attitude in the forthcoming years — 1871 to 1875 — that lead up to the end of Reconstruction efforts in Mississippi. This chapter chronicles these years. It documents the evolution of public schools and how blacks sought to use their acquired learning to progress their overall livelihood and how whites would respond to these black initiatives.

Regardless of the gains made by African Americans in emancipation, most whites still regarded freedpeople as inferior, even subhuman, and accordingly deemed them to be, at best, freed laborers rather than slaves. It was a nearly impossible to get whites to accept African Americans as a people deserving of equality under the law. African Americans were their laborers and nothing more, and the recent public school initiatives threatened to dismantle these pseudosociological characterizations and economic expectations whites assumed of blacks. Schools challenged the very foundation upon which white culture and opportunities in Mississippi were built upon. Emancipation may have freed African Americans, but schools — if allotted the proper attention and resources — threatened to make African Americans citizens equal to whites. This result seemed inevitable if whites continued to disregard the educational aspirations of blacks and allowed northerners and former slaves to determine the future direction of schools for African Americans. No newspaper illustrated this fear of blacks gaining equality better than the *Hinds County Gazette*. "We have it on good authority that the public school teachers imported from the North into several of the counties," asserted the editor of the *Gazette*, "are Radical emissaries in disguise, who not only insidiously inculcate the political creed of that party, but are propagandist of its social equality doctrines."[1]

Still no evidence corroborates the *Gazette*'s theory of the intent or efforts on the part of teachers from the North to "inculcate social equality doctrines" among blacks. At best, they encouraged black children to think for themselves, value self-sufficiency and thrift, and to use their educational training to improve their personal and professional conditions. What most likely prompted the persistent distrust white Mississippians had of northern teachers were the intimate social relations most maintained with their students and their families. Northern-born public school teachers frequently boarded with respectable black families when they were unable to secure boarding from antagonistic whites. While innocent in nature, this persistent practice of white women taking up residence under the roof of even "good colored folk" piercingly disregarded the social expectations and mannerisms that firmly established Mississippi's color line. Thus, it should come as no surprise, Stuart Grayson Noble remarked, that the actions of these teachers "quite reasonably fell under suspicion of Southerners unused to such intimacy with the colored race."[2]

What continued to frustrate white Mississippians even more were the new taxes imposed on them for the support of public schools, especially those for black children. Superintendent H. R. Pease, in some ways agreed with the frustrations of whites regarding the new tax system. He recognized that some county officials were not properly collecting or distributing the funds raised for schools. In his mind, the system of taxation adopted in Mississippi was flawed because there was no uniformity. But Pease, unlike disgruntled whites, was far more concerned with the way taxes were levied and collected than with who benefited from these funds. Still, in defense of the new burden white taxpayers endured, Pease said:

> The organic law requires taxation for all State purposes to be uniform. Experience shows, that the present system of special county taxation is not uniform in its operation. Some counties levy a tax sufficient to defray the school expenses, others levy none at all. In many instances, the school tax levied has been absolutely burdensome upon the people. Again, there are counties in the State where, if the maximum limit of taxes were levied upon the assessed value of taxable property, it would not afford revenue enough to support the schools twenty days during the year.[3]

Pease well understood the endemic economic crisis in Mississippi and its property owners' displeasure with financing a public school system that catered very little to their personal or profession self-interests. His remarks were more of a plea than a suggestion for the state legislature to revamp the way they obtained funds for public schools. He wanted them to abandon the common school fund model borrowed from northern states and adjust the state's school law so that public schools would be supported through government expenditures and not primarily through local taxation.[4] He believed this would ultimately make public schools more appealing to all Mississippians and would allow more black and white children the opportunity to attend one.

The disapproval whites had of public schools, however, had as much to do with who attended them as it did with who funded them. Whites simply contested the idea of blacks receiving any type of academic instruction. Reconstruction traditionalists who have devoted any attention to this subject have argued differently, however. They maintained that the state's tax system, and not the idea of universal schooling for African Americans, was the primary reason whites objected to the state's first comprehensive public school system.[5] Yet this interpretation is woefully incorrect, because it dismissed the fact that much of the debate over school taxes centered on landowning white farmers having to support a system of public schools for former slaves. Moreover, these histories ignored or minimized the repeated acts of violence specifically directed toward blacks, their children, and their schools.

The reality was that race was a motivating factor in every aspect of Mississippi's postbellum political economy. Therefore, the majority of the state's public school critics candidly disapproved of white taxpayers having to support the establishment and maintenance of schools for black children. White taxpayers might have been satisfied with a public school system that collected and distributed taxes based solely on the proportion raised by each racial group. Congressman Charles E. Hooker, a Democrat, epitomized this sentiment when he argued that Mississippi and many other southern states were being unduly taxed to support the establishment and maintenance of a dual public school system. He concluded that Mississippi should be granted the legislative privilege that a few northern states exercised, which was to collect and distribute school funds in proportion to the amount each racial group paid.[6]

This proportional distribution proposition probably would not have silenced the many public school critics in Mississippi. In addition to their disapproval of white landowners funding schools for black children, they continually compared the state's new taxes to the amount collected and distributed prior to the war. Taxes levied for the common school fund, while significantly higher than those collected during the antebellum era, were relatively insignificant when compared to the total tax revenue. The common school fund was not the only, or even the primary, purpose of taxation as most of the monies collected and spent went toward the rebuilding of levies and railroads and the restoration of Jackson, the state capital. But it was the first time in Mississippi history that landed white elites did not politically decide its current tax structure and were concomitantly required to pay taxes for concerns beyond their immediate responsibilities. White property owners for the first time paid taxes for general purposes, such as the improvement of towns and cities, roads, streets, public buildings, water, gas, and the state's overall repair from the Civil War; damages many white landholders — most ex-Confederates — were greatly responsible for creating.

Thus, while the postbellum tax rates might have appeared high or excessive to "old property-holders of the South, accustomed to aristocratic governments, conducted by property-holders," who maintained similar interests, they were not excessive when compared to the taxes levied and collected in other southern states or even northern states with smaller or comparable populations.[7] Moreover, those who repeatedly complained of the high taxes for public schools, especially schools for African American children, disregarded the funds collected from the poll tax, which blacks readily paid. This money constituted the largest proportion of the common school funds collected in majority-black counties when county supervisors could not efficiently collect revenue from white property holders. As important, disgruntled landholders overlooked the fact that despite the limited property ownership of blacks, their labor created property — cotton — and produced the wealth that white farmers used to pay their taxes. By this latter observation alone, African Americans — at the very least — were entitled to have a system of free public schools on their behalf.

Still, few white Mississippians acknowledged the parallels between black labor, public schools for African Americans, and white wealth. Additionally, most discounted the poll tax contributions made by blacks and continued to look to the antebellum past to rationalize the state's ever-increasing taxes and for what purposes they were being levied. This outlook only produced greater frustration among landowning whites still attempting to recover their losses from the war. This was especially true of white small farmers, who were barely beginning to record a profit a half decade after the Civil War. Historian J. Mills Thorton illustrated that the postbellum tax structure — regardless of how it compared to other states — was a particular burden to white small farmers in Mississippi because they were "paying 2 to 4 percent of their total cash income, and from 8 to 10 percent of their discretionary income in taxes."[8] Some had their property confiscated because of their inability to pay their taxes. Adding to their frustrations was another cotton crop failure, the third in the past five years. In late 1870, when only a fraction of the cotton harvest could be salvaged, most of the state's planters refused to pay their black laborers, let alone a school tax designated to improve the status of their children.

This frustration, in the latter part of 1870 and the early months of 1871, went well beyond the typical verbal accusations of "Radical corruption" and manifested into terrorism and violence as the state's Ku Klux Klan chapters and other disgruntled whites waged a "taxpayers' revolt." They commenced to murdering and whipping any and every person that seemed to favor the current political, economic, and social conditions. These disorders largely prevailed in the state's northern counties and its easternmost counties, bordering Alabama; and they included, but were not exclusive to, the counties of Alcorn, Chickasaw, Choctaw, Itawamba, Kemper, Lauderdale, Leake, Lee, Lowndes, Monroe, Noxubee, Oktibbeha, Pontotoc, Prentiss, Tippah, Tishomingo, Union, and Winston.[9] The actions of the Klan and other white militia groups represented the brutal embodiment of disillusioned Democrats and white property owners, even if they despised the Klan or were not members themselves. In any case, as Allen Trelease has asserted, these whites, whether by active participation or not, used the Klan as their vehicle of protest "against the newfangled ideas and costs of Radical Reconstruction."[10]

Not surprisingly, Mississippi public schools, in particular public schools and teachers for black children, were the primary targets. The Klan's assault on black schooling was symbolic because it signified their censure of blacks and their schools as the primary reason for their current difficulties. In their minds, black schools cost money, teachers and furnishings for these schools cost money, and the fact that blacks were attending school and not at work in cotton fields cost white landholders money. The Klan's attack on schools for African Americans also indicated the various successes in the schools, as blacks continued to use them to achieve full citizenship.

The violence was swift and brutal. Colonel A. P. Huggins, school superintendent of Monroe County, testified at the state's Ku Klux Klan hearings that Mississippi Klansmen "were entirely opposed to the free-school system."[11] Huggins knew this because the Klan paid him a visit late one evening to inform him to discontinue public school operations in Monroe County. When he asked them what the county's children would do for schooling, one Klansmen replied, "whites could do as they had always done before; they could educate their own children; and so far as Negroes were concerned, they did not need educating, only work."[12] When Huggins ignored their warning, he was nearly beaten to death by the Klan and forced to leave the county for being "the instrument for collecting the taxes" and because he hired "foreign-born social equality propagandists" as teachers.[13]

Without question Klan violence was particularly damaging to the new public school opportunities of blacks. In Monroe County, for example, in addition to Huggins being beaten and run out of town, Klan violence closed all twenty-six schools by early March 1871.[14] A month later, the Klan threatened to harm the board of school directors if they too did not leave town, and the terrorist group refused to allow them to collect any school-related funds.[15] Among those "called upon" by the Klan was Sarah Allen, a white American Missionary Association (AMA) teacher from Illinois who stayed in Monroe County when the AMA discontinued her grassroots school. Approximately eighty Klansmen terrorized her during the midnight hour and warned her to leave the county or suffer the consequences. To the surprise of many she stayed, but southern-born Congregationalist and fellow public school teacher Rev. Thomas S. Galloway promptly left the county after his Klan warning.[16] In fact, most schoolteachers left in fear, sometimes deprived of their pay, after receiving a warning from the Klan.

Similar assaults occurred in the counties of Lowndes, Noxubee, and Pontotoc during the first year of public schooling. White terrorism was so prevalent in Lowndes County that J. N. Bishop, the county superintendent, lamentably informed Pease that "to give you each and every case of unlawful disturbance against our free public schools in this county would swell my communication to an unexpected length."[17] He noted that three of the county's schools for black children were compelled to close because of Klan intimidation, and that the Klan had visited and threatened several of his teachers.[18] The intimidation and violence was so pervasive, Lowndes County blacks refused to send their children to school until local and school authorities subdued the hostilities.

In 1870–71, white terrorism was so extensive in Noxubee County that it forced an unspecified number of blacks to migrate elsewhere for safety, better work conditions, and schooling opportunities. As County Superintendent Charles B. Ames noted, Noxubee County "freedmen preferred working and living in parts where their children" could have the "benefit of attending school" free of hostilities.[19] Pontotoc County Superintendent, St. Clair Laurence, understood Ames's frustrations and further articulated the hindrance the Klan and other white vigilantes had on the schooling opportunities of black children. "There exists much prejudice," stated Laurence, "against the public school system . . . [and] efforts were made, in June last, to close all the colored schools by the Ku Klux."[20] Laurence, like every other county superintendent, found it virtually impossible to secure and keep teachers in schools for African Americans. This was especially true after the Klan repeatedly visited and intimidated every teacher of black children in the county. Even after the assaults ceased, Laurence found only three individuals willing to teach black children the following year.

In Winston County, the Klan chapter burned down every school for African Americans as a demonstration of their disapproval of blacks having the same rights as whites to attend a public school. The same was true in Chickasaw County. Besides burning down the three schoolhouses for black children — one a black church, the other two were constructed and paid for by Chickasaw blacks — the Klan was dead set on making an example of their schoolteachers. Cornelius McBride, a young Scot, and F. B. Emmens, a Chickasaw white, were terribly beaten by the Klan for instructing black children.[21] Attempting to explain these assaults to his superior, County Superintendent A. J. Jamison, stated that he was "unable to account for these outrages," aside from "local whites' severe opposition to colored schools."[22]

In 1871, white violence and the Klan were so destructive that Governor Alcorn contemplated the establishment of an all-black militia to combat the lawlessness. Alcorn instead created a seven-man secret service team to infiltrate these organizations and put an end their activities. However, before year's end, limited resources and personnel, coupled with the Klan's extensive activities and white Mississippians' resistance to the secret service team, abruptly upended this initiative.[23] In April 1871, Congress passed the Enforcement Act, better known as the Ku Klux Klan Act, which accompanied this secret service initiative. The Ku Klux Klan Act outlawed all unauthorized militia activity and threatened to imprison any member of these organizations.[24] In Mississippi, this decree proved to be much more effective than the seven-man secret service team, as a number of Klansmen were arrested and indicted. Few were ever prosecuted by their peers for their actions, however.

These legal measures did not halt white terrorism or future Klan assaults against blacks and their schools. In fact, they may have exacerbated them. In Amite County, for example, despite the new laws, Klan members continued to threaten and assault all persons associated with the county's schools for

African Americans.[25] In Choctaw County, Superintendent R. B. Wooley reported that the new law did nothing to deter the violence, as many of the county's schools for black children were still being disrupted or destroyed by the Klan. The terrorist group set fire to four of the thirteen schoolhouses for black children in the county; two were churches.[26] In Oktibbeha County, the Klan chapter set a school for African Americans on fire while in session. As the teacher rushed his students from the burning structure, Klansmen attempted to deter his efforts by pelting the children with stones as they blindly hurried out of the burning smoke-filled structure.[27]

The nation's ban of the Klan and other clandestine organizations was wholly ineffective without the willingness of local authorities to enforce the law. Schools for black children were still being destroyed or upended without fear of repercussion, and teachers working in a school for African Americans were still being assaulted without recourse. Throughout the state, teachers and students continued to work and learn in fear for their lives. For instance, well after the enactment of the Ku Klux Klan Act, teachers of black children in Warren County continued to be harassed by the Klan. Teachers and advocates of black education received elaborate and threatening letters by the Klan advising them to leave the county or suffer the consequences. William Snider, who taught a school for black children, would never forget the letter he received. The Klan sent him a letter that found him guilty of "associating with Negroes in preference to the white race, as God ordained" and guilty of being an active Republican.[28] It stated that if Snider did not want the Klan to "visit" him he had three days to leave the county forever. Snider promptly left.

Calvin Holly and D. Webster received similar written threats. Holly, a northern-born black who taught black schoolchildren in Meridian refused to heed the demands stated in his letter, so the Klan promptly burned down the black church that housed his school. The same thing happened to D. Webster, who also taught black schoolchildren in Meridian. Webster, who was African American and a native son to Meridian, refused to be intimidated by the county's Klan chapter, so they made an example of Webster and burned down his schoolhouse. When Meridian blacks rebuilt the school in defiance of the Klan assault, the Klan returned and promptly burned it down again; they also beat Webster nearly to death.[29] Similar assaults on blacks, their teachers, and schools occurred in Meridian well after the passing of the Ku Klux Klan Act. The violence forced a number of teachers to leave or discontinue their work. It also forced a number of black parents to keep their children away from schools.[30]

Additional examples of the damaging effects that the Klan and other white terrorist groups had on the schooling of blacks could readily be provided; however, they would only serve as supplementary illustrations. At the heart of all these examples is the fact that the Klan severely disrupted the already limited schooling opportunities established for African Americans. The continued violence should help contextualize some of the data illustrated in chapter 4 that showed why few African American children attended a public school during the inaugural year. Intimidation and violence made African Americans rethink their attitudes toward sending their children to school, and they made teachers rethink their decisions to teach in Mississippi. Even if African Americans and teachers in schools for black children never witnessed or experienced a Klan attack, the ever-present fear of it was enough to keep them away from schools. And while the Klan represented the ambitions and actions of only a small minority of whites in Mississippi, they nonetheless roamed the state at will. Most white Mississippians detested the Klan and its activities, but few objected to its results. Klan chaos solidified the continuation of a racial caste system and secured to whites many of the privileges they enjoyed during the antebellum era. They kept blacks from voting, renting or purchasing land, and from collectively exercising their newfound liberties. They stunted the growing economic leverage of Mississippi blacks and shifted control over their labor choices back into the hands of landowning whites. Concomitantly, their presence terrified whites supportive of emancipation, black suffrage, or public schools for African Americans. As James Lusk Alcorn recalled shortly before his appointment as Mississippi governor, "Several plantations and buildings were seen burning as a punishment to benevolent whites for renting land to freedmen."[31] These attacks served as daily reminders to whites and blacks alike that under no circumstances was support for the reconstruction of Mississippi or the advancement of African Americans to be tolerated.

. . .

By the fall of 1871, the terror that plagued blacks and their public school opportunities abruptly ended with the arrival of additional Union troops in the most destructive parts of the state. Consequently, the 1871–72 academic year opened with very little outside interference. School officials pressed forward with a dual public school system at the taxpayers' expense. They built additional schoolhouses, hired more teachers, and continued to adjust the educational bureaucracy to make it more efficient. This progress occurred despite continued tacit resistance on the part of white property holders to contribute their apportionment of the school taxes. Between 1872 and 1875, there were many general improvements to public schools in Mississippi. During the 1871–72 academic year, an additional 432 schoolhouses were built and many more rented. This expansion increased the total number of public schools from 3,450 to 4,650; an increase of approximately 35 percent.[32] The growth in schools also meant a growth in teachers. The number of public school teachers increased almost 33 percent, from 3,193 to 4,800, and this occurred in spite of an eight-dollar-a-month decrease in teacher pay.[33] There were additional costs as well. Numerous public schools, destroyed by the violence, had to be rebuilt. In some ways, schools for African Americans were starting all over again, as there would be few gains considering the loss of so many teachers and school facilities.

By 1874, it appeared that the state, for the most part, had a functional public school system. In total the expended finances for the construction of schoolhouses, school buildings, or their repairs was just over $35,000. This sum was $141,858 less than the previous year. The lack of attacks on public schools most likely was the reason for the lower expenditure. Between 1872 and 1875, perhaps the most challenging task that confronted Mississippi's public school system was how to become more uniform and efficient. The length of the school term and the types of textbooks that each school used were major problems, because they varied from county to county during the first decade of the system's existence. However, more pressing to school officials than this recurring problem was how to reduce the unnecessary expenses associated with the governance and management of public schools. In the system's first year, a small, but nonetheless significant, portion of the common school fund was mismanaged, misappropriated, and in some cases, embezzled by county directors. Moreover, the cost of keeping county directors exceeded their value.[34] An estimated $58,000 in the 1870–71 school year and almost $70,000 in the 1871–72 academic year went toward just the travel reimbursement and *per diem* of the county directors.[35] This cost did not include their salary. As early as the beginning of the 1871–72 school year, Superintendent Pease recommended abolishing the current system of county supervision. "Experience proves that the system of County Directors," explained Pease, "now in operation, is productive of much evil, without advantage, and very expensive."[36] By the opening of the 1873–74 school year, Pease reorganized the system's bureaucracy. The county boards of directors were abolished, and their duties and responsibilities were bestowed upon the board of supervisors. Pease additionally amended the school law so that county superintendents received a fixed salary and teachers were paid according to certification.[37] The 1874 school laws declared that the assessed valuation of the taxable state property was to be no more than four mills on the dollar.[38] This provision spoke directly to Pease's discontent with the structure of the common school fund and his attempt to relieve taxpayers of the added pressure of additional or higher taxes. These changes remained undisturbed until 1876 when the state's new Democratic government abolished and revised the school laws.

The length of the school term, as mentioned, was also a major concern for Mississippi's school officials. Public schools were supposed to remain in session at least four months out of the year. However, as Pease noted, most schools never achieved this requirement. This was particularly true among schools for black children. Schools for black children in Bolivar, Lee, and Leake counties barely stayed opened twenty days.[39] In many ways economic demands determined a school term as African Americans — young and old — were expected to be in the fields during the critical months of the cotton season. In Alcorn County, for example, the school term was four months in 1870–71 and five months in 1871–72, but its schools were only conducted during the "leisure months" of the cotton cycle, that was, before the planting and after the gathering of crops.[40] In Amite County, labor demands and poverty, according to County Superintendent William H. Yeandle, forced many struggling black and white parents to keep their children away from the schools and at home to work in the fields.[41] These observations regarding the duration of public school terms were not exceptional. Between 1871 and 1875, the typical school term for most public schools for black children were conducted in the manner expressed by Benton County's superintendent, G. N. Dickerson. Dickerson was quick to note that most of the schools for blacks did not run quite four months because of economic demands. Black students in Benton County, said Dickerson, "like most black pupils in the state . . . had to stop to labor, so I thought it best to stop the schools in consequence."[42]

Creating a structured and uniformed curriculum was an equally vexing challenge. The biggest dilemma was how to achieve this goal on an already meager budget. School officials soundly believed that a uniformed curriculum across the state would most efficiently abolish high illiteracy rates and lead to the overall education of Mississippi's poorest. They further believed that the curriculum, for the most part, should be classically, and not industrially, centered. This meant that greater emphasis should be placed on teaching and learning the rudiments of reading, writing, arithmetic, and the humanities, rather than on a specific agricultural or mechanical trade. This expectation was written into both the 1870 and 1874 school laws. Second-grade schools—primary, grammar, and most mixed-grade schools—were expected to teach orthography, reading, writing, grammar, geography, and rudimentary arithmetic.[43] First-grade schools—mostly high schools, but some grammar schools—in addition to a more advanced level of the aforementioned subjects, would also teach U.S. history and English composition.[44] While a number of historians of education identify industrial education as the primary curriculum for African Americans in the South, in Mississippi, it would not take root until after the mid-1880s.

At the county level, the call for a standard curriculum was a request few counties could achieve due to a lack of funds; accordingly, black and white parents were asked to contribute. Once again blacks were at a disadvantage, because the only text available in the black home that would provide any semblance of uniformity was the Bible or New Testament tracts that the AMA distributed in previous years. The same was true in poor white households. But this was something top school officials, arguably, already knew. In 1870, the school law stated explicitly that "the Bible shall not be excluded from the Schools of the State."[45] The rationale was simple. The Bible was available in virtually every Mississippi home and until standardized textbooks could be uniformly distributed across school districts, it would be available for use as the school's primary reader. Notwithstanding, the 1874–75 annual school report accounted for a variety of texts used in the state's school system, and this lends credence to the argument that school officials had not yet established a uniform curriculum. For example, there were three blueback spellers to choose from: Webster's Speller, the Union Speller, and the Holmes Speller; Wilson, McGuffey, Sanders, and Holmes comprised the four readers available; there were five grammar books to choose from; three geography textbooks, four history textbooks, and three arithmetic texts.[46] While it is nearly impossible to assess the utility and effectiveness of these textbooks in the classroom, Stuart Grayson Noble noted that many of these texts were interchangeably used well into the 1890s.[47]

The positive changes within public schools did not redirect the fear and antagonism whites continued to maintain toward them. In 1873–74, public schools would once more come under attack from landowning whites. The new concern was ensuing talk of compulsory attendance. If this initiative passed, it would have crippled Mississippi's still struggling economy, because it would have required all children between the ages of five and fifteen to be in school rather than at work. School officials felt that compulsory attendance was the most efficient means to promote the advancement of schools in Mississippi. In early 1873, Pease devoted almost sixteen pages of his annual report to the necessity of "obligatory education"; he pointed out that only half of the state's 400,000 educable children were currently enrolled in a public school.[48] Knowing how volatile the issue was, Pease neglected to illustrate statistics demonstrating the extremely low enrollment of black children and instead concentrated his examples on the low enrollment of white youth. In 1874, Thomas W. Cardozo, the second superintendent of education in the state, offered a more congenial and middle-ground approach to compulsory schooling to whites. "There is no doubt," stated Cardozo, "that the compulsory education laws that have worked so well in other States might be with us introduced."[49] He continued, "There would be little difficulty in having all children between the ages of five and fifteen attend the schools for three months of the year without seriously interfering with their labors."[50] His proposition lowered the school term by one month—from four months to three—and directly catered to the economic interests of the state's planters and landed elite. If they saw that their own economic self-interests were not threatened by mandating a compulsory school law, Cardozo believed the state could, with public support, implement his proposal. Cardozo offered one additional appeal in the hopes of gaining enough support for compulsory education. He drew a parallel between the state's rising crime rate and continued widespread illiteracy and concluded that it would be better and more cost-efficient for Mississippi to "provide school-houses for the accommodation of children under a compulsory system, than provide jails for them when they become adults."[51] Despite his appeals, his proposal, much like Pease's, was ultimately rejected.

What truly upset whites were the overall advancements and opportunities afforded to blacks. The knowledge and confidence blacks received from freedom and attending school were finally materializing in the form of greater opportunities for them as state citizens. The events that shaped the year 1873 and its outcomes proved this. Their hard work, sacrifice, determination, and perseverance were both seen and rewarded. White fears of blacks being considered as equals was affirmed when the state passed a civil rights bill that forbade discrimination in all public institutions. The bill in theory guaranteed blacks equal access to "all places of public entertainment."[52] Moreover, the 1873 legislation coincided with the reelection of Adelbert Ames as governor, Alexander K. Davis, a freeborn African American from Mississippi as his lieutenant governor, and Thomas W. Cardozo, a freeborn African American also from Mississippi, as superintendent of education. These three events caused a major uproar among whites, who once again felt their racial status threatened. For the most part, whites were responsible for these developments. Their collective refusal to participate in the 1873 election easily secured Ames's victory over Alcorn, who had alienated the black vote in favor of the conservative politics of state Democrats. Alcorn became so unpopular among blacks that even the African Americans that labored his plantation, as Eric Foner indicated, voted against him.[53] To Mississippi whites the election of Ames as governor was a major setback. As provisional military governor four years earlier, Ames made it very clear that he strongly favored suffrage rights, equality, and the advancement of African Americans.

Adding to the concerns of whites was the fact that the black vote had substantially increased the representation of blacks in the state legislature and had "consolidated" their hold on local offices throughout the black belt. When state lawmakers assembled for the fall session they chose a black Speaker of the House and a black U.S. senator. The Speaker was John Roy Lynch of Natchez, and the senator was Blanche K. Bruce.[54] Bruce was the former county superintendent of education in Bolivar County. As the 1873 election drew to a close, Mississippi blacks held four of the seven major state appointments (see the appendix), and the black vote, loyal to the party of Abraham Lincoln, proved to have an unprecedented strength. Blacks catered to the Republican Party not out of blind faith, but because Republicans continued to support their suffrage rights, education, desires for self-improvement, and their overall advancement.

The educational statistics from the 1876–77 academic year substantiate

TABLE 14. School Population, Enrollment, and Average Attendance
of Educable Children, 1870–1871 and 1876–1877

Race	Educable Children (Ages 5–21)	Number of Children Enrolled in Schools	Percent of Children Enrolled	Average Attendance of Enrolled Children	Average Attendance as a Percentage of Enrolled Children
1870–1871					
Black	126,769	45,429	35.8	36,040	79.3
White	120,073	66,257	55.1	49,290	74.4
Total	246,842	111,686	45.2	85,330	76.4
1876–1877					
Black	184,857	90,178	48.7	68,580	76
White	171,062	76,026	44.4	65,384	86
Total	355,919	166,204	46.6	133,964	80.6

Sources: Adapted from *Annual Report of the Superintendent of Public Education of the State of Mississippi
for the Year Ending December, 1871* (Jackson, Miss.: Kimball, Kaymond, State Printers, 1872), 124–31;
*Annual Report of the State Superintendent of Public Education to the Legislature of Mississippi for the Year
1876* (Jackson, Miss.: Power & Barksdale, State Printers, 1877), 93–94.

the argument that the political voice of Mississippi blacks had a direct effect
on their educational opportunities.[55] Although these statistics were not collected nor tabulated with the same specificity as prior annual reports, they
nonetheless illustrate that the schooling opportunities of blacks were on the
rise. In 1876, as table 14 demonstrates, there were 355,919 educable children in
Mississippi, 53 percent being black. Since 1870, this was an increase of 109,077
educable children, or approximately 31 percent. However, the percentage of
children to enroll in a public school had increased by less than 2 percent from
1870 to 1876—from 45.2 percent to 46.6 percent.

Still, when the state's 1876–77 statistics are disaggregated by race, it is
clear that more black youth were benefiting from public schools than ever
before. As table 14 further exemplifies, black children—for the first docu-

mented time in the state's brief public school history—enrolled in a public school at a higher rate than white children. Approximately 48.7 percent of all black children, or 90,178 children, were enrolled in a public school, and 76 percent of them attended on a daily basis. Equally notable, however, was the fact that in 1876, almost 45,000 more black children attended school than in the inaugural year. This outcome occurred in spite of the hostility some whites directed toward blacks and their schools.

By contrast, there was a sharp decline in the enrollment of white youth. By the 1876 school year, white pupil enrollment decreased by 11 percent. Nevertheless, of the white children enrolled in a public school, roughly 80 percent regularly attended. White children's lower enrollment was not due to an increase in white private schools. In fact, there were fewer white private schools in 1876 than there were six years earlier. In studying the selected majority-black counties analyzed in chapter 4, it is somewhat plausible that the lower enrollment of white children had to do with fewer white public schools in these counties. In 1876–77, as table 15 shows, schools for white children in those majority-black counties averaged forty-one pupils per school. However, this higher pupil per school ratio does not fully explain why white children had a lower enrollment, because these counties' black public schools averaged sixty-three pupils per school and enrolled over 16,000 more students. Lack of enthusiasm is a possibility, but given the limited material evidence on the subject, this question may be unanswerable. What is discernable is that a lack of schooling opportunities or resources was not a sufficient reason for the lower public school enrollment of white children in these counties.

Similar developments happened in the selected majority-white counties used for analysis. As table 16 indicates, enrollment for both black and white children increased. However, 808 new black children enrolled in a public school, while the number of enrolled white children decreased by 6,837. This occurred in spite of the addition of only four new public schools for blacks in these counties in six years. Public schools for black children in Covington and Itawamba counties remained virtually unchanged six years after their opening. This was reflective in the black pupil per school ratio. Schools for black children in these counties averaged approximately forty-eight pupils, an increase of about one pupil per school in comparison to the year they first went into operation. By contrast, 177 fewer public schools for whites were

TABLE 15. Enrollment, Number of Schools, and Number of Enrolled Pupils per School in Fifteen Majority-Black Counties, 1876–1877

County	Enrolled Youth		Number of Public Schools		Number of Enrolled Pupils per School	
	Black	White	Black	White	Black	White
Adams	2,214	581	58	13	38	45
Carroll	1,116	1,207	24	25	47	48
Claiborne	1,336	646	27	30	49	21
DeSoto	2,591	1,352	39	34	66	40
Hinds	5,100	3,500	60	50	85	70
Holmes	—	—	—	—	—	—
Lowndes	2,282	875	23	20	99	44
Marshall	1,913	1,620	47	62	41	26
Noxubee	4,131	927	43	39	96	24
Panola	4,453	2,698	56	57	80	47
Tallahatchie	1,165	952	25	26	47	37
Tunica	787	125	—	—	—	—
Warren	3,293	1,078	43	21	77	51
Wilkinson	1,484	1,160	30	9	49	129
Yazoo	2,500	950	59	44	42	22
Total	34,365	17,671	534	430	63	41

Source: Adapted from *Annual Report of the Superintendent of Public Education to the Legislature of Mississippi for the Year 1876* (Jackson, Miss.: Power & Barksdale, State Printers, 1877), 93–94.

TABLE 16. Enrollment, Number of Schools, and Number of Enrolled
Pupils per School in Fifteen Majority-White Counties, 1876–1877

County	Enrolled Youth		Number of Public Schools		Number of Enrolled Pupils per School	
	Black	White	Black	White	Black	White
Alcorn	—	—	—	—	—	—
Choctaw	391	861	15	26	26	33
Coahoma	1,300	300	29	11	45	27
Covington	104	844	2	29	52	29
Itawamba	159	1,502	5	40	32	38
Jackson	—	—	—	—	—	—
Leake	863	2070	23	60	38	35
Lee	1,019	1,776	—	—	—	—
Montgomery	939	1,459	18	40	52	36
Pontotoc	185	720	6	39	31	18
Smith	29	299	—	13	—	23
Scott	149	222	5	8	30	28
Tishomingo	170	1,728	5	48	34	36
Tippah	662	2,168	15	58	44	37
Wayne	164	145	4	5	41	29
Total	6,134	14,094	127	377	48	37

Source: Adapted from Annual Report of the Superintendent of Public Education to the Legislature of Mississippi for the Year 1876 (Jackson, Miss.: Power & Barksdale, State Printers, 1877), 93–94.

established in these selected majority-white counties, and public schools for white children averaged about thirty-seven students.

. . .

However, the strides made by blacks in a full decade after slavery's demise were about to hastily change. The year 1875, and the outcome of that year's election, abruptly stifled the opportunities that blacks had secured for themselves and others as countless whites rallied behind a white supremacist political campaign to rid the state of Republican politics and its influential black vote. By the end of 1874, it had become more and more evident that whites had grown tired of the people and policies that appeared to overlook, if not harm, their overall self-interests. To paraphrase historian William C. Harris, who best summarized this collective sentiment, Republicans fortuitously miscalculated the financial situation and prospects of postbellum Mississippi. They continued to place inordinate demands upon the state's limited tax resources, hoping for a near-complete restoration of one of the nation's hitherto richest states.[56] But the cotton economy that gave Mississippi its sobriquet King Cotton never returned to relieve the state of its struggling economy and the costs accrued by Republican Reconstruction policy. "Perhaps more than any other reasons," Harris concluded, "including the endemic race issue and the emotionalism generated by Reconstruction politics, the problem of finance proved the undoing of the Republican dream" in postwar Mississippi.[57]

What occurred in 1875 was a "counter Reconstruction," as historian John Hope Franklin says, or a counterattack by disenchanted whites on the state's primarily Republican Reconstruction policies and postemancipation expectations and gains of Mississippi blacks.[58] White Democrats premised their political campaign on the state's racial color line and strongly urged all whites to join them in order to carry the state election of 1875. They repeatedly slandered the increased political presence and gains of blacks after the 1873 election, and offered propaganda such as "Do you want the bottom rail to remain on top?" to whites frustrated with the advancements of blacks.[59] The language of violence and intimidation characterized the political atmosphere, speeches, and dialogue of white Democrats. Rally cries of "Carry the election peacefully if we can, forcibly if we must" or "This is a white man's country and government" were catchphrases at most Democrat conventions, local barbecues, and political picnics. Newspapers reinforced these racially charged catchphrases as they too called for white solidarity and advocated for the return of the Democrat party to best avoid a repeat of the 1873 election.[60]

Many whites responded to the rally cries by practicing intimidation, social coercion, and violence. For example, white physicians in Lafayette County pledged they would not serve or cater to the medical needs of blacks that did not vote the Democrat ticket. Additionally, the wives and friends of known black and white Republicans were boycotted from using numerous commercial areas.[61] Throughout the state, planters fired or displaced employees known to vote Republican and refused to hire any black supporting the Republican ticket. They instead hired blacks willing to either vote Democrat or not at all.[62] This economic burden, more than anything else, forced many Mississippi blacks to reevaluate the necessity of using their newfound franchise.

The racial propaganda and white supremacist platform of Democrats inspired some white males to formally establish White Leagues—another militia organization determined to uphold the ideals of the antebellum past—and reinvigorated the Klan in many parts of Mississippi. While Blanche K. Bruce informed the U.S. Senate in 1876 that members in these terrorist organizations were little more than "a ferocious minority," and were not representative of white Mississippians in general, they nonetheless significantly dictated the direction and outcome of the state's 1875 election.[63] By early 1875, white terrorism of some sort was organized in virtually every county with the sole intent of ridding Mississippi of Republican politics and policies, and obliterating the political, social, and economic leverage blacks had gained since emancipation. Vigilantes broke up or prevented the political meetings of blacks; they diverted and intimidated African Americans from registering to vote, and they repeatedly threatened, and sometimes took the lives of, advocates of the Republican Party or black advancement. On the eve of the election, white militia groups established outposts on every road that led to voting booths.[64] They were determined to make sure African Americans did not use their franchise to once again determine the future of Mississippi. Consequently, before votes were even submitted for the state election of 1875, African Americans and their Republican allies were politically silenced and disfranchised. When the votes were finally counted, white Democrats—with minimal opposition—regained statewide control.

The intimidation and violence that ensued in the months before the election illustrated the extent that whites opposed and feared the possible consequences of African Americans living and voting as equals. It also demonstrated the enduring defenselessness and vulnerable position of blacks, regardless of emancipation, their majority population, or strength in voting almost a full decade after the war. Lawlessness, not civility, determined the future status of African Americans in Mississippi since emancipation. Whites had the power to kill, and do so unmercifully, without the slightest concern of law authorities stopping them. African Americans had no recourse, no law officials to turn to for protection; all they could do was hope that the violence stayed clear of them or someone they loved. Historian Vernon Lane Wharton illustrates this sad point as he describes the violence that led up to the state elections of 1875. In Austin, Wharton says,

> Negroes raised violent objection to the release of a white man who, in shooting at a Negro man, had killed a Negro girl. In the quarrel which followed, six Negroes were killed; no whites were wounded. . . . In Vicksburg, where a white militia had overthrown Republican control . . . about thirty-five Negroes were killed; two whites met death, one by accident. . . . [In] Water Valley an unknown number of Negroes were killed; no whites wounded. In August, a group of whites near Macon, including more than a hundred horsemen from Alabama, found a black church and fired into the crowd. Twelve or thirteen Negroes were killed; no white was hurt. . . . In Yazoo City, white militia took charge of the county, and systematically lynched the Negro leaders in each supervised district. . . . In Clinton, [whites] scoured the surrounding country killing Negro leaders. Estimates of the number killed varied between ten and fifty. . . . At Columbus . . . on the night before the election, a crowd of young whites attacked a Negro parade . . . four were killed and several were wounded; no whites were hurt.[65]

Appeals for military protection to ensure the safety of black voters at critical voting designations and in riot-prone cities went ignored by local authorities, state officials, Congress, and northern sympathizers. In the words of President Ulysses S. Grant's attorney general, Edward Pierrepont, the "whole public tired of these annual autumnal outbreaks in the South."[66] Blacks and state Republicans were expected to resolve these acts of violence themselves or learn to endure their existence. On election day "thousands of black Republicans," professed historian Michael Perman, "demonstrated remarkable courage and determination by still appearing to support their beleaguered and demoralized party."[67] This extraordinary display of loyalty and political involvement, as Perman concluded, however did very little to offset the more numerous votes cast for the candidates running on the Democratic ticket and the restoration of a political party determined to re-claim Mississippi and restore it to its glory days before the Civil War.[68]

. . .

The propaganda and violence used in the state election of 1875 illustrate the extent whites would go to reestablish the semblance of an antebellum status quo and the overall subjugation of blacks. Their effects resonated in the political, social, and economic lives of blacks in the following years. This was especially true throughout the South, not just in Mississippi. Southern whites—within a decade's time—would regain control over their states' general affairs and southern blacks would abruptly lose their political voice, support, and ability to effectively negotiate a livelihood better than second-class citizenship. Yet with regard to public schools for black children in Mis-sissippi this latter contention was not as immediately evident. In fact, as tables 14, 15, and 16 illustrate, schools for black children not only survived the malicious assaults in 1875, but expanded. This is a lasting testimony of how ingrained an institution like public schools had become in Mississippi's postbellum landscape. It is also a testament to how blacks, despite their obvi-ous losses, saw education as a fundamental acquisition. Education, alongside landownership and the right to vote, were the three principles that defined freedom and full citizenship to freedpeople. These acquisitions had greatly improved the lives of countless blacks and assisted them in their transition from slavery to freedom.

While landownership and the vote were abruptly upended after the state election of 1875, schools remained, and this outcome served as a permanent indicator that African Americans were slaves no more. African American slaves stepped out of cotton field and into schools, and their actions in the first decade of emancipation dramatically altered Mississippi society and its treatment and consideration of them. It would take brute force and extreme violence to return Mississippi to its olden days of whites on top and blacks on the bottom. By 1880, the educational opportunities of black children would be circumscribed, defined, and impeded by whites as they continually re-vamped public schools to appease their own self-interests. Taxes for school purposes and salaries for teachers were reduced, and various provisions were ratified that specified school funds could only be used for the salaries of school teachers and officials and not toward the improvement of public schools.[69] The schools that African American children would attend from 1880 until the late 1960s would primarily educate them for a life of second-class citizenship and servitude.

Nonetheless, between 1870 and 1875, universal schooling for African Americans arose in a postbellum society extremely antagonistic to its establishment. While there were many debates over who would administer and control these schools and how schools would be funded, blacks were never overly concerned with these issues. They provided their input when possible and made the most of the opportunities before them. In the greater scheme of things they had achieved one of their primary goals and that was to establish schools for themselves, their children, and future generations of black children to be born and raised in Mississippi. They did their best to challenge their limited and circumscribed schooling opportunities, the persistent opposition, the violence, and their abrupt removal of civic life and leadership. Had they had any real support and protection as citizens of Mississippi and the United States during these formative years of public schooling, one could only fathom what the outcome of their lives and of the state of Mississippi would have been.

Still, Mississippi blacks were slaves no more. They made their former owners change their attitudes and actions toward them and, to some degree, recognize them as citizens. They repeatedly forced Mississippi's ruling and landed elite to acknowledge their majority presence and demanded — to the best of their ability — that they be granted the same access, consideration, and treatment as whites. Their recognition and arrival as citizens was never more apparent than in 1873 when incumbent governor Adelbert Ames in his inaugural address thanked African Americans. Because of their unwavering support and belief in a more democratic Mississippi, "the colored citizen," Ames said, "would never be less citizens than they are today."[70] Conversely, this recognition of them as citizens also carried over into the state election of 1875, as antagonistic whites refused to allow a repeat of the advancements made by blacks in previous elections and years. Their fear of African Americans gaining equality (or more) made them resort to a level of unprecedented violence to ensure that Mississippi would forever be for whites only.

EPILOGUE

In June 2002, a family gathered in the college town of Urbana, Illinois, for a high school graduation. It was not your typical graduation; the graduate was a sixty-nine-year-old woman by the name of Johnnie Mae Dorris. The local newspaper carried the story and the front page headline read: "From Cotton Field to Cap, Gown." She was the oldest graduate of Urbana High School. She recalled for the newspaper how she grew up on a cotton farm in Tallahatchie County, Mississippi, where formal schooling was severely limited. "From December, when all the cotton was picked," Dorris told the newspaper staff writer, "to about April, when it was time to plant again, rural children met in a little country church where a family tried to pass on what education they had." She continued, "If the regular teacher couldn't be there, her sister or niece might show up to lead the class." Mrs. Dorris learned how to read and write, but, as she concluded, "I don't even consider it a school now that I know better."[1]

Dorris was born Johnnie Mae Sheperd in 1932. As she came of age, she learned that her life was to be different because of the color of her skin, that, as a native daughter of Mississippi, she should not expect much in life beyond the bare necessities, and that when she went to school, she might, at best, get an eighth grade education. At the time George Washington Albright was retelling his activities to the editors of the *Daily Worker*, Johnnie Mae would have been six years old and ready to start school. The irony would be that the school she attended as a young child was very much reminiscent of the type of school Albright taught in when he emerged from slavery, and that Ida B. Wells, Belle Caruthers, and others would recall attending as young children in the first decade of emancipation. Nearly seventy years later, African Americans like Johnnie Mae, still attended school around the cotton cycle, in small cramped spaces in back rooms of black churches, and were taught by people who, in some cases, knew only a little bit more than their students. The African Americans who emerged from Mississippi cotton fields in slavery, who struggled in the first decade of freedom to ensure that their children and grandchildren would have opportunities denied to them, would within their own lifetime see these dreams slowly erode away.

Notwithstanding H. R. Pease's request in 1871 for the establishment of high schools for all adolescents in the state, from 1890 to 1965, Mississippi paid only lip service to the establishment of high schools for African Americans. Instead the state developed a system of schools, not just high schools, for whites at the expense of blacks. In principle, schools remained antithetical to the expectations whites had of African Americans, especially the high school. The main goal of high schools was to prepare youths for college, citizenship, leadership, and employment in society. By their very nature and design, high schools had the potential to prepare blacks in ways and for opportunities whites in did not want. Mississippi never developed a system of high schools for blacks prior to the *Brown v. Board of Education* decision of 1954. In 1916, Thomas Jessie Jones of the federal Bureau of Education believed that there were probably only nine to eleven schools "above the elementary grades" that taught African Americans in Mississippi.[2] If they were high schools, this would have been an increase of only five to seven since 1871. In 1940, of the 115,000 educable black children of high school age, only 9,473 were enrolled in a high school. By contrast, there were 575 high schools for white adolescents and they enrolled 62,747 students.[3] In the late 1940s, when Johnnie Mae would have been high school age, Mississippi school officials had done very little to advance high school educational opportunities for African Americans. By 1950, there were, according to the assistant supervisor of Negro schools, P. H. Easom, just 261 schools throughout Mississippi "doing some high school work."[4] Even if Johnnie Mae wanted to attend a high school in her home county, her limited formal school experiences as a child would have greatly hindered her ability to effectively complete school.

Nevertheless, the determination on the part of Dorris to go back to school after fifty-odd years to get her high school diploma is a testament to the longstanding fervor African Americans in Mississippi had for knowledge. Whites, who controlled the state's public school system from 1875 and beyond, systematically stifled the schooling opportunities for blacks. In many ways they halted the momentum that former slaves and their children carried out during the first decade of emancipation to use schools to obtain freedom, citizenship, and equality. Their schools may have been stifled, but the aspirations on the part of African Americans were passed down from one generation to the next. When Johnnie Mae and her kin came of age, their elders would have told them of the importance and value of schools and knowledge, even though they themselves could never take advantage of these long-held beliefs. Their hope was that a young Johnnie Mae, her fraternal twin brother, and other siblings and kin could. When Dorris realized she could not fulfill her aspirations of using school to earn freedom and equality in Jim Crow Mississippi, she would pass this cultural value down to her children and grandchildren. As she raised her seven children from Mississippi to Tennessee to Illinois, she stressed to them the importance of an education. "I always encouraged them," she said, "and all of them completed high school and most went to college."[5]

The story of Johnnie Mae Dorris, my wife's grandmother, my son's great-grandmother, in many ways captures the hopes and frustrations of countless blacks from emancipation well into the twentieth century. The dreams of former slaves in 1865 to use schools to achieve freedom, citizenship, and equality, to make a name for themselves and their families, to live right and do right by others, were the dreams of my grandmother-in-law and every African American—before and after her generation—who struggled and hoped to live as free men and women with dignity, opportunities, and equality. Nearly one hundred years would elapse before African Americans in Mississippi would taste the semblance of freedom and equality and attend schools without legal restraints. Even so, the denial of these most basic dignities did not deter them from believing in and striving for a better tomorrow for their children and grandchildren. They made the most of their lives and of the resources before them, they "made change from pennies" as the famed Mississippi poet Sterling Plumpp once wrote, and they bided their time until their days of glory would come.[6] As I watched my grandmother-in-law literally jump with jubilation on the graduation platform as they called her name and awarded her a high school diploma, tears filled my eyes and my heart felt a joy I had never felt before or since. I understood better the history and aspirations of the people I was writing about, and I appreciated so much more the opportunity to tell their story. All the years of denied opportunity, forced patience, second-class citizenship, humming of hymns like "Do Lord, Do Lord, Remember Me," and an endless belief that better days were ahead, unequivocally expressed itself in a shower of emotions on this special graduation day. Four generations of relatives—siblings and kin, children, grandchildren, and great-grandchildren—all cried as she walked across that platform to accept her high school diploma. The audience gave her a standing ovation and countless people—family, friends, and otherwise—who understood the moment, her struggle to prove to herself that she could do it, applauded and wept. She proved to everyone in attendance that all dreams, even those long deferred, were possible.

When asked by the paper how does it feel to finally graduate from high school, Dorris responded in a way that gave closure to one of her life's greatest aspirations. "It's like a dream," she said, "and I haven't woken up yet. . . . Sometimes I cry thinking about it—I just can't believe it's happened."

APPENDIX · KNOWN AFRICAN AMERICAN POLITICIANS AND LEGISLATORS IN MISSISSIPPI DURING RECONSTRUCTION, 1870–1875

U.S. SENATE

. . .

Rev. Hiram R. Revels, 1870–71
Blanche K. Bruce, 1875–81

STATE SENATE, 1870

. . .

Charles Caldwell (Hinds County)
Robert Gleed (Lowndes County)
Rev. T. W. Stringer (Warren County)
Rev. William Gray (Washington County)

STATE HOUSE OF REPRESENTATIVES, 1870

. . .

Adams County: John R. Lynch and Henry P. Jacobs
Bolivar County: C. M. Bowles
Chickasaw County: Ambrose Henderson

Adapted from Monroe N. Work, "Some Negro Members of Reconstruction Conventions and Legislatures and of Congress," *Journal of Negro History* 5 (1920): 73–74; Eric Foner, *Reconstruction America's Unfinished Revolution, 1863–1877* (New York: Harper & Row, 1988), 353.

Claiborne County: M. T. Newsom

Copiah County: Emanuel Handy

Hinds County: Henry Mayson and C. F. Norris

Holmes County: Edmund Scarborough and Cicero Mitchell

Issaquena County: Richard Griggs

Jefferson County: Merrimon Howard

Lauderdale County: J. Aaron Moore

Lawrence County: George Charles

Lowndes County: J. F. Bolden

Madison County: Dr. James J. Spellman

Monroe County: William Holmes

Noxubee County: Isham Stewart, Nathan McNeese, and A. R. Davis

Oktibbeha County: David Higgins

Panola County: C. A. Yancy and J. H. Piles

Warren County: Charles P. Head, Peter Barrow, and Albert Johnson

Washington County: John Morgan, and Dr. Stiles

Wilkinson County: H. M. Faley and George W. White

Yazoo County: W. H. Fonte

STATE HOUSE OF REPRESENTATIVES, 1871

. . .

Adams County: Henry P. Jacobs and John R. Lynch

Amite County: Rueben Kendrick

Bolivar County: G. W. Gayles

Claiborne County: Joseph Smothers

Copiah County: Emanuel Handy

DeSoto County: H. H. Johnson and Thomas McCain

Hinds County: Monroe Bell, William Johnson, and Charles Reese

Holmes County: Perry Howard, F. Stewart, and H. H. Truehart

Issaquena County: Richard Griggs and R. W. Houston

Jefferson County: James D. Cessar and William Landers

Madison County: Alfred Handy and Dr. James J. Spelman

Marshall County: James Hill

Monroe County: Arthur Brooks and William Holmes

Noxubee County: A. K. Davis and Isham Stewart

Oktibbeha County: Randle Nettles

Panola County: John Cocke and James H. Piles

Tunica County: Gilbert Smith

Warren County: Charles W. Bush, H. C. Carter, W. H. Mallory, and I. D. Shadd

Washington County: J. H. Morgan and John D. Webster

Wilkinson County: H. M. Foley and George W. White

Yazoo County: James M. Dixon and F. D. Wade

SECRETARY OF STATE

· · ·

James Lynch, 1869–72

Hiram Revels, 1872–73

Hannibal C. Carter, 1873

M. M. McCleod, 1874

James Hill, 1874–78

SUPERINTENDENT OF EDUCATION

· · ·

Thomas W. Cardozo, 1874–76

LIEUTENANT GOVERNOR

· · ·

Alexander K. Davis, 1874–76

NOTES

INTRODUCTION

1. Immediately following the Civil War, George Washington Albright was a state legislator from Marshall County. His narrative can be found in George P. Rawick's compilation of slave narratives, undertaken for the Works Progress Administration (WPA). From 1936 to 1938, Federal Writers' Project (FWP) writers and journalists, under the aegis of the WPA, interviewed over 2,300 former slaves from across the American South. These former slaves, most born in the concluding years of slavery, provided accounts of their experiences. These narratives remain an unrivaled resource for understanding the lives of America's 4 million slaves. The interviews themselves present some problems as historical data and have been a persistent source of contention for historians, who debate their validity and usefulness in understanding American slavery and the slave's worldview. An ex-slave's account would be influenced by his or her interviewer's age, professional inexperience, race, and regional bias. Yet, as Charles T. Davis and Henry Louis Gates Jr. properly insist, such shortcomings should not dismiss the tremendous value these interviews maintain as valuable resources on the American slave experience (Charles T. Davis and Henry Louis Gates Jr., *The Slave's Narrative: Text and Context* [New York: Oxford University Press, 1985], xvi). Albright's narrative was reprinted from the *Daily Worker*, June 18, 1937. The *Daily Worker* was an East Coast weekly newspaper of the American Communist Party. From 1948 through the 1950s, the paper was under constant surveillance from the FBI. George P. Rawick, *The American Slave: A Composite Autobiography* 19 vols. (Westport, Conn.: Greenwood Press, 1977): 8–19, quote on 16–17. The historian Neil McMillen indirectly questions the accuracy of Albright's comment on the funding disparity between black and white schoolchildren during the 1930s. McMillen's data indicate that Albright's estimates were too high; on average only *seven* cents of every educational dollar went toward black education in Mississippi during this decade. Still, McMillen's assessment of the funding disparities regarding

black and white education in Mississippi may not be in conflict with Albright and his estimates. McMillen might not have included—which Albright could have—the additional funds and taxes Mississippi blacks volunteered for their children's educational advancement. For educational funding disparities in Jim Crow Mississippi, see Neil McMillen, *Dark Journey: Black Mississippians in the Age of Jim Crow* (Urbana: University of Illinois Press, 1989), 72–108. For funds volunteered by southern blacks in the cause of African American schools, see James D. Anderson, *The Education of Blacks in the South, 1860–1935* (Chapel Hill: University of North Carolina Press, 1988); Vanessa Siddle Walker, *Their Highest Potential: An African American School Community in the Segregated South* (Chapel Hill: University of North Carolina Press, 1996); and Heather Andrea Williams, *Self-Taught: African American Education in Slavery and Freedom* (Chapel Hill: University of North Carolina Press, 2005).

2. According to the 1860 census approximately 436,631 enslaved African Americans, 773 free blacks, and 354,674 whites resided in Mississippi. At the start of the Civil War, less than 1 percent of African Americans residing in Mississippi were classified as "free." Census data from 1790 to 1960 can now be obtained at http://fisher.lib .virginia.edu/census/.

3. Rawick, *The American Slave*, 16–17.

4. Ibid., 17.

5. Ibid., 8–19. The interviewer and the editor appeared to have had some difficulty believing Albright's recollections, which was why they dismissed much of his testimony. While there is no way of knowing, I believe that the interviewer and editor had a hard time understanding Albright, perhaps because of his dialect. For example, the paper quoted Albright as saying "Hollis Springs," which should have been recognized as Holly Springs. There is no way of telling whether the interviewer had difficulty understanding Albright's pronunciation, whether the paper intentionally misrepresented Albright, or whether Albright's memory was the problem. This is also the case where Albright's narrative misrecords the number of black delegates who participated in the Mississippi constitutional convention. The *Daily Worker* states that Albright declared seventy-four out of one hundred delegates at the 1868 convention were black. In actuality, only seventeen of the one hundred delegates were African American. Once again this could have been a case of vernacular misunderstanding. The editors also assumed that Albright exaggerated the number of schools built by and for African Americans in Marshall County. Albright states that African Americans built forty schools, which, according to the 1870–71 superintendent's annual report, is nearly accurate. The report states that thirty-nine schools were established for African Americans in Marshall County in the inaugural year of public schooling; although it does not specify who built these schools. See *Annual Report of the Superintendent of Public Education of the State of Mississippi for the Year Ending December 31, 1871* (Jackson, Miss.: Kimball, Kaymond, State Printers, 1872), 124–31.

6. W. E. B. Du Bois, *Black Reconstruction in America* (repr., Cleveland: World Publishing, 1964), 638.

7. Extensive scholarship details the educational motivations of ex-slaves during the Reconstruction era. Most notable are the following: Anderson, *The Education of Blacks in the South*, 4–16; Ronald E. Butchart, *Northern Schools, Southern Blacks, and Reconstruction* (Westport, Conn.: Greenwood Press, 1980); Eric Foner, *Reconstruction: America's Unfinished Revolution, 1863–1877* (New York: Harper & Row, 1988), 96–102; Herbert Gutman, "'Schools for Freedom': The Post-Emancipation Origins of Afro-American Education," in *Major Problems in African American History*, ed. Thomas Holt and Elsa Barkley Brown (New York: Houghton Mifflin, 2000), 1:388–401; Jacqueline Jones, *Soldiers of Light and Love: Northern Teachers and Georgia Blacks, 1865–1873* (Chapel Hill: University of North Carolina Press, 1980); Robert C. Morris, *Reading, 'Riting, and Reconstruction: The Education of Freedmen in the South, 1862–1870* (Chicago: University of Chicago Press, 1981); Christopher M. Span, "'I Must Learn Now or Not At All': Social and Cultural Capital in the Educational Initiatives of Formerly Enslaved African Americans in Mississippi, 1862–1869," *Journal of African American History* 87 (2002): 22–31; Randy J. Sparks, "'The White People's Arms Are Longer than Ours': Blacks, Education, and the American Missionary Association in Reconstruction Mississippi," *Journal of Mississippi History* 54 (1992): 1–27; Williams, *Self-Taught*.

8. William Leon Woods, "The Travail of Freedom: Mississippi Blacks, 1862–1870" (Ph.D. diss., Princeton University, 1979), 152. Despite the critique and efforts of Woods, he too offered only minimal discussion on African American education in postbellum Mississippi. Nevertheless, his analysis was much more congenial to the perspective of former slaves and more representative to the available evidence than the analyses of other historians, who, he declared, had written very little on the subject.

9. Garner devoted only a few pages and select passages to the origins and development of schools for African Americans in Mississippi in his Reconstruction history. Wharton, who challenged Garner, did little more in his analysis and summary of African American education in postbellum Mississippi. In the single chapter he devoted to African American education, Wharton relied heavily on the interpretations and publications of early-twentieth-century Reconstruction traditionalists, who had only made mention of, and not effectively researched, the history of African American education in this era. Wharton's reliance on the interpretations proffered by these early traditionalists (see n. 12 below for those interpretations) distorted his assessment of the origins and purpose of schools for African Americans in Reconstruction Mississippi. As for Harris, he offered only a superficial discussion of the educational opportunities that arose for African Americans and made no mention of the role former slaves played in the grassroots or legislative development of schools for themselves or their children. James Garner, *Reconstruction in Mississippi* (New

York: Macmillan Press, 1901); Vernon Lane Wharton, *The Negro in Mississippi, 1865–1890* (repr., New York: Harper & Row, 1965), 243–55; William C. Harris, *The Day of the Carpetbagger: Republican Reconstruction in Mississippi* (Baton Rouge: Louisiana State University Press, 1979), 311–53. Also see William C. Harris, *Presidential Reconstruction in Mississippi* (Baton Rouge: Louisiana State University Press, 1967).

10. Stuart Grayson Noble, *Forty Years of the Public Schools in Mississippi: With Special Reference to the Education of the Negro* (New York: Teachers College, Columbia University Press, 1918).

11. W. H. Hardy, "Recollections of Reconstruction in East and Southeast Mississippi," *Publications of the Mississippi Historical Society* 8 (1904): 150–51.

12. As mentioned, Stuart Grayson Noble wrote the first and—at present—only in-depth educational history of African Americans in Mississippi. However, Noble, like the early traditionalists cited below, repeatedly and unabashedly inserted his own bias about the era's outcome and the people he researched, oftentimes with little or no evidence to support his contentions. Noble's publication characterized the efforts of the overwhelming majority of southern historians writing about the South and the era of Reconstruction. These writers did not hesitate to voice their personal opposition to the persons, policies, and practices of the era, especially if they felt these did a disservice to the white South. They offered a very denigrating portrayal of African Americans, characterizing them as incompetent, lazy, and corrupt. They approved, or even celebrated, the murder of African Americans by Klansmen or other members of a white militia. Moreover, they gave little, if any, recognition to the part African Americans played in the restoration and advancement of postbellum Mississippi. These early studies characterized the times as an era when "Vindictives" and "Radicals" in Congress "silenced" President Johnson and the Supreme Court and "imposed" "Carpetbag" (northern-born Republican), "Scalawag" (southern-born Republican), and "Negro" governments in the South at the political and economic "expense" of "loyal" white southerners. To them, any hostile or violent response on the part of southern whites to a northern migrant, a southern loyalist, or an African American was an act of "self-defense." The major traditionalist Reconstruction histories of Mississippi are M. G. Abney, "Reconstruction in Pontotoc County," *Publications of the Mississippi Historical Society* 11 (1910): 240–69; Robert Bowman, "Reconstruction in Yazoo County," *Publications of the Mississippi Historical Society* 7 (1903): 115–30; W. H. Braden, "Reconstruction in Lee County," *Publications of the Mississippi Historical Society* 10 (1909): 135–46; Thomas Battle Carroll, "Historical Sketches of Oktibbeha County," *Historical Publications on Mississippi* (Gulfport, Miss.: Dixie Press, 1931); Rowland Dunbar, "The Rise and Fall of Negro Rule in Mississippi," *Publications of the Mississippi Historical Society* 2 (1898): 189–200; Garner, *Reconstruction in Mississippi*; Hardy, "Recollections of Reconstruction in East and Southeast Mississippi"; J. H. Jones, "Reconstruction in Wilkinson County," *Publications of*

the Mississippi Historical Society 8 (1904): 153–75; Nannie Lacey, "Reconstruction in Leake County," *Publications of the Mississippi Historical Society* 11 (1910): 271–94; Hattie Magee, "Reconstruction in Lawrence and Jefferson Davis County," *Publications of the Mississippi Historical Society* 11 (1910): 163–204; J. S. McNeily, "From Organization to Overthrow of Mississippi's Provisional Government, 1865–1868," *Publications of the Mississippi Historical Society*, centenary series 1 (1918); J. S. McNeily, "Climax and Collapse of Reconstruction in Mississippi," *Publications of the Mississippi Historical Society* 12 (1912): 283–474; J. S. McNeily, "The Enforcement Act of 1871 and the Ku Klux Klan in Mississippi," *Publications of the Mississippi Historical Society* 9 (1906): 109–72; J. S. McNeily, "War and Reconstruction in Mississippi, 1863–1890," *Publications of the Mississippi Historical Society*, centenary series 1 (1917): 9–403; Irby Nichols, "Reconstruction in DeSoto County," *Publications of the Mississippi Historical Society* 11 (1910): 295–316; Noble, *Forty Years*; E. F. Puckett, "Reconstruction in Monroe County," *Publications of the Mississippi Historical Society* 11 (1910): 103–60; Jesse Thomas Wallace, *A History of the Negroes in Mississippi from 1865 to 1890* (repr., New York: Johnson Reprint, 1970); Ruth Watkins, "Reconstruction in Newton County," *Publications of the Mississippi Historical Society* 11 (1910): 205–28; Ruth Watkins, "Reconstruction in Marshall County," *Publications of Mississippi Historical Society* 12 (1912): 155–213.

13. Leon Litwack, *Trouble in Mind: Black Southerners in the Age of Jim Crow* (New York: Vintage, 1999), 219. The term "Jim Crow" dates back to the early antebellum era. Thomas "Daddy" Rice, a white minstrel, popularized the term. Litwack writes, "Using burned cork to blacken his face, attired in the ill-fitting, tattered garment of a beggar, and grinning broadly, Rice imitated the dancing, singing, and demeanor generally ascribed to Negro character" (*Trouble in Mind*, xiv). By the 1830s Jim Crow was part of the American vocabulary, and by the 1840s northern abolitionist papers were using the term to describe the setting up of separate railroad cars for African Americans and whites in the North.

14. The last chapter of Du Bois's *Black Reconstruction* is entitled "The Propaganda of History." The chapter challenged the historiography of his day pertaining to the Civil War, the Reconstruction era, and the role African Americans played in these formative years. Du Bois remarked, "How the facts of American history have in the last half century been falsified because the nation was ashamed. The South was ashamed because it fought to perpetuate human slavery. The North was ashamed because it had to call in the black men to save the Union, abolish slavery and establish democracy" (*Black Reconstruction*, 711).

15. Litwack, *Trouble in Mind*, xiii.

16. Du Bois, *Black Reconstruction*. For first quote see page 641; for remaining quotes see p. 645.

17. *Selma Times*, 30 June 1866.

18. Walter L. Fleming, ed., *Documentary History of Reconstruction: Political, Military,*

Religious, Educational and Industrial, 1865 to 1906, 2 vols. (repr., New York: McGraw-Hill, 1966), 2:165.

19. Only two other ex-Confederate states, South Carolina and Louisiana, did not specify in their educational amendments that the public school system would be segregated. Like Mississippi, South Carolina and Louisiana were both black-majority states, meaning that more than 50 percent of the population was African American.

20. The power of the black vote in Mississippi was never more evident than in the 1873 elections. In November 1873, Alexander K. Davis was elected lieutenant governor in Adelbert Ames's administration, James Hill was elected secretary of state, and Thomas W. Cardozo was appointed superintendent of public education — all African Americans. In 1875, Blanche Kelso Bruce was elected to the United States Senate, only the second African American to join the Senate (the other, Hiram Revels, was also from Mississippi). One year earlier, I. D. Shadd had been elected Speaker of the Lower House of the Mississippi legislature. John Roy Lynch, a former slave from Adams County, continued his appointment as Speaker of the House. Lynch was first elected in 1872. In addition to these appointments African Americans in Mississippi "won 55 of the 115 seats in the house and 9 out of 37 seats in the senate — 42 percent of the total number." For quote and for more information on African American representatives in Mississippi during the Reconstruction era, see Lerone Bennett Jr., *Before the Mayflower: A History of Black America* (repr., New York: Johnson Reprint Co., 1988), 495.

21. According to the 1860 census, 490,865 slaves and 52,128 slaveholders resided in Virginia and 462,198 slaves and 41,084 slaveholders resided in Georgia. Alabama had a slave and slaveholder population comparable to Mississippi's. In 1860, there were 435,080 slaves and 33,730 slaveholders in Alabama; there were 436,631 enslaved African Americans in Mississippi and 30,943 slaveholders. For census data, see http://fisher.lib.virginia.edu/census/.

22. The Thirteenth Amendment was rejected (and subsequently not ratified) by Mississippi in 1865. State lawmakers refused to ratify the amendment because they felt that they should have been paid compensation for the value of their freed slaves. One hundred and thirty years would pass before Mississippi would officially ratify the Thirteenth Amendment. On March 16, 1995, Mississippi became the last state to abolish slavery. See "Mississippi Legislators Set to Abolish Slavery," *Jet* March 1995, 6; "Mississippi Finally Bans Slavery," *Jet* April 1995, 6.

23. W. E. B. Du Bois, "Strivings of the Negro People," *The Atlantic Monthly*, August 1897, 196; W. E. B. Du Bois, *The Souls of Black Folk* (repr., New York: Dover Publications, 1994), 4.

CHAPTER I

1. Linda O. McMurray, *To Keep the Waters Troubled: The Life of Ida B. Wells* (New York: Oxford University Press, 1998); John Eaton Jr., *Grant, Lincoln, and the Freedmen* (New York: Longmans, Green, 1907), 2.

2. McMurray, *To Keep the Waters Troubled*, 5.

3. W. E. B. Du Bois, *Black Reconstruction in America* (repr., Cleveland: World Publishing, 1964), 638. Du Bois was born February 23, 1868, in Great Barrington, Massachusetts.

4. For discussion on Du Bois's teaching activities among African Americans in rural Tennessee, see David Levering Lewis, *W. E. B. Du Bois: Biography of a Race, 1868–1919* (New York: Henry Holt, 1993), 56–78; W. E. B. Du Bois, *The Souls of Black Folk* (repr., New York: Dover, 1994), 37–45.

5. Alfreda M. Duster, ed., *Crusade for Justice: The Autobiography of Ida B. Wells* (Chicago: University of Chicago Press, 1970), 9.

6. George Washington Williams, *A History of the Negro Race in America, 1619–1880*, 2 vols. (repr., New York, Arno Press, 1968), 2:180–81. According to Williams, who in 1883 became the first African American to write and publish a comprehensive history of the African American past, African Americans — enslaved or free — in Virginia were prohibited from attending school. In March 1819, an act was passed in the state prohibiting "all meetings or assemblages of slaves, or free negroes, or mulattoes" for the purposes of schooling. Schools were regularly kept, nonetheless, for African Americans in Virginia until the Nat Turner insurrection in 1831. Thereafter, whites in Virginia rigidly enforced the law. For additional discussion of antiliteracy laws against African Americans in the antebellum era, see Christopher M. Span, "Knowledge is Light, Knowledge is Power: African American Education in Antebellum America," in *Surmounting All Odds: Education, Opportunity & Society in the New Millennium*, ed. Carol Camp Yeakey and Ronald D. Henderson, 2 vols. (Greenwich, Conn.: Information Age Press, 2003), 1:1–29; Heather Andrea Williams, *Self-Taught: African American Education in Slavery and Freedom* (Chapel Hill: University of North Carolina Press, 2005), 203–13.

7. W. E. B. Du Bois believed that the first school for Virginia freedmen to be opened during the Civil War was Peake's establishment, reporting that it commenced on September 17, 1861, in the town of Hampton under the auspices of the American Missionary Association (AMA). Peake would manage this school for only about half a year, however. In the midst of her activities she would die of consumption in the spring of 1862 at the early age of thirty-nine. See Du Bois, *Black Reconstruction*, 642; Herbert Gutman, "Schools for Freedom: The Post-Emancipation Origins of Afro-American Education," in *From Slavery to Freedom, 1619–1877*, vol. 1 of *Major Problems in African American History*, ed. Thomas Holt and Elsa Barkley Brown, 389 (New York:

Houghton Mifflin, 2000); and Lewis C. Lockwood, "Mary S. Peake, The Colored Teacher at Fortress Monroe," in *Two Black Teachers during the Civil War*, ed. William Loren Katz (New York: Arno Press, 1969).

8. National Freedmen's Aid Union, *The Industry of the Freedmen of America* (Birmingham, Eng.: The National Freedmen Aid Union, 1867), 4.

9. Emancipation League, *Facts Concerning the Freedmen: Their Capacity and Their Destiny* (Boston, 1863), 5.

10. John W. Alvord, *Fourth Semi-Annual Report on Schools for Freedmen, July 1, 1867* (Washington, D.C.: Government Printing Office, 1867), 15.

11. Gutman, "'Schools for Freedom,'" 390–91. At the start of the Civil War, Tennessee law did not prohibit the teaching of African Americans although the educational bill passed in 1838 did designate only "white children over the age of six and under sixteen" were eligible to attend public schools. Albeit, in 1840, a second educational amendment was passed that did not specify color distinctions. It stated, "All children between the ages of six and twenty-one years shall have the privilege of attending the public schools." Daniel Watkins, from Davidson County, Tennessee, was an influential educator and organizer of Tennessee's first state convention for African Americans in 1865. For quotes in note, see Williams, *History of the Negro Race*, 180; for a brief synopsis of the activities and expectations of Watkins see, Philip S. Foner and George E. Walker, eds., *Proceedings of the Black National and State Conventions, 1865–1900* (Philadelphia: Temple University Press, 1986), 115–29.

12. John W. Alvord, *Eighth Semi-Annual Report on Schools for Freedmen, July 1, 1869* (Washington, D.C.: Government Printing Office, 1869), 62.

13. John W. Alvord, *First Semi-Annual Report on Schools and Finances of Freedmen, January 1, 1866* (Washington, D.C.: Government Printing Office, 1866), 9. See also Gutman, "Schools for Freedmen," 391.

14. Foner and Walker, *Proceedings*, 228.

15. Ibid., 227–28. This 1866 state convention for African Americans was not the first of its kind in Maryland. Unlike that of other slave states at the start of the Civil War, Maryland's free black population almost equaled its enslaved populace. Of the 171,131 African Americans in Maryland in 1860, 83,942 were classified as free. Most of the enslaved were concentrated on the Eastern Shore and in southern Maryland; free blacks resided almost exclusively in Baltimore and the Eastern Shore. The number of free blacks in Maryland produced a different set of standards and liberties for African Americans. Accordingly, prior to the Civil War, Maryland was the only slave state to allow, according to Foner and Walker, "the holding of a black convention, which met in Baltimore, July 27–28, 1852." For census data on Maryland, see Du Bois, *Black Reconstruction*, 564; and http://fisher.lib.virginia.edu/census/, where census data from 1790 to 1960 can be easily obtained.

16. James M. McPherson, *The Negro's Civil War: How American Negroes Felt and Acted during the War for the Union* (New York: Pantheon Books, 1965), 139.

17. Alvord, *Fourth Semi-Annual Report*, 14.

18. Quote from Eaton can be found in McPherson, *The Negro's Civil War*, 142.

19. Foner and Walker, *Proceedings*, 194.

20. Alvord, *First Semi-Annual Report*, 8.

21. Ibid., 10.

22. John. W. Alvord, *Third Semi-Annual Report on Schools for Freedmen, January 1, 1867* (Washington, D.C.: Government Printing Office, 1867), 5.

23. Ibid.

24. Randy J. Sparks, "'The White People's Arms are Longer than Ours': Blacks, Education, and the American Missionary Association in Reconstruction Mississippi," *Journal of Mississippi History* 54 (1992): 3.

25. Clifford Ganus Jr., "The Freedmen's Bureau in Mississippi" (Ph.D. diss., Tulane University, 1953), 301.

26. Sparks, "'The White People's Arms,'" 3.

27. Du Bois, *Black Reconstruction*, 646–47; Sparks, "'The White People's Arms,'" 3; Vernon Lane Wharton, *The Negro in Mississippi* (repr., New York: Harper & Row, 1965), 45–46, 243–56; Eric Foner, *Reconstruction: America's Unfinished Revolution, 1863–1877* (New York: Harper & Row, 1988), 98; Ganus, "The Freedmen's Bureau in Mississippi," 301–3. William Leon Woods, "Travail of Freedom: Mississippi Blacks, 1862–1870" (Ph.D. diss., Princeton University, 1979), 168.

28. James E. Yeatman, *A Report of the Conditions of the Freedmen of the Mississippi, Presented by the Western Sanitary Commission, December 17, 1863* (St. Louis: Western Sanitary Commission, 1864), 11.

29. Ibid.

30. Ibid.

31. George Rawick, ed., *The American Slave: A Composite Autobiography*, vol. 6, *Mississippi Narratives* (Westport, Conn.: Greenwood Press, 1977), pt. 1, 365; Williams, *Self-Taught*, 18.

32. Rawick, *Mississippi Narratives*, pt. 1,365.

33. James W. Garner, *Reconstruction in Mississippi* (New York: Macmillan, 1901), 354.

34. Ganus, "The Freedmen's Bureau in Mississippi," 155.

35. Woods, "Travail of Freedom," 8.

36. *Statistics of the Operations of the Executive Board of Friends' Association of Philadelphia and its Vicinity for the Relief of Colored Freedmen, As Presented to a Public Meeting of Friends, Held at Arch Street Meeting House, Philadelphia, 1st Month 19th, 1864* (Philadelphia: Inquirer Printing Office, 1864), 19.

37. Ibid., 14.

38. James T. Currie, "Freedmen at Davis Bend, April 1964," *Journal of Mississippi History* 46 (1984): 126.

39. Whitelaw Reid, *After the War: A Southern Tour, May 1, 1865 to May 1, 1866* (Cincinnati: Wilstach and Baldwin, 1866), 285.

40. Ibid., 283.

41. Ibid.

42. Currie, "Freedmen at Davis Bend," 126.

43. Martha Mitchell Bigelow, "Vicksburg: Experiment in Freedom," *Journal of Mississippi History* 26 (1964): 41.

44. Currie, "Freedmen at Davis Bend," 126.

45. Sparks, "'The White People's Arms,'" 2.

46. Ibid.

47. Rawick, *Mississippi Narratives*, pt. 3, 1226–42.

48. Rawick, *Mississippi Narratives*, 1237–38.

49. Rawick, *Mississippi Narratives*, pt. 5, 2401.

50. Rawick, *Mississippi Narratives*, pt. 4, 1878.

51. J. P. Bardwell to M. E. Strieby, January 5, 1865, in the American Missionary Association Archives microfilmed records from the Amistad Research Center, Tulane University, New Orleans. Hereafter referred to as the AMA Papers (Miss.).

52. Rawick, *Mississippi Narratives*, pt. 3, 1157.

53. Sparks, "'The White People's Arms,'" 2.

54. Ibid., 3; Bell Irvin Wiley, *Southern Negroes, 1861–1865* (repr., New Haven, Conn.: Yale University Press, 1965), 278.

55. Alvord, *Third Semi-Annual Report*, 20.

56. Joseph Warren to Stuart Eldridge, November 15, 1865. Bureau of Refugees, Freedmen, and Abandoned Lands, Mississippi, Records Group 105. Manuscripts obtained from the Mississippi Department of Archives and History. All Freedmen's Bureau documents hereafter referred to as BRFAL, Miss., RG 105. Warren replaced John Eaton Jr. in December 1865 when Eaton resigned from the Freedmen's Bureau. Eaton's stint with the bureau was very brief. He joined it at the close of the war when the bureau commissioner, General O. O. Howard, requested that Eaton serve as the assistant commissioner for the District of Columbia and parts of Maryland. After resigning from the bureau, Eaton returned to Memphis, where he edited the *Memphis Post*. In 1867, he would become the state superintendent of education in Tennessee. He resigned from this post in 1870 to serve as the head of the Bureau of Education for President Ulysses S. Grant. For more information on Eaton, see Eaton, *Grant, Lincoln, and the Freedmen*, ix–xxxiv.

57. Joseph Warren to Stuart Eldridge, November 15, 1865, BRFAL, Miss., RG 105.

58. Ibid.

59. Ibid.

60. Alvord, *First Semi-Annual Report*, 14.

61. *Statistics*, 20.

62. Ibid., 21.

63. Yeatman, *A Report on the Conditions of the Freedmen*, 16.

64. Ibid., 14.

65. Alvord, *Eighth Semi-Annual Report*, 46.

66. Ganus, "The Freedmen's Bureau in Mississippi," 392–93. This total was aggregated from an appendix table offered by Ganus. Bureau and missionary aid collected in this same timespan approximately $47,857.14. The total amount collected, inclusive of known freedmen contributions, was $71,833.24.

67. Ibid., 311.

68. Woods, "Travail of Freedom," 147.

69. Ibid.

70. James W. C. Pennington, *The Fugitive Blacksmith; or, Events in the History of James W. C. Pennington, Pastor of a Presbyterian Church, New York, Formerly a Slave in the State of Maryland, United States* (London: Charles Gilpin, 1849), 56–57. James W. C. Pennington's narrative can also be obtained online at http://docsouth.unc.edu/neh/penning49/menu.html.

71. Ibid.

72. Anderson, *Education of Blacks in the South*, 5.

73. Quoted in Walter L. Fleming, ed., *Documentary History of Reconstruction: Political, Military, Social, Religious, Educational and Industrial, 1865 to 1906*, 2 vols. (repr., New York: McGraw-Hill, 1966), 2:174.

74. Du Bois, *Black Reconstruction*, 641.

75. Quoted in Leon Litwack, *Trouble in Mind: Black Southerners in the Age of Jim Crow* (New York: Vintage, 1998), 56.

76. Wharton, *The Negro in Mississippi*, 45.

77. A. Hutchinson, comp., *Code of Mississippi: Being an Analytical Compilation of the Public and General Statutes of the Territory and State, with Tabular References to the Local and Private Acts, from 1798–1848* (Jackson, Miss.: Price and Fall State Printers, 1848); Williams, *Self-Taught*, 205.

78. Du Bois, *Black Reconstruction*, 641.

79. Litwack, *Trouble in Mind*, 53.

80. Yeatman, *A Report on the Condition of the Freedmen*, 3.

81. Foner, *Reconstruction*, 97.

82. *Statistics*, 28.

83. Donald Nieman, "The Freedmen's Bureau and the Mississippi Black Code,"

The Journal of Mississippi History 40 (1978): 93–94; David Sansing, "The Failure of Johnsonian Reconstruction in Mississippi, 1865–1866," *The Journal of Mississippi History* 34 (1972): 378–87.

84. John Dennett, *The South as It Is: 1865–1866* (New York: Harcourt Brace, 1965), 304.

85. Anderson, *Education of Blacks in the South*, 15.

CHAPTER 2

1. John Eaton Jr., *Grant, Lincoln, and the Freedmen* (New York: Longmans, Green, 1907), 4.

2. Ibid., 5–6.

3. Ibid., 13. The contraband camp at Grand Junction was not the first of its kind. In May 1861, Brigadier General Benjamin F. Butler initiated the efforts that led the military to assign fugitive or freedom-seeking enslaved African Americans to work at the government's expense. At Fortress Monroe in Virginia, Butler instituted a system that provided wage employment to able-bodied men and women, rations to the most destitute, and a fund to wage-earning African Americans so they could set aside money for the elderly and disabled. In Autumn 1861, at Port Royal, South Carolina, Edward L. Pierce, and his successor, General Rufus Saxton, carried on similar efforts by providing relief, employment, and education for enslaved African Americans. Such considerations toward African Americans were not as favorable in the western military campaigns. In November 1861, General H. W. Halleck, in "General Order No. 3," excluded freedom-seeking blacks from entering Union lines. By March 1863, however, Halleck would have a change in attitude. He conferred with Grant and deduced that "the character of the war has very much changed within the last year. There is no possible hope of reconciliation with the rebels. . . . There can be no peace but that which is forced by the sword." Within six months, Halleck would urge Grant to use enslaved African Americans who came into Union lines as laborers against the South. By this time, Grant had already commanded Eaton to take charge of this activity. For quote in note and further discussion of these developments, see Eaton, *Grant, Lincoln, and the Freedmen*, 51, 46–61.

4. Ira Berlin et al., eds., *The Destruction of Slavery*, ser. 1, vol. 1 of *Freedom: A Documentary History of Emancipation, 1861–1867* (New York: Cambridge University Press, 1985), 256.

5. Henry Swint, *The Northern Teacher in the South, 1862–1870* (Nashville: Vanderbilt University Press, 1941); Jacqueline Jones, *Soldiers of Light and Love: Northern Teachers and Georgia Blacks, 1865–1873* (Chapel Hill: University of North Carolina Press, 1980).

6. Edward Norris Kirk, *Educated Labor, or, Our Duty in Regard to the Americo-African*

Race: An Address Delivered before the American Missionary Association, Homer, N.Y., October 17, 1867 (New York: Holt Brothers, 1868), 7.

7. John W. Alvord, *Eighth Semi-Annual Report on Schools for Freedmen, July 1, 1869* (Washington, D.C.: Government Printing Office, 1869), 46.

8. George Rawick, ed., *Mississippi Narratives*, vol. 6 of *The American Slave: A Composite Autobiography*, 19 vols. (Westport, Conn.: Greenwood Press, 1977), pt. 1, 74.

9. Ibid., 95.

10. Ibid., 443.

11. Ibid., 303.

12. Eaton, *Grant, Lincoln, and the Freedmen*, 19.

13. Bell Irvin Wiley, *Southern Negroes, 1861–1865* (repr., New Haven, Conn.: Yale University Press, 1965), 269.

14. Vernon Lane Wharton, *The Negro in Mississippi, 1865–1890* (repr., New York: Harper & Row, 1965); Noralee Frankel, *Freedom's Women: Black Women and Families in Civil War Era Mississippi* (Bloomington: Indiana University Press, 1999), 31.

15. *Statistics of the Operations of the Executive Board of Friends' Association of Philadelphia and its Vicinity, for the Relief of Colored Freedmen, as Presented to a Public Meeting of Friends, Held at Arch Street Meeting House, Philadelphia, 1st Month 19th, 1864* (Philadelphia: Inquirer Printers Office, 1864), 4.

16. Ibid., 9.

17. Eaton, *Grant, Lincoln, and the Freedmen*, 18.

18. Ibid., 19.

19. Quoted in David M. Oshinsky, *"Worse than Slavery": Parchman Farm and the Ordeal of Jim Crow Justice* (New York: Free Press, 1996), 15.

20. *Statistics*, 4.

21. William Leon Woods, "Travail of Freedom: Mississippi Blacks, 1862–1870" (Ph.D. diss., Princeton University, 1979), 8.

22. For quote, see John Eaton Jr., "Report of the U.S. Army, Department of Tennessee for 1864," BRFAL, Miss., RG 105. While this quote offers a good illustration of the significant number of the freedom-seeking African Americans seeking safety in the Union army, it vastly underestimates the rationale of black Mississippians to seek shelter within Union-occupied areas. Their decision to flee enslavement toward the Union army was not instinctual or "without reason," but purposeful and empowering; they assumed Union soldiers would be supportive of and sympathetic to their desire to be free.

23. Annie E. Harper Papers, October, 1876. Manuscript division, Mississippi Department of Archives and History, 2450F. Hereafter referred to as MDAH. Not to dismiss the validity of this stark recollection, but the observation that 11,000 African Americans lay dead and buried may overestimate the total number witnessed by

Harper. It is clear from the available material evidence that a significant number of blacks died during these years, especially in Natchez, but Harper's estimate seems particularly high, and no other material evidence can corroborate its accuracy. If it is accurate, however, that would mean that in Harper's single observation, approximately 3 percent of Mississippi's total black population lay dead in one city. The entire black population, according to the 1860 census, in Adams County—where Natchez resides—was 9,920. Still, this observation does raise an important demographic question for future consideration. What effects did the Civil War have on the life opportunities of enslaved blacks?

24. Quoted in Martha Mitchell Bigelow, "Vicksburg: Experiment in Freedom," *Journal of Mississippi History* 26 (1964): 40.

25. Quoted in Frankel, *Freedom's Women*, 32.

26. *New England Freedmen Aid Society: Second Annual Report* (Boston: Office of the Society, 1864), 38. To the best of my understanding, a study systematically assessing the death toll of enslaved blacks during this epoch of American history has not been done. Such stark recollections, as those mentioned, raise a critical question for historians of the Civil War, demography, the South, and the African American experience to explore in order to better understand how the South's enslaved black populace fared amid the confusion and devastation of a nation at war.

27. John Eaton Jr. to Levi Coffin, July 5, 1864, BRFAL, Miss., RG 105.

28. Northwestern Freedmen's Association, "An Urgent Appeal to the People of the Northwest," January 10, 1864 American Missionary Association Archives, Amistad Research Center, Tulane University, roll 1. Hereafter referred to as the AMA Papers (Miss.).

29. Joseph Warren, *Reports Relating to Colored Schools in Mississippi, Arkansas, and Western Tennessee, April 1865* (Memphis: Freedmen Press, 1865), 18–20.

30. *New England Freedmen Aid Society*, 37.

31. *Statistics*, 16.

32. *New England Freedmen Aid Society*, 37; James E. Yeatman, *A Report of the Conditions of the Freedmen of the Mississippi, Presented by the Western Sanitary Commission, December 17, 1863* (St. Louis: Western Sanitary Commission, 1864), 13.

33. Northwestern Freedmen's Association, "An Urgent Appeal to the People of the Northwest," January 10, 1864, AMA Papers (Miss.), roll 1.

34. Yeatman, *A Report of the Conditions of the Freedmen*, 13.

35. Woods, "The Travail of Freedom," 11.

36. Ibid., 57.

37. *Statistics*, 17.

38. Yeatman, *A Report of the Conditions of the Freedmen*, 6.

39. Clifford Ganus Jr. documents that of all the southern states that received missionary and governmental medical assistance, Mississippi ranked last in freedpeople

being treated, despite their immediate need for attention. A total of 4,905 black Mississippians were treated, in comparison to 7,493 in Louisiana, 25,907 in Virginia, 15,767 in North Carolina, 9,523 in Georgia, and 48,575 in South Carolina. See Clifford Ganus Jr., "The Freedmen's Bureau in Mississippi" (Ph.D. diss., Tulane University, 1953), 389.

40. Rev. S. F. Porter to Rev. L. W. Magile, March 18, 1864, AMA Papers (Miss.), roll 1.

41. Wiley, *Southern Negroes*, 268.

42. Ibid.

43. *Statistics*, 17.

44. Correspondence of AMA teachers found in the AMA papers of Mississippi provides a host of examples that illustrate the additional duties and responsibilities of northern-born teachers. The correspondence explains in detail daily practices of teachers, which included countless tasks in addition to offering instruction to freedpeople.

45. G. M. Carruthers to George Whipple, September 12, 1863, AMA Papers (Miss.), roll 1.

46. Rev. S. G. Wright to Rev. C. H. Fowler, February 1, 1864, AMA Papers (Miss.), roll 1.

47. Rev. S. G. Wright to George Whipple, December 10, 1863, AMA Papers (Miss.), roll 1.

48. Joseph Warren to Lt. Stuart Eldridge, December 11, 1865, BRFAL, Miss., RG 105.

49. Rev. S. F. Porter to Rev. George Whipple, March 5, 1864, AMA Papers (Miss.), roll 1.

50. Monthly school reports from Lily Grandison, a former ex-slave in Natchez, and Clara Freeman, a native free black of Natchez, illustrate this practice. See monthly school reports of Miss Lily Grandison for February, 1866, April, 1866, June, 1866; monthly school reports for Clara Freeman for February, 1866; superintendent report for Palmer Litts, March 1866. All can be found in the AMA Papers (Miss.), roll 1.

51. J. A. Hawley to Colonel Lorenzo Thomas, June 20, 1865, BRFAL RG 105.

52. Northwestern Freedmen's Association, "An Urgent Appeal to the People of the Northwest," January 10, 1864, AMA Papers (Miss.), roll 1.

53. John Eaton Jr. to Rev. George Whipple, June 29, 1863, AMA Papers (Miss.), roll 1.

54. Ibid.

55. Ronald E. Butchart, *Northern Schools, Southern Blacks, and Reconstruction: Freedmen's Education, 1862–1875* (Westport, Conn.: Greenwood Press, 1980), 128–30.

56. In fact, the 1866 semiannual report of Alvord illustrates that Tennessee had 125 teachers, Maryland had 101 teachers, Georgia had 113 teachers, South Carolina had

148 teachers, North Carolina had 135 teachers, and Virginia had 200 teachers. See John W. Alvord, *Second Semi-Annual Report on Schools and Finances of Freedmen, July 1, 1866* (Washington, D.C.: Government Printing Office, 1868), 2.

57. Ganus, "The Freedmen's Bureau in Mississippi," 303–17.

58. Randy J. Sparks, "'The White People's Arms are Longer than Ours': Blacks, Education, and the American Missionary Association in Reconstruction Mississippi," *Journal of Mississippi History* 54 (1992): 10.

59. J. A. Hawley to Colonel Lorenzo Thomas, June 20, 1865, BRFAL, Miss., RG 105. These missionary-supported schools for freedpeople reported by Joseph Warren in table 2 are not inclusive of the unspecified, but nonetheless significant, number of relatively independent black schools scattered throughout Mississippi as discussed in chapter 1. Thus, this table only illustrates the reported schools acknowledged by Joseph Warren, and not the total number of schooling opportunities for black Mississippians.

60. Rev. S. G. Wright to George Whipple, January 29, 1864, AMA Papers (Miss.), roll 1.

61. Warren, *Reports Relating to Colored Schools*, 4.

62. Ibid.

63. G. M. Carruthers to Rev. George Whipple, September 12, 1863, AMA Papers (Miss.), roll 1.

64. Warren, *Reports Relating to Colored Schools*, 4.

65. John Eaton Jr. to Rev. George Whipple, September 11, 1863, AMA Papers (Miss.), roll 1.

66. Ganus, "The Freedmen's Bureau in Mississippi," 303.

67. Instruction in mental rather than written arithmetic most likely had to do with the limited writing materials (pens, paper, chalk and chalkboards) and apparatuses (desks, tables, boards) in schools than with freedpeople's inability to write. Similar observations have been identified in the teaching of geography. Rather than identify or write specific geographic locations, freedpeople were instructed to memorize or recite these locations. Again, limited school materials, not limited ability on the part of freedpeople or limited expectations or interest on the part of teachers, was the cause of this pedagogical approach.

68. "Monthly School Report of Miss Eleis Spell," June 1864, AMA Papers (Miss.), roll 1.

69. "Monthly School Report of Miss Clara Spees," June 1865, AMA Papers (Miss.), roll 1.

70. "Monthly School Report of Miss A. C. Hardwood," September 1865, AMA Papers (Miss.), roll 1.

71. "Monthly School Report of Miss Sarah P. Hulburt," April 1866, AMA Papers (Miss.), roll 1.

72. Yeatman, *A Report of the Conditions of the Freedmen*, 2.

73. In late August 1865, 8,784 of the 10,193 Union soldiers (86 percent) in Mississippi were black. Nevertheless, by mid-April 1866, local whites opposing the presence of black troops because of their association with the general freed black population demanded their immediate dismissal. William C. Harris in *Presidential Reconstruction in Mississippi* commented that local whites asserted that black troops "threatened white control of blacks and offered poor examples for local blacks" as many white Mississippians wished to keep African Americans in a subordinate position. Consequently, to maintain a peaceful and working relationship with whites and to continue forward with the federal government's Reconstruction policy in Mississippi, President Johnson offered an honorable discharge to all black Union servicemen in Mississippi and dismissed them from their military duties. By the end of April 1866, all black servicemen in Mississippi were appropriately discharged. See William C. Harris, *Presidential Reconstruction in Mississippi* (Baton Rouge: Louisiana State University Press, 1967), 63, 70–71; C. Peter Ripley, ed., *The Black Abolitionist Papers*, vol. 5, *The United States, 1859–1865* (Chapel Hill: University of North Carolina Press, 1992), 402–3; Rev. J. P. Bardwell to George Whipple, April 11, 1866, AMA Papers (Miss.), roll 2.

74. By far the best account of African American legislators in Mississippi during the Reconstruction era is Vernon Lane Wharton's publication, *The Negro in Mississippi, 1865–1890*. His biographical sketch of these legislators was drawn primarily from traditionalists' early twentieth-century Reconstruction histories and contemporary newspaper accounts. Nevertheless, Wharton illustrated that the significant majority of African American legislators during the Reconstruction era, state and local, were former slaves, not freeborn blacks. See Wharton, *The Negro in Mississippi*, 138–80. Historian Eric Foner, in his quintessential Reconstruction study, confirmed Wharton's findings and added that the majority of Mississippi's African American legislators were ex-slave army veterans or an immediate relative of these veterans. See Eric Foner, *Reconstruction: America's Unfinished Revolution* (New York: Harper & Row, 1988), 112.

75. Heather Andrea Williams, *Self-Taught: African American Education in Slavery and Freedom* (Chapel Hill: North Carolina Press, 2005), 50.

76. Monthly School Report Miss Anna M. Somers for September 1865, AMA Papers (Miss), roll 1.

77. Rev. A. D. Olds to George Whipple, April 16, 1863, AMA Papers (Miss.), roll 1.

78. Sparks, "'The White People's Arms,'" 17.

79. Many AMA letters reported a somewhat standard lesson plan in Sabbath schools. The majority of schools commenced early in the morning, around 8 A.M. and ended around noon. This was particularly true during the summer months. The singing of hymns, prayer, and Bible lessons — reading, recitation, and explanation of scriptures — accordingly followed. A number of Sabbath schools were reported as

having extensive book collections. A Sabbath school in Natchez had an excess of 200 books in its collection. Freedpeople eager to develop their literacy skills most likely made good use of these reading materials.

80. Unlike the other black-majority states — South Carolina and Louisiana — Mississippi had a relatively insignificant free black population before the war. Its peak was approximately 1,300 in 1840; however, by 1860 the census recorded just 773 free blacks. The majority of free blacks resided in the southwestern portion of the state (225 resided in Adams County alone) and over 600 were classified as "mulatto." That would mean that approximately 77 percent of all free blacks in Mississippi prior to the Civil War were biracial. For additional information on free blacks in Mississippi prior to the Civil War see Wharton, *The Negro in Mississippi*, 12.

81. Ganus, "The Freedmen's Bureau in Mississippi," 325.

82. The Freedmen's Bureau Act of March 3, 1865, made no provision for the establishment of schools, and President Johnson had vetoed a revised Freedmen's Bureau bill introduced by Senator Lyman Trumbull on January 12, 1866, which would have empowered Oliver. O. Howard, the bureau commissioner, to erect buildings for dependent freedpeople. Upon the veto, Congress modified the requisition and passed another Freedmen's Bureau bill. President Johnson vetoed this bill as well; nonetheless, Congress passed the bill over Johnson's veto on July 16, 1866. This bill provided for an appropriation of $521,000 to be used in constructing, renting, and repairing school buildings throughout the South. See Paul Skeels Peirce, The *Freedmen's Bureau: A Chapter in the History of Reconstruction* (Iowa City: University of Iowa Press, 1904), 63; Ganus, "The Freedmen's Bureau in Mississippi," 339.

83. Ganus, "The Freedmen's Bureau in Mississippi," 304.

84. Circular No. 4, July 25, 1865, BRFAL, Miss., RG 105; Joseph Warren to G. W. Buckley, July 8, 1865, BRFAL, Miss., RG 105. Bureau-sponsored schools were the missionary or private black schools already in operation. After the arrival of the Freedmen's Bureau, these schools, if they wanted to partake in the incentives offered by the bureau, would report directly to the Freedmen's Bureau. By 1869, nearly 3,000 schools serving over 150,000 pupils, throughout the South, reported to the bureau, and, as Eric Foner points out, these figures do not include many evening and private schools operated by missionary societies and by freedpeople themselves. See Foner, *Reconstruction*, 144.

85. Sparks, "'The White People's Arms,'" 10.

86. Roger L. Ransom and Richard Sutch, One Kind of Freedom: The Economic Consequences of Emancipation (Cambridge: Cambridge University Press, 1977), 40–55.

87. J. J. Knox to Samuel Hunt, May 25, 1866, AMA Papers (Miss.), roll 2.

88. Joseph Warren to Stuart Eldridge, August 31, 1865, BRFAL, Miss., RG 105; Joseph Warren to Stuart Eldridge, January 2, 1866, BRFAL, Miss., RG 105.

89. Joseph Warren to Stuart Eldridge, August 31, 1865, BRFAL, Miss., RG 105.

90. J. P. Bardwell to Rev. S. Hunt, November 2, 1866, AMA Papers (Miss.), roll 2.

91. J. P. Bardwell to George Whipple, January 2, 1867, AMA Papers (Miss.), roll 2.

92. Woods, "The Travail of Freedom," 165.

93. This story was related to Joseph Warren from Reverend Palmer Litts. See Joseph Warren to Lt. Stuart Eldridge, November 15, 1865, BRFAL, Miss., RG 105.

94. Ibid.

95. Gen. E. O. C. Ord to O. O. Howard, January 27, 1867, BRFAL, Miss., RG 105.

96. J. W. Alvord, *Fourth Semi-Annual Report on Schools for Freedmen, July 1, 1867* (Washington, D.C.: Government Printing Press, 1867), 43.

97. Woods, "The Travail of Freedom," 193; Ganus, "The Freedmen's Bureau in Mississippi," 392–95; Wharton, *The Negro in Mississippi*, 244.

98. Sparks, "'The White People's Arms,'" 25.

99. Ibid., 26.

100. "Report of Dr. Mayo to the Bureau of Education," in John Eaton Jr., *Report of the General Superintendent of Freedmen, Department of the Tennessee and Arkansas, for 1864*, 21 (Memphis: Freedmen Press Printing, 1865).

101. Sparks, "'The White People's Arms,'" 7.

102. "Report of the Commissioner," *Executive Documents*, no. 11, 39th cong., sess. 1, 34. Moreover, this declaration was made understanding that the Bureau Act of 1865 provided no provision for the educational needs or demands of freedpeople.

103. Ganus, "The Freedmen's Bureau in Mississippi," 337.

104. Col. Wood to Bishop Spalding, November 26, 1866, BRFAL, Miss., RG 105.

105. *New England Freedmen Aid Society*, 40.

106. Ibid.

107. Foner, *Reconstruction*, 144.

108. Ibid., 158.

109. *Vicksburg Journal*, August 5, 1865.

110. Ibid.

111. John E. Bryant's quote was telegraphed to the *Vicksburg Journal*, August 13, 1865.

112. Ibid.

113. *The Vicksburg Journal*, August 15, 1865.

114. Ibid.

115. *The Vicksburg Journal*, December 10, 1866.

116. Ibid.

117. Ibid.

118. Foner, *Reconstruction*, 144.

119. Merrimon Howard to O. O. Howard, April 7, 1866, BRFAL, Miss., RG 105.

120. Ibid.

121. William Preston Vaughn, *Schools for All: The Blacks & Public Education in the South, 1865–1877* (Lexington: University Press of Kentucky, 1974), 15. See also Henry Swint, *Dear Ones at Home: Letters from Contraband Camps* (Nashville: Vanderbilt University Press, 1966), 144.

122. S. G. Wright to George Whipple, June 25, 1864, AMA Papers (Miss.), roll 1. This situation was similar across the South. In Savannah, Georgia, for example, the AMA waged a long campaign against the independent black-controlled school system and finally succeeded in taking control of it. See Jacqueline Jones, *Soldiers of Light and Love* (Chapel Hill: University of North Carolina Press, 1980), 68–76 and Joe Richardson, *Christian Reconstruction: The American Missionary Association and Southern Blacks, 1861–1870* (Athens: University of Georgia Press, 1986), 246–50.

123. Foner, *Reconstruction*, 100.

124. H. R. Pease to Gen. O. O. Howard, February 1, 1868, BRFAL, Miss., RG 105.

125. Sparks, "'The White People's Arms,'" 10.

126. Ibid.

127. Ibid., 27.

CHAPTER 3

1. Ira Berlin, *Generations of Captivity: A History of African American Slaves* (Cambridge, Mass.: Harvard University Press, Belknap Press, 2003), 263.

2. Ibid., 254.

3. Ruth Watkins, "Reconstruction in Marshall County," *Publications of the Mississippi Historical Society* 12 (1912): 156.

4. Michael Wayne, *The Reshaping of Plantation Society, The Natchez District, 1860–1880* (Urbana: University of Illinois Press, 1983), 10.

5. Ibid. See chapter 1 for a more detailed analysis of the wealth in the lower Mississippi River valley.

6. Watkins, "Reconstruction in Marshall County," 156.

7. Ibid.

8. Ibid.

9. The white population of the county was reduced by almost 10,000 for two primary reasons: first, the loss of life in the Civil War, and second, the formation of two new counties—Lee (1866) and Union (1870). See M. G. Abney, "Reconstruction in Pontotoc County," *Publications of the Mississippi Historical Society* 11 (1910): 259.

10. Hattie Magee, "Reconstruction in Lawrence and Jefferson Counties," *Publications of the Mississippi Historical Society* 11 (1910): 165.

11. Ruth Watkins, "Reconstruction in Newton County," *Publications of the Mississippi Historical Society* 11 (1910): 207.

12. Whitelaw Reid, *After the War: A Southern Tour* (Cincinnati: Wilstach and Baldwin, 1866), 283.

13. Wayne, *The Reshaping of Plantation Society*, 31.

14. U.S. Congress, House, *Report of the Joint Select Committee to Inquire into the Condition of Affairs in the Late Insurrectionary States, Made to the Two Houses of Congress, February 19, 1872,* 42d Cong., 2d sess., H. Rep. 22 (Washington, D.C.: Government Printing Office, 1872), 179.

15. Eric Foner, *Nothing but Freedom: Emancipation and Its Legacy* (Baton Rouge: Louisiana State University Press, 1983), 3.

16. Quoted in ibid., 44.

17. The Freedmen's Bureau recorded numerous instances of labor contracts and agreements throughout the South, especially in Mississippi. See Records of the Bureau of Refugees, Freedmen, and Abandoned Lands, National Archives, Micro E185.2 Reel 24, M803. All Freedmen's Bureau documents hereafter referred to as BRFAL, Miss., RG 105.

18. Wayne, *The Reshaping of Plantation Society*, 196.

19. See Garner, *Reconstruction in Mississippi* (New York: Macmillan, 1901), 104; J. S. McNeily, "War and Reconstruction in Mississippi," *Publications of the Mississippi Historical Society*, centenary series, 1 (1917): 326.

20. Watkins, "Reconstruction in Marshall County," 205.

21. Wayne, *The Reshaping of Plantation Society*, 123.

22. This was a privilege few free blacks in Mississippi had before the war. By contrast, Thomas Holt in *Black over White*, recognized free black South Carolinians as a notable "small minority" in the antebellum era. "Conceding all the oppressions and indignities of their 'quasi-free' status under the old regime," Holt opined, free blacks "had generally enjoyed an economic freedom, in fact if not in law, that enabled many of them to live comfortable and in some cases wealthy lives." Charles Vincent's volume on Louisiana's black Reconstruction legislators also highlights that the state, in particular New Orleans, historically had a large, wealthy, and well-educated free black antebellum population. This reality ensured a progressive number of black legislators who made sure state statutes addressed the concerns of freedmen in slavery's aftermath. See Vernon Lane Wharton, *The Negro in Mississippi* (repr., New York: Harper & Row, 1965); Thomas Holt, *Black over White: Negro Political Leadership in South Carolina during Reconstruction* (Urbana: University of Illinois Press, 1977); Charles Vincent, *Black Legislators in Louisiana during Reconstruction* (Baton Rouge: Louisiana State University Press, 1976).

23. George P. Rawick et al., eds., *The American Slave: A Composite Autobiography*, vol. 8, supplement series 1 (Westport, Conn.: Greenwood Press, 1977), 1348.

24. Quoted in Wayne, *The Reshaping of Plantation Society*, 45.

25. David L. Cohn, *The Life and Times of King Cotton* (New York: Oxford University

Press, 1956), 155; William Charles Sallis, "The Color Line in Mississippi Politics, 1865–1915" (Ph.D. diss., University of Kentucky, 1967), 3 (freedman's quote).

26. David M. Oshinsky, *"Worse than Slavery": Parchman Farms and the Ordeal of Jim Crow Justice* (New York: Free Press, 1996), 19.

27. Wayne, *The Reshaping of Plantation Society*, 31–52.

28. National Freedmen's Aid Union, *The Industry of the Freedmen* (Birmingham, Eng.: The National Freedmen's Aid Union, 1866), 18–9.

29. Foner, *Nothing but Freedom*, 47.

30. Irby Nichols, "Reconstruction in DeSoto County," *Publications of the Mississippi Historical Society* 11 (1910): 312.

31. E. F. Puckett, "Reconstruction in Monroe County," *Publications of the Mississippi Historical Society* 11 (1910): 140.

32. Lucy M. Cohen, "Entry of Chinese to the Lower South from 1864 to 1870: Policy Dilemmas," *Southern Studies* 27 (1978): 5–38; Vernon Lane Wharton, *The Negro in Mississippi*, 97–98, 125; James W. Loewen, *The Mississippi Chinese: Between Black and White* (Cambridge, Mass.: Harvard University Press, 1971), 1–2, 22–31.

33. Quoted in Wayne, *The Reshaping of Plantation Society*, 61.

34. Michael Wayne gives a good illustration of a plantation wage. Most consisted of a trivial monetary amount and yearly food and shelter. Such wages, Wayne contends, easily appealed to the newly freed slave, but not an urban-born immigrant. See Wayne, *The Reshaping of Plantation Society*, 69; see also, Rowland Berthoff, "Southern Attitudes toward Immigration, 1865–1914," *Journal of Southern History* 17 (1951): 328–60.

35. Reid, *After the War*, 563.

36. Southerner, "Agricultural Labor at the South," *The Galaxy* 12 (1871): 328.

37. Walter Lynn Fleming, ed., *Laws Relating to Freedmen, 1865–6* (Morgantown: University of West Virginia Press, 1904), 1. Fleming adhered to the traditional perspective of Reconstruction that sympathized with the defeated southern Confederacy and the North's ill-treatment of the South during this era. This perspective is most apparent in Fleming's repeated description of the black codes, as the "so-called black codes", or "so-called Black Laws."

38. Ibid.

39. Donald Nieman, "The Freedmen's Bureau and the Mississippi Black Code," *The Journal of Mississippi History* 40 (1978): 93–94; David Sansing, "The Failure of Johnsonian Reconstruction in Mississippi, 1865–1866," *The Journal of Mississippi History* 34 (1972): 378–87.

40. Nieman, "The Freedmen's Bureau and the Mississippi Black Code," 94.

41. Ibid.

42. Woods, "Travail of Freedom: Mississippi Blacks, 1862–1870" (Ph.D. diss., Princeton University, 1979), 144.

43. Lt. Stuart Eldridge to Gen. Thomas J. Wood, February 3, 1866, BRFAL, Miss., RG 105.

44. John J. Knox to Capt. E. Bamberger, March 10, 1866, BRFAL, Miss., RG 105.

45. Thomas Holt contends in *Black over White* that South Carolina's black codes, which were enacted approximately one month after Mississippi instituted its statutes, not only threatened the ex-slave to accept a serfdom status, but also threatened the ultimate survival of South Carolina's free black population as a distinct social class. "The Black Codes may have restricted the newly won freedoms of the ex-slaves," Holt asserts, but "they struck still harder at the more traditional privileges of the antebellum free class" (19–21). However, Leon Litwack suggests, "To make too much of the pretentiousness exhibited by members of these small elites would be to overlook the degree to which most mulattos, free Negroes, and former slaves had always worked and lived together, sharing a common condition and plight and generally too preoccupied with survival in a hostile white society to cultivate any caste pretensions." See Leon Litwack, *Been in the Storm So Long: The Aftermath of Slavery* (New York: Vintage, 1980), 514.

46. Oshinsky, *"Worse than Slavery"*, 18.

47. *Laws of Mississippi, 1865* (Jackson, Miss.: J. J. Shannon, 1866), 90; Fleming, *Laws Relating to Freedmen*, 11–12.

48. Oshinsky, *"Worse than Slavery"*, 21.

49. Ronald Davis, *Good and Faithful Labor: From Slavery to Sharecropping in the Natchez District, 1860–1890* (Westport, Conn.: Greenwood Press, 1982), 6.

50. Quoted in F. W. Loring and C. F. Atkinson, *Cotton Culture and the South Considered with Reference to Emigration* (Boston: Houghton Mifflin, 1869), 32.

51. Eugene Genovese, *Roll Jordan Roll: The World the Slaves Made* (New York: Vintage, 1974).

52. James H. Matthews to George D. Reynolds, January 7, 1866, BRFAL, Miss., RG 105.

53. Col. Samuel Thomas to Gen. Oliver Otis Howard, December 25, 1865, BRFAL, Miss., RG 105.

54. Ibid.

55. Col. Samuel Thomas to Gen. Oliver Otis Howard, September 21, 1865, BRFAL, Miss., RG 105.

56. Foner, *Nothing but Freedom*, 45.

57. Roger L. Ransom and Richard Sutch, *One Kind of Freedom: The Economic Consequences of Emancipation* (New York: Cambridge University Press, 1977), 40–55.

58. For a detailed quantitative analysis of the withdrawal of black labor in the cotton-South, see chapter 3 of Ransom and Sutch, *One Kind of Freedom*.

59. McNeily, "War and Reconstruction in Mississippi," 236; Woods, "The Travail of Freedom," 212.

60. William C. Harris, *Presidential Reconstruction in Mississippi* (Baton Rouge: Louisiana State University Press, 1970), 228–45.

61. Wharton, *The Negro in Mississippi*, 139.

62. More recently James D. Anderson has written on the role race played in the drafting and enactment of the Fourteenth Amendment. See James D. Anderson, "Race-Conscious Educational Policies versus a 'Color-Blind Constitution': A Historical Perspective," *Educational Researcher* 36 (2007): 249–57.

63. *Jackson Weekly Clarion*, March 28, 1867.

64. Ibid.

65. *Natchez Democrat*, June 22, 1867.

66. Wharton, *The Negro in Mississippi*, 120.

67. Woods, "The Travail of Freedom," 212.

68. *Natchez Democrat*, April 6, 1867.

69. The sixteen African American delegates were John C. Brinson (Rankin County), Charles Caldwell (Hinds County), William T. Combash (Washington County), Amos Drane (Madison County), Charles W. Fitzhugh (Wilkinson County), Emanuel Handy (Copiah County), Henry P. Jacobs (Adams County), Amos Johnson (Warren County), Wesley Lawson (Lawrence County), William Leonard (Yazoo County), Henry Mason (Hinds County), Cyrus Meyers (Rankin County), Matthew Newson (Claiborne County), Isham Stewart (Noxubee County), Doctor Stites (Claiborne County), T. W. Stringer (Warren County). For additional information on the sixteen black delegates of the 1868 Constitutional Convention, see James Currie, "Conflict and Consensus: Creating the 1868 Mississippi Constitution" (M.A. thesis, University of Virginia, 1969); Woods, "The Travail of Freedom," 224.

70. *Journal of the Proceedings of the Constitutional Convention of the State of Mississippi, 1868* (Jackson, Miss.: J. J. Shannon, 1868), 46.

71. Ibid., 47.

72. Ibid.

73. Woods, "The Travail of Freedom," 230.

74. U. Ozanne to Representative Thaddeus Stevens, July 9, 1868, BRFAL, Miss., RG 105.

75. George Corliss to O. D. George, July 4, 1868, BRFAL, Miss., RG 105.

76. *Hinds County Gazette*, October 5, 1868.

77. Joseph Warren to Lt. Stuart Eldridge, November 15, 1865, BRFAL, Miss., RG 105.

78. Ibid.

79. Quoted in Stuart Grayson Noble, *Forty Years of the Public School in Mississippi: With Special Reference to the Education of the Negro* (New York: Teachers College, Columbia University Press, 1918), 6.

80. Ibid.

81. Thomas Battle Carroll, *Historical Sketches of Oktibbeha County* (Gulfport, Miss.: Dixie Press, 1931), 115; Clifford Ganus, "The Freedmen's Bureau in Mississippi," (Ph.D. diss., Tulane University, 1953), 338.

82. Joseph Warren to R. L. Preston, July 10, 1866, BRFAL, Miss., RG 105.

83. Ibid.

84. Henry Swint, *Northern Teachers in the South* (Nashville: Vanderbilt University Press, 1941), 123, 136; Ganus, "The Freedmen's Bureau in Mississippi," 336-37.

85. Swint, *Northern Teachers in the South*, 136.

86. H. R. Pease to Gen. O. O. Howard, November 1, 1867, BRFAL, Miss., RG 105.

87. Ibid.

88. *Panola Star*, April 8, 1866. The *paper's* inclusion of this information had more to do with discrediting illustrations by northern newspapers of the intense antagonism whites maintained toward school for African Americans than it had to do with the paper's respect for these schools.

89. *Oxford Falcon*, June 14, 1866.

90. *The Jackson Daily Clarion*, February 9, 1866.

91. *The Jackson Daily Clarion*, January 3, 1866. This commonwealth, as surmised in this newspaper, was not inclusive of the expectations Mississippi blacks had in slavery's aftermath, but was indicative of the expectations Mississippi whites had of blacks in slavery's aftermath.

92. *Hinds County Gazette*, February 13, 1866.

93. Ibid.

94. *Hinds County Gazette*, February 16, 1866.

95. Joseph Warren to Lt. Stuart Eldridge, November 15, 1865, BRFAL, Miss., RG 105.

96. Joseph Warren to Lt. Stuart Eldridge, December 11, 1865, BRFAL, Miss., RG 105.

97. J. P. Bardwell to George Whipple, April 20, 1866, in the American Missionary Association Archives microfilmed records from the Amistad Research Center, Tulane University. Hereafter referred to as the AMA Papers (Miss.).

98. J. P. Bardwell to George Whipple, March 10, 1866, AMA Papers (Miss.), roll 2.

99. H. R. Pease to Gen. O. O. Howard, November 1, 1867, BRFAL, Miss., RG 105.

100. S. G. Wright to George Whipple, March 14, 1866, AMA Papers (Miss.), roll 2.

101. J. P. Bardwell to George Whipple, March 10, 1866, AMA Papers (Miss.), roll 2.

102. Robert C. Morris, "Educational Reconstruction," in *The Facts of Reconstruction: Essays in Honor of John Hope Franklin*, ed. Eric Anderson and Alfred A. Moss Jr. (Baton Rouge: Louisiana State University Press, 1991), 151.

103. Wharton, *The Negro in Mississippi*, 213.

104. H. R. Pease to Gen. O. O. Howard, November 1, 1867, BRFAL, Miss., RG 105.

105. Ibid.

106. Ibid.

107. Joseph Warren to Stuart Eldridge, March 15, 1865, BRFAL, Miss., RG 105.

108. Ibid.

109. Ibid.

110. Swint, *Northern Teachers in the South*, 35–76, 142.

111. Abney, "Reconstruction in Pontotoc County," 265; Magee, "Reconstruction in Lawrence and Jefferson Counties," 202; Watkins, "Reconstruction in Newton County," 226.

112. Carl Schurz, *Speeches, Correspondence, and Political Papers of Carl Schurz*, ed. Frederic Bancroft, 6 vols. (New York: G. P. Putnam's Sons, 1913), 1:329.

113. As quoted in H. R. Pease to Gen. O. O. Howard, November 1, 1867, BRFAL, Miss., RG 105.

114. Ibid.

115. Ibid.

116. Ibid.

117. Ross Moore, "Social and Economic Conditions in Mississippi during Reconstruction" (Ph.D. diss., Duke University, 1938), 54.

118. Ganus, "The Freedmen's Bureau in Mississippi," 325.

119. Joseph Warren to the editor of the *Sunny South* February 27, 1866, BRFAL, Miss., RG 105.

120. Joseph Warren to R. L. Moore, May 18, 1866, BRFAL, Miss., RG 105.

121. John Alvord to Gen. O. O. Howard, January 1, 1866, BRFAL, Miss., RG 105.

122. Ganus, "The Freedmen's Bureau in Mississippi," 358.

123. Ibid.

124. Ibid., 330.

125. Randy J. Sparks, "'The White People's Arms Are Longer than Ours': Blacks, Education, and the American Missionary Association in Reconstruction Mississippi," *Journal of Mississippi History* 54 (1992): 21.

126. Ganus, "The Freedmen's Bureau in Mississippi," 331.

127. Ibid.; W. F. Du Bois to Warren, February 14, 1866, BRFAL, Miss., RG 105.

128. H. R. Pitts to George Whipple, February 22, 1867, AMA Papers (Miss.), roll 2.

129. Ibid.

130. Woods, "The Travail of Freedom," 173–74.

131. Ibid.

132. Knox to Thomas C. Norton, May 30, 1866, BRFAL, Miss., RG 105.

133. Ibid.

134. Helen M. Jones to Rev. Samuel Hunt, June 1, 1866, AMA Papers (Miss.), roll 2.

135. Ibid.

136. Ganus, "The Freedmen's Bureau in Mississippi," 332.

137. Helen M. Jones to Rev. Samuel Hunt, June 1, 1866, AMA Papers (Miss.), roll 2.

138. M. E. Gill to E. P. Smith, June 14, 1869, AMA Papers (Miss.), roll 3.

139. Allen Trelease, *White Terror: The Ku Klux Klan Conspiracy and Southern Reconstruction* (New York: Harper & Row, 1971), 276.

140. Ibid.

141. Oshinsky, *"Worse than Slavery"*, 25.

142. Joseph Bishop, "Lynching," *The International Quarterly* 8 (1903): 203.

143. Richard Taylor, *Destruction and Reconstruction: Personal Experiences* (New York: D. Appleton, 1879), 250.

144. Eric Foner, *Reconstruction: America's Unfinished Revolution* (New York: Harper & Row), 120.

CHAPTER 4

1. Stuart Grayson Noble, *Forty Years of the Public Schools in Mississippi: With Special Reference to the Education of the Negro* (New York: Teachers College, Columbia University Press, 1918), 32.

2. "Colored" included all persons not legally defined as "white." Thus African Americans, Native Americans, Latinos, and Asian Americans were all "colored" according to the law. In Mississippi, however, African Americans were the majority of the "colored" population. The 1860 census documents only *two* Native Americans in all of Mississippi; the 1870 census documents 16 Asian Americans and 809 Native Americans. On the other hand, the 1870 census documented more than 444,000 African Americans in Mississippi. Accordingly, during these years, "colored" meant African American in Mississippi, and therefore "black" or "African American" will be used to describe this population rather than "colored."

3. Carl F. Kaestle, *Pillars of the Republic: Common Schools and American Society, 1780–1860* (New York: Hill & Wang, 1983), 62–103.

4. Ibid.

5. *Speech of Honorable Cassius D. Landon of Warren County on the Subject of Public Education June 14, 1870* (Jackson, Miss.: Power & Barksdale State Printers, 1870), 9; however, Landon's public school statement was somewhat incorrect. Nita Katherine Pyburn's study on public schools in Mississippi prior to 1860 illustrates that 1,116 public schools existed in 1860 with an annual income of $385,679 ($29,689 from school

taxes; $21,225 from endowments; $107,947 from public funds; and $226,818 from other unnamed sources). Historian William D. McCain confirms this finding, as did Reconstruction traditionalist Elise Timberlake nearly forty years earlier in her publication. Their data was gathered from the 1860 census, which also reported that 1,116 public schools were operational in Mississippi in this year. Not challenged, however, was the number of blacks who attended an antebellum public school. See Nita Katherine Pyburn, "Public Schools in Mississippi before 1860," *Journal of Mississippi History* 21 (1959): 113–30; William D. McCain, "Education in Mississippi in 1860," *Journal of Mississippi History* 22 (1960): 156; Elise Timberlake, "Did the Reconstruction Regime Give Mississippi Her Public Schools," *Publications of the Mississippi Historical Society* 12 (1912): 76.

6. W. E. B. Du Bois, *Black Reconstruction in America* (repr., Cleveland: World Publishing, 1964), 640.

7. Pyburn, "Public Schools in Mississippi before 1860," 122.

8. McCain, "Education in Mississippi in 1860," 156.

9. Timberlake, "Did the Reconstruction Regime Give Mississippi Her Public Schools," 82.

10. Ibid.

11. See chapter 2 for additional statistics.

12. William Charles Sallis, "The Color Line in Mississippi Politics, 1865–1915," (Ph.D. diss., University of Kentucky, 1967), 151.

13. Noble, *Forty Years*, 28–29.

14. Governor Alcorn (1870–73) and Senator Blanche K. Bruce (1874–78) give an excellent summary of the attempts and successes on the part of blacks to purchase private property. Their assessments directly challenged the notion that whites would be the sole state taxpayers. In seven counties, Washington, Madison, Holmes, Rankin, Neshoba, Jones, and Lauderdale, 69 blacks owned real estate to a gross value of $30,680; 3,798 blacks owned personal property to a gross value of $630,860; and 178 blacks owned both real and personal property at a gross valuation of $220,700. See *The Mississippi Election: A Speech by the Hon. Blanche K. Bruce of Mississippi in the United States Senate, March 31, 1876* (Washington, D.C.: Government Printing Office, 1876), 9. Moreover, Loren Schweninger, using the United States census of 1870, assessed that 23,665 black Mississippians—about 5 percent—were property owners, with an estimated $8,248,100 in total property holdings. In the primary Deep South states, Schweninger indicated that Mississippi had the highest number of black property owners. See Loren Schweninger, "Black Economic Reconstruction in the South," in *The Facts of Reconstruction: Essays in Honor of John Hope Franklin*, ed. Eric Anderson and Alfred A. Moss Jr. (Baton Rouge: Louisiana State University Press, 1991), 183.

15. Allen Trelease, *White Terror: The Ku Klux Klan Conspiracy and Southern Reconstruction* (New York: Harper & Row, 1971), 294.

16. Alvord, *Eighth Semi-Annual Report on Schools for Freedmen, July 1, 1869* (Washington, D.C.: Government Printing Office, 1869), 3.

17. *Journal of the Proceedings of the Constitutional Convention of the State of Mississippi, 1868* (Jackson, Miss.: J. J. Shannon, 1868), 148. Hereafter referred to as *Proceedings*.

18. Ibid., 316.

19. Noble, *Forty Years*, 10.

20. Ibid.

21. *Daily Clarion*, February 9, 1868.

22. *Daily Clarion*, February 21, 1868.

23. Ibid.; This quote was reprinted in the March 11, 1868, edition as well.

24. Noble, *Forty Years*, 17.

25. *Proceedings*, 47.

26. John Roy Lynch, *Civil Rights Speech of Hon. John Roy Lynch of Mississippi in the House of Representatives, February 3, 1875* (Washington, D.C.: Government Printing Office, 1875), 10.

27. *Laws for the Establishment and Government of the Common Schools of Mississippi, 1870* (Jackson, Miss.: Kimball, Kaymond, State Printers, 1870), 19.Hereafter referred to as *Laws, 1870*.

28. Noble, *Forty Years*, 12.

29. Ibid.

30. *Journal of the Senate, 1870* (Jackson, Miss.: E. Stafford, 1870), 436.

31. In many ways the expenditures of Mississippi's public school system was a microcosm of the reconstruction expenditures of the state. John Roy Lynch accurately said, "All of the public buildings in the state had to be repaired, some of them rebuilt" after the war. Moreover, as with the establishment of a working educational bureaucracy, the entire state government, and all its branches, had to be reconstructed to once again function as a centralized unit. Unfortunately, all of these measures had to be accomplished with little money in the treasury, because the bulk of the state's fiscal surplus went toward the war. According to Lynch, the government functioned on a "credit basis—that is by the issuing of notes or warrants based on the credit of the state" until the state's economy rebounded from its wartime losses. See William C. Harris, ed., *John Roy Lynch, The Facts of Reconstruction* (New York: Oxford University Press, 1970), 48–49.

32. Noble, *Forty Years*, 22.

33. *Annual Report of the Superintendent Public Education of the State of Mississippi for the Year Ending December 31, 1871* (Jackson, Miss.: Kimball, Kaymond, State Printers, 1872), 126–28. Hereafter referred to as *Superintendent's Annual Report, 1871*.

34. Ibid.

35. *Laws, 1870*, 6–13.

36. Noble, *Forty Years*, 32. This contention by Noble is misleading because it ignored

the fact that most of the leading Democrats in the state were systematically disfran-chised from voting or holding public office because of their participation in the Con-federacy. The Reconstruction Acts of 1867 disfranchised them. The appointments by General Ames were due to the fact that Mississippi remained under military control with a provisional military governor until it was deemed "reconstructed" by adopt-ing a state constitution that included the Thirteenth and Fourteenth Amendments. Although the formal adoption of the 1869 draft of the state's constitution repealed this legislative measure, it was not implemented until late December of 1869; two months after Ames's appointments. For a percentage of native-born white county superintendents, county school directors, and local officers, see *Superintendent's An-nual Report, 1871*, 43–48.

37. Noble, *Forty Years*, 32.

38. *Superintendent's Annual Report, 1871*, 34.

39. William Henington Weathersby, *A History of Educational Legislation in Missis-sippi from 1796 to 1860* (Chicago: University of Chicago Press, 1921), 112.

40. *Hinds County Gazette*, October 12, 1870. Much of the argument centered around the state's Democrats' lack of involvement in drafting the educational provisions out-lined at the Constitutional Convention, and the educational appointees of Governor Ames. In both scenarios, Mississippi Democrats felt their concerns were disregarded because of partisan politics. While this contention held some truth, it overlooked the fact that Mississippi Democrats at the convention decidedly adopted, according to John Roy Lynch, a policy of "masterly inactivity." In essence, they refrained from taking part in any election in which "colored men were allowed to vote." This action resulted in migrant and native-born Republicans constituting an overwhelming ma-jority of delegates at the convention, and they accordingly framed the state's consti-tution anew with little contribution from Democrats. See Harris, ed., *The Facts of Reconstruction*, 18.

41. *Hinds County Gazette*, October 12, 1870. See also Noble, *Forty Years*, 14. In 1876, Thomas S. Gathright was elected state superintendent of education in Mississippi.

42. *Hinds County Gazette*, October 12, 1870. This contention was grossly inaccurate and illustrated the extent of dissension some leading Mississippi whites had toward public schools, particularly for African Americans. Noxubee's county superinten-dent, Charles B. Ames, abstained from establishing the number of public schools needed because of, in his words, the "white people's distaste of public schooling." Noxubee County was a predominantly black county and blacks outnumbered whites nearly three to one. The superintendent's report of 1871 demonstrated that just over $7,000 ($4,166.53 from the common school fund and $3000 from poll taxes) was raised for the county's school system. The poll tax was based on the number of adults in the county. Because of the black-white ratio of three to one, nearly three-fourths of the county's poll tax was drawn exclusively from Noxubee blacks. However, the

aggravated value of the county's public school property was just $320. Moreover, only 21 public schools for the 1,482 black children were established in the county. By comparison, 26 public schools were established for the county's 900 white children. Equally interesting, however, was the aggravated value of the county's white private school property, which was reportedly estimated at $20,000. If this estimate is accurate, this property received little usage because there were only two private schools for whites in the entire county and none for blacks. See *Superintendent's Annual Report, 1871*, 75, 127, 130, 139, and 143.

43. M. G. Abney, "Reconstruction in Pontotoc County," *Publications of the Mississippi Historical Society* 11 (1910): 258; Randy J. Sparks, "'The White People's Arms Are Longer Than Ours': Blacks, Education, and the American Missionary Association in Reconstruction Mississippi," *Journal of Mississippi History* 54 (1992): 22-23.

44. Nannie Lacey, "Reconstruction in Leake County," *Publications of the Mississippi Historical Society* 11 (1910): 287.

45. Noble, *Forty Years*, 16. Reconstruction traditionalist Hattie Magee raised a similar point and based her argument on the fact that one of the three Mississippi whites to teach in a black school was forced by her father to do so out of sheer need of money. See Hattie Magee, "Reconstruction in Lawrence and Jefferson Counties," *Publications of the Mississippi Historical Society* 11 (1910): 195.

46. Julia Brown, "Reconstruction in Yalobusha and Grenada Counties," *Publications of the Mississippi Historical Society* 12 (1912): 264.

47. While Tougaloo was Mississippi's first black normal school, it was not the first attempt to establish a normal school for blacks in Mississippi. In May 1868, as historian Clifford Ganus Jr. noted, the Ohio Yearly Meeting of Friends applied to the Freedmen's Bureau for assistance in establishing a normal school in Jackson. However, they did not convince the bureau's state superintendent of educational affairs, H. R. Pease, that the school would be a permanent institution. Additionally, in August 1868, the Indiana Yearly Meeting of Friends also expressed a sincere desire to open a normal school in Jackson. However, the bureau, after the passing of the 1867 Freedmen's Bureau Bill, which extended the bureau's ability to continue its operations in the South, assisted the AMA only in finding a suitable location for the establishment of a normal school for African Americans, because of the AMA's intent to make the normal school a permanent institution. Columbus was the AMA's first choice, primarily because they had so many teachers working in the town, but with some convincing from Colonel A. P. Huggins, a bureau agent, the AMA established the state's first normal school for African Americans in Tougaloo, a small town ten miles north of Jackson. See Clifford Ganus Jr., "The Freedmen's Bureau in Mississippi" (Ph.D. diss., Tulane University, 1953), 360-62; Joe M. Richardson, *Christian Reconstruction: The American Missionary Association and Southern Blacks, 1861-1890* (Athens: University of Georgia Press, 1986), 134-39.

48. For additional discussion on Rust and Shaw universities, see Ruth Watkins, "Reconstruction in Marshall County," *Publications of the Mississippi Historical Society* 12 (1912): 199.

49. Edward Smith to Charles H. Howard, April 2, 1870, AMA Papers (Miss.), roll 2; William Leon Woods, "The Travail of Freedom: Mississippi Blacks, 1862–1870," (Ph.D. diss., Princeton University, 1979), 191; Robert C. Morris, *Reading 'Riting, and Reconstruction: The Education of Freedmen in the South, 1861–1870* (Chicago: University of Chicago Press, 1981), 124–25.

50. Morris, *Reading, 'Riting, and Reconstruction*, 124–25.

51. Josephine Posey, *Against Great Odds: The History of Alcorn State University* (Jackson: University Press of Mississippi, 1994).

52. *Superintendent's Annual Report, 1871*, 5–6, 124.

53. Ibid., 6.

54. Ibid., 7.

55. These fifteen counties were selected because they had the largest African American populations in the state.

56. See James D. Anderson, *The Education of Blacks in the South, 1860–1935* (Chapel Hill: University of North Carolina Press, 1988), 4–16; Ronald E. Butchart, *Northern Schools, Southern Blacks, and Reconstruction* (Westport, Conn.: Greenwood Press, 1980), 166–79; W. E. B. Du Bois, *Black Reconstruction in America, 1860–1880* (repr., Cleveland: World Publishing, 1964), 640; Eric Foner, *Reconstruction: America's Unfinished Revolution, 1863–1877* (New York: Harper & Row, 1988), 96–102; Jacqueline Jones, *Soldiers of Light and Love: Northern Teachers and Georgia Blacks, 1865–1873* (Chapel Hill: University of North Carolina Press, 1980), 58–62; Morris, *Reading, 'Riting, and Reconstruction*; Sparks, "'The White People's Arms'"; Heather Andrea Williams, *Self-Taught: African American Education in Slavery and Freedom* (Chapel Hill: University of North Carolina Press, 2005).

57. *Superintendent's Annual Report, 1871*, 2.

58. If every African American parent in these counties petitioned for their child to attend a public school, the ratio would have been an astonishing 182 pupils per available school. If every white parent petitioned for their child to attend a public school, the ratio would have been 77 pupils per available school. This coincidentally was the black pupil per school ratio in Holmes County.

59. To meet the petitions of parents who enrolled their children in the state's public schools, as specified by the state's common school laws, every county needed to establish additional schools. The formula for the additional schools needed to accommodate enrolled students is: ([# of enrolled students/25] – # of established schools). Below are the numbers of black and white schools each of the state's fifteen predominantly black counties needed to reach this goal. Adams County: 17 black and 2 white; Carroll County: 22 black and 33 white; Claiborne County: 22 black

and 7 white; DeSoto County: 9 black and 34 white; Hinds County: 33 black and 29 white; Holmes County: 65 black and 23 white; Lowndes County: 59 black and 19 white; Marshall County: 52 black and 17 white; Noxubee County: 38 black and 10 white; Panola County: 12 black and 18 white; Tallahatchie County: 8 black and 5 white; Tunica County: 9 black and 1 white; Warren County: 57 black and 21 white; Wilkinson County: 24 black and 0 white; Yazoo County: 9 black and 17 white.

60. *Superintendent's Annual Report, 1871,* 124–31.

61. Of the 444,000 African Americans in Mississippi, it was estimated that 80,755 adult males, 87,278 adult females, and nearly 121,000 black children were illiterate. See *Superintendent's Annual Report, 1871,* 233–35.

62. Timberlake, "Did the Reconstruction Regime Give Mississippi Her Public Schools," 80–81.

63. *Superintendent's Annual Report, 1871,* 127.

64. Ibid.

65. Ibid., 53.

66. These fifteen counties were selected because they had the largest white populations in the state. Nevertheless, there are incomplete data for the counties of Itawamba, Tishomingo, and Tippah.

67. The total revenue collected for public schooling in predominantly black counties doubled the amount collected in predominantly white counties. Black counties collected a common school fund and a state poll tax that amounted to $102,679.20 for the 1870–71 school year. White counties' total common school fund and poll tax was $50,612.37. See *Superintendent's Annual Report, 1871,* 81, 142–45.

68. Trelease, *White Terror,* 294.

69. If all the educable white children in these counties attended a public school, the white pupil per school ratio would still be lower than the black pupil per school ratio in Wayne County. It would have averaged eighty pupils to a school.

70. To meet the petitions of parents who enrolled their children in the state's public schools, as specified by the state's common school laws, every county needed to establish additional schools. The formula for the additional schools needed to accommodate enrolled students is: ([# of enrolled students/25] − # of established schools). Below are the numbers of black and white schools each of the state's fifteen predominantly white counties would have needed to establish to reach this goal. Alcorn County: 3 black, 33 white; Choctaw County: 12 black, 100 white; Coahoma County: 18 black, 1 white; Covington County: 1 black, 1 white; Jackson County: 1 black, 5 white; Leake County: 16 black, 32 white; Lee County: 9 black, 42 white; Montgomery County: 30 black, 39 white; Pontotoc County: 7 black, 29 white; Scott County: 1 black, 11 white; Tippah County: (report incomplete for blacks and whites); Tishomingo County: (report incomplete for blacks), 86 white; Wayne County: 9 black, 0 white.

71. *Superintendent's Annual Report, 1871*, 128–31; *Annual Report of the State Superintendent of Public Education of the State of Mississippi for the Scholastic Year 1874* (Jackson, Miss.: Pilot Publishing Company, State Printers, 1875), 12.

CHAPTER 5

1. *Hinds County Gazette*, March 15, 1871.

2. Stuart Grayson Noble, *Forty Years of the Public Schools in Mississippi* (New York: Teachers College, Columbia University Press, 1918), 15.

3. *Annual Report of the Superintendent Public Education of the State of Mississippi for the Year Ending December 31, 1871* (Jackson, Miss.: Kimball, Kaymond, State Printers, 1872), 33. Hereafter referred to as *Superintendent's Annual Report, 1871*.

4. Ibid., 33–35.

5. Stuart Grayson Noble contended that "the chief ground for [whites'] opposition was undoubtedly the expense" of establishing and maintaining a new system of schools. He later added, however, that this development was not so much a problem of white taxpayers paying for white children to attend school, but of white taxpayers having to pay for blacks to also attend school at the taxpayer's expense. Elise Timberlake makes a similar argument and added that white farmers' dependence on black labor, and not blacks acquiring an education, forced them to oppose the state's efforts to establish a system of public schools inclusive of African Americans. See Noble, 36–37; and Elise Timberlake, "Did the Reconstruction Regime Give Mississippi Her Public Schools," *Publications of the Mississippi Historical Society* 12 (1912): 87–88.

6. The northern states that Hooker was referring to were Indiana, Illinois, and Kansas. In Indiana, the state still referred to an 1860 statute that declared, "Negroes and mulattoes were not liable to school taxes, nor entitled to the benefit of school funds in Indiana." In Illinois, an 1858 statute was still being applied in 1870, and it stated that "persons of color were to have no other interest in the common school taxes except such amount as they paid themselves." Likewise, Kansas law excluded African Americans from the common schools altogether until 1872. See Charles E. Hooker, *On Relation between the White and Colored People of the South: A Speech of Hon. Chas. E. Hooker of Mississippi Delivered in the United States House of Representatives, June 15, 1876* (Washington, D.C.: Government Printing Office, 1876), 9, 14–16.

7. In 1860, taxes levied for the state was $945,806. In 1870, the taxes levied for the state amounted to $3,544,831, and the state tax for school purposes amounted to $400,000. As demonstrated, the greater portion of this amount went toward the construction of schoolhouses and the hiring of teachers. The county property taxes averaged about 1 percent of its value, but in many counties it reached 2 percent, and in several 3 percent. According to the Joint Select Committee Report of the House

of Representatives, county debts and the necessity of erecting or repairing county buildings caused exceptional rates. By comparison, the taxes levied in Mississippi were lower than most northern states with smaller or similar populations. For example, in 1870 the taxes levied on Connecticut's 537,454 residents was $6,064,843, with $1,621,397.76 expended for public schools; the taxes levied on New Jersey's 906,096 residents was $7,416,724, with $2,364,441.58 expended for public schools; and the taxes levied on Maine's 626,915 residents were $5,348,645, with $917,364 expended toward public schools. See *Superintendent's Annual Report, 1871*, 232; *Report of the Joint Select Committee to Inquire into the Condition of Affairs in the Late Insurrectionary States, Made to the Two Houses of Congress, February 19, 1872* (Washington, D.C.: Government Printing Office, 1872), 231, 241. Hereafter referred to as the *Joint Select Committee Report, 1872*.

8. J. Mills Thorton, "Fiscal Policy and the Failure of Radical Reconstruction in the Lower South," in *Region, Race, and Reconstruction: Essays in Honor of C. Vann Woodward*, ed. J. Morgan Kousser and James M. McPherson (New York: Oxford University Press, 1982), 381.

9. *Joint Select Committee Report, 1872*, 73.

10. Allen Trelease, *White Terror: The Ku Klux Klan Conspiracy and Southern Reconstruction* (New York: Harper & Row, 1971), 293.

11. *Joint Select Committee Report, 1872*, 76.

12. Ibid.

13. Noble, *Forty Years*, 15.

14. *Superintendent's Annual Report, 1871*, 72; Trelease, *White Terror*, 294; *Joint Select Committee Report, 1872*, 77.

15. *Superintendent's Annual Report, 1871*, 72. As historian Allen Trelease nas noted, Monroe County had the "rare distinction" of having black Ku Klux Klan members. There were five total: three (Joe Davis, Henry Hatch, and Jehu Wolf) were forced to join against their will, and two black Democrats (Mike Forshee and Jeffrey Willis) voluntarily participated. See Trelease, *White Terror*, 296–97. For additional specifics of black Ku Klux Klan activity in Mississippi, see *Full Report of the Great Ku Klux Klan Trial in the U.S. District Court at Oxford, Mississippi: Evidence of Witnesses, Arguments of Counsel, Decision and Rulings of Judge Hill, Incidents, &c.* (Memphis: William J. Mansford, 1871), 46.

16. *Joint Select Committee Report, 1872*, 77.

17. *Superintendent's Annual Report, 1871*, 68.

18. Ibid.

19. Ibid., 76.

20. Ibid., 87.

21. Ibid., 67.

22. Ibid.

23. William Blain, "Challenge to the Lawless: The Mississippi Secret Service, 1870–1871," *Journal of Mississippi History* 40 (1978): 119–31; Otis Singletary, *Negro Militia and Reconstruction* (Austin: University of Texas Press, 1957), 11; Eric Foner, *Reconstruction: America's Unfinished Revolution, 1863–1877* (New York: Harper & Row, 1988), 439.

24. J. S. McNeily, "The Enforcement Act of 1871 and the Ku Klux Klan in Mississippi," *Publications of the Mississippi Historical Society* 9 (1906), 109–71.

25. *Superintendent's Annual Report, 1871*, 67.

26. Ibid.

27. Ibid.

28. Ibid., 69.

29. Ibid., 72; *Joint Select Committee Report, 1872*, 83.

30. *Superintendent's Annual Report, 1871*, 73.

31. Foner, *Reconstruction*, 429.

32. *Annual Report of the State Superintendent of Public Education of the State of Mississippi for the Scholastic Year 1874* (Jackson, Miss.: Pilot Publishing, State Printers, 1875), 9. Hereafter referred to as *Superintendent's Annual Report, 1874*.

33. Noble, *Forty Years*, 42.

34. *Superintendent's Annual Report, 1871*, 33.

35. Noble, *Forty Years*, 42.

36. *Superintendent's Annual Report, 1871*, 90.

37. *Laws of the State of Mississippi in Relation to Education, 1874* (Jackson, Miss.: Powers & Barksdale, State Printers, 1874), 6. Hereafter referred to as *Laws, 1874*.

38. Ibid., 9.

39. *Superintendent's Annual Report, 1871*, 8, 34, 36.

40. Ibid., 6.

41. Ibid., 7.

42. Ibid., 15.

43. *A Law for the Establishment and Government of the Common Schools of Mississippi* (Jackson, Miss.: Kimball, Kaymond, State Printers, 1870), 12, 19 (hereafter referred to as *Laws, 1870*); *Laws, 1874*, 11.

44. Noble, *Forty Years*, 44.

45. *Laws, 1870*, 19.

46. Ibid.; *Superintendent's Annual Report, 1874*, 8.

47. Noble, *Forty Years*, 44.

48. Ibid., 46.

49. *Superintendent's Annual Report, 1874*, 8.

50. Ibid.

51. Ibid.

52. Vernon Lane Wharton, *The Negro in Mississippi, 1865–1890* (repr., New York: Harper & Row, 1965), 175.

53. Davis was not the first or only African American to be named lieutenant governor of a southern state during Reconstruction. The striking fact is that every African American who held this position resided in a black-majority state. In Louisiana there were three: Oscar J. Dunn, 1868–71; P. B. S. Pinchback, 1871–72; and Caesar C. Antoine, 1873–77. In South Carolina there were two: Alonzo J. Ransier, 1871–73 and Richard H. Gleaves, 1873–77. Similarly, Cardozo was not the only African American to hold the position of superintendent of education in a southern state. Joseph C. Corbin held the position in Arkansas from 1873–74. Jonathan C. Gibbs was superintendent of education in Florida from 1873–75. William G. Brown held the post in Louisiana from 1873–77. For comment on Alcorn, see Foner, *Reconstruction: America's Unfinished Revolution*, 539; for discussion in note, see Foner, *Reconstruction: America's Unfinished Revolution*, 353.

54. Foner, *Reconstruction: America's Unfinished Revolution*; William C. Harris, *The Day of the Carpetbagger: Republican Reconstruction in Mississippi* (Baton Rouge: Louisiana State University Press, 1979), 160; James W. Garner, *Reconstruction in Mississippi* (New York: Macmillan, 1901), 307–8.

55. While the 1874 annual report of State Superintendent Thomas W. Cardozo is available, its data were not disaggregated by race or gender, making it virtually impossible to offer a feasible estimate of the schooling opportunities of black children. That being the case, the educational statistics from the 1876–77 academic year are used as a supplement.

56. Harris, *The Day of the Carpetbagger*, 333, 352.

57. Ibid., 352.

58. John Hope Franklin, *Reconstruction: After the Civil War* (Chicago: University of Chicago Press, 1961), 153.

59. J. S. McNeily, "Climax and Collapse of Reconstruction in Mississippi," *Publications of the Mississippi Historical Society* 12 (1912): 285. This reference was mostly directed toward Blanche K. Bruce, Alexander K. Davis, Thomas W. Cardozo, John Roy Lynch, and James Hill, secretary of state.

60. Wharton, *The Negro in Mississippi*, 187.

61. Julia Kendel, "Reconstruction in Lafayette County," *Publications of Mississippi Historical Society* 13 (1912): 251.

62. Wharton, *The Negro in Mississippi*, 184.

63. *The Mississippi Election: A Speech by the Hon. Blanche K. Bruce of Mississippi in the United States Senate, March 31, 1876* (Washington, D.C.: Government Printing Office, 1876), 10.

64. Ibid.

65. Wharton, *The Negro in Mississippi*, 190–93.

66. J. S. McNeily, "Climax and Collapse of Reconstruction," 397.

67. Michael Perman, "Counter Reconstruction," in *The Facts of Reconstruction:*

Essays in Honor of John Hope Franklin, ed. Eric Anderson and Alfred A. Moss Jr. (Baton Rouge: Louisiana State University Press, 1991), 134.

68. Ibid.

69. For additional details see *Biennial Report of the State Superintendent of Public Education to the Legislation of Mississippi for the Years 1882–83* (Jackson, Miss.: J. L. Power, State Printer, 1884).

70. "Administration of Governor Correspondence," Adelbert Ames Papers, RG 27, no. 27. Mississippi Department of Archives and History, Jackson, Mississippi.

EPILOGUE

1. "From Cotton Fields to Cap, Gown," *News-Gazette,* June 2, 2002.

2. Neil McMillen, *Dark Journey: Black Mississippians in the Age of Jim Crow* (Urbana: University of Illinois Press, 1989), 347.

3. *Biennial Report and Recommendations of the State Superintendent of Public Education to the Legislature of Mississippi for the Scholastic Years, 1949–1950 and 1950–1951* (Jackson, Miss.: Division of Administration and Finance, 1952), 55.

4. *Biennial Report and Recommendations of the State Superintendent of Public Education to the Legislature of Mississippi for the Scholastic Years 1939–1940 and 1940–1941* (Jackson, Miss.: Division of Information and Statistics, 1941), 16.

5. "From Cotton Fields to Cap, Gown."

6. Sterling Plumpp, *Blues Narratives* (Chicago: Tia Chucha, 1999), 12.

BIBLIOGRAPHY

PRIMARY SOURCES

Manuscripts and Archives

Jackson, Miss.
   Mississippi Department of Archives and History
      Adelbert Ames Papers
      Annie E. Harper Papers
      Benjamin G. Humphreys Papers
      Bureau of Refugees, Freedmen, and Abandoned Lands Papers,
         Record Group 105
New Orleans, La.
   Amistad Research Center, Tilton Hall, Tulane University
      American Missionary Association Papers, Mississippi, 1863–1873

Newspapers and Periodicals

Daily Worker
De Bow's Review
Hinds County Gazette
Jackson Daily Clarion and Standard
Jackson Weekly Clarion
Jet Magazine
Natchez Democrat

National Freedmen
News-Gazette (East Central Illinois)
Oxford Falcon
Panola Star
Selma Times
Vicksburg Journal

Published Works

Addresses of Rev. Drs. Wm. Hague and E. N. Kirk, at the Annual Meeting of the
    Educational Commission for Freedmen, at the Old South Church, May 28, 1963. Boston:
    David Clapp, 1863.
Alvord, John W. Eighth Semi-Annual Report on Schools for Freedmen, July 1, 1869.
    Washington, D.C.: Government Printing Office, 1869.
———. Fifth Semi-Annual Report on Schools for Freedmen, January 1, 1868.
    Washington, D.C.: Government Printing Office, 1868.
———. First Semi-Annual Report on Schools and Finances of Freedmen, January 1, 1866.
    Washington, D.C.: Government Printing Office, 1866.
———. Fourth Semi-Annual Report on Schools for Freedmen, July 1, 1867. Washington,
    D.C.: Government Printing Office, 1867.
———. Inspector's Report of Schools and Finances. Washington, D.C.: Government
    Printing Office, 1866.
———. Letters for the South Relating to the Conditions of the Freedmen, Addressed
    to Major General O. O. Howard, Commissioner, Bureau of Refugees, Freedmen, and
    Abandoned Lands. Washington, D.C.: Howard University Press, 1870.
———. Ninth Semi-Annual Report on Schools for Freedmen, January 1, 1870.
    Washington, D.C.: Government Printing Office, 1870.
———. Second Semi-Annual Report on Schools and Finances of Freedmen, July 1, 1866.
    Washington, D.C.: Government Printing Office, 1868.
———. Seventh Semi-Annual Report on Schools for Freedmen, January 1, 1869.
    Washington, D.C.: Government Printing Office, 1869.
———. Sixth Semi-Annual Report on Schools for Freedmen, July 1, 1868. Washington,
    D.C.: Government Printing Office, 1868.
———. Tenth Semi-Annual Report on Schools for Freedmen, July 1, 1870. Washington,
    D.C.: Government Printing Office, 1870.
———. Third Semi-Annual Report on Schools for Freedmen, January 1, 1867.
    Washington, D.C.: Government Printing Office, 1867.
Annual Report of the State Superintendent of Public Education of the State of Mississippi
    for the Scholastic Year 1874. Jackson, Miss.: Pilot Publishing, State Printers, 1875.
Annual Report of the State Superintendent of Public Education to the Legislature of
    Mississippi for the Year 1876. Jackson, Miss.: Power & Barksdale, State Printers,
    1877.
Annual Report of the Superintendent of Public Education of the State of Mississippi for the
    Year Ending December 31, 1871. Jackson, Miss.: Kimball, Kaymond, State Printers,
    1872.
Berlin, Ira, et al. The Black Military Experience. Ser. 2 of Freedom: A Documentary
    History of Emancipation, 1861–1867. New York: Cambridge University Press, 1982.

————. *The Destruction of Slavery*. Ser. 1, vol. 1 of *Freedom: A Documentary History of Emancipation, 1861–1867*. New York: Cambridge University Press, 1985.

————. *Free at Last: A Documentary History of Slavery, Freedom, and the Civil War*. New York: New Press, 1992.

————. *The Wartime Genesis of Free Labor: The Lower South*. Ser. 1, vol. 3 of *Freedom: A Documentary History of Emancipation, 1861–1867*. New York: Cambridge University Press, 1990.

————. *The Wartime Genesis of Free Labor: The Upper South*. Ser. 1, vol. 2 of *Freedom: A Documentary History of Emancipation, 1861–1867*. New York: Cambridge University Press, 1993.

Biennial Report and Recommendations of the State Superintendent of Public Education to the Legislature of Mississippi for the Scholastic Years 1939–1940 and 1940–1941. Jackson, Miss.: Division of Information and Statistics, 1941.

Biennial Report and Recommendations of the State Superintendent of Public Education to the Legislature of Mississippi for the Scholastic Years, 1949–1950 and 1950–1951. Jackson, Miss.: Division of Administration and Finance, 1952.

Biennial Report of the State Superintendent of Public Education to the Legislature of Mississippi for the years 1882–83. Jackson, Miss.: J. L. Power, State Printer, 1884.

Brown, William Wells. *The Negro in the American Rebellion: His Heroism and his Fidelity*. Boston: Lee & Shepard, 1867.

Bruce, Blanche K. *The Mississippi Election: A Speech by the Hon. Blanche K. Bruce of Mississippi in the United States Senate, March 31, 1876*. Washington, D.C.: Government Printing Press, 1876.

Eaton, John, Jr. *Building for the Children in the South*. Washington, D.C.: Government Printing Office, 1884.

————. *Grant, Lincoln, and the Freedmen*. New York: Longmans, Green, 1907.

————. *Report of the General Superintendent of Freedmen, Department of the Tennessee and Arkansas, for 1864*. Memphis: Freedmen Press, 1865.

————. *Reports Relating to Colored Schools in Mississippi, Arkansas, and Western Tennessee, April 1865*. Memphis: Freedmen Press, 1865.

Emancipation League. *Facts Concerning the Freedmen: Their Capacity and Their Destiny*. Boston, 1863.

Foner, Philip S., and George E. Walker, eds. *Proceedings of the Black National and State Conventions, 1865–1900*. Philadelphia: Temple University Press, 1986.

Full Report of the Great Ku Klux Klan Trial in the U.S. District Court at Oxford, Mississippi: Evidence of Witnesses, Arguments of Counsel, Decision and Rulings of Judge Hill, Incidents, &c. Memphis: William J. Mansford, 1871.

Hooker, Charles E. *On Relation between the White and Colored People of the South: A Speech of Hon. Chas. E. Hooker of Mississippi Delivered in the United States House of*

Representatives, June 15, 1876. Washington, D.C.: Governmental Printing Office, 1876.

Howard, Oliver Otis. *Report of Brevet Major General O. O. Howard, Commissioner, Bureau of Refugees, Freedmen, and Abandoned Lands, to the Secretary of War, October 20, 1869.* Washington, D.C.: Governmental Printing Office, 1869.

———. *Report of the Commissioner of the Bureau of Refugees, Freedmen and Abandoned Lands, December 2, 1867.* Washington, D.C.: Governmental Printing Office, 1868.

Hutchinson, A., comp. *Code of Mississippi: Being an Analytical Compilation of the Public and General Statutes of the Territory and State, with Tabular References to the Local and Private Acts, from 1798-1848.* Jackson, Miss.: Price and Fall State Printers, 1848.

Journal of the Proceedings and Debates in the Constitutional Convention of the State of Mississippi, August 1865, By Order of the Convention. Jackson, Miss.: D. M. Yerger, State Printer, 1865.

Journal of the Proceedings of the Constitutional Convention of the State of Mississippi, 1868. Jackson, Miss.: J. J. Shannon, 1868.

Journal of the Senate, 1870. Jackson, Miss.: E. Stafford, 1870.

Journal of the Senate of the State of Mississippi Sitting as a Court of Impeachment, in the Trials of Adelbert Ames, Governor, Alexander K. Davis, Lieutenant Governor, Thomas W. Cardozo, Superintendent of Public Education. Jackson, Miss.: Power & Barksdale, State Printers, 1876.

Kirk, Edward Norris. *Educated Labor, or, Our Duty in Regard to the Americo-African Race: An Address Delivered before the American Missionary Association, Homer, N.Y., October 17, 1867.* New York: Holt Brothers, 1868.

A Law for the Establishment and Government of the Common Schools of Mississippi. Jackson, Miss.: Kimball, Kaymond, 1870.

Laws of Mississippi, 1865. Jackson, Miss.: J. J. Shannon, 1866.

Laws of the State of Mississippi in Relation to Education, 1874. Jackson, Miss.: Powers & Barksdale, State Printers, 1874.

Lockwood, Lewis C. "Mary S. Peake, The Colored Teacher at Fortress Monroe." In *Two Black Teachers during the Civil War,* edited by William Loren Katz, 1–53. New York: Arno Press, 1969.

Loring, F. W., and C. F. Atkinson. *Cotton Culture and the South Considered with Reference to Emigration.* Boston: Houghton Mifflin, 1869.

Lynch, John Roy. *Civil Rights Speech of Hon. John Roy Lynch of Mississippi in the House of Representatives, February 3, 1875.* Washington, D.C.: Government Printing Office, 1875.

———. *The Facts of Reconstruction.* New York: Neale, 1913.

———. *Southern Question — Reply to Mr. Lamar. Speech of Hon. John R. Lynch, of*

Mississippi, in the House of Representatives, August 12, 1876. Washington, D.C.: Government Printing Office, 1876.

Mayes, Edward. *History of Education in Mississippi.* Washington D.C.: Government Printing Press, 1899.

Mayo, Amory D. "Common School Education in the South from the Beginning of the Civil War to 1870–1876." In vol. 1 of *Report of the U.S. Commissioner of Education for the Years 1900–1901.* Washington, D.C.: Government Printing Office, 1902.

————. *The Educational Situation in the South.* N.p., n.d.

National Freedmen's Aid Union. *The Industry of the Freedmen of America.* Birmingham, Eng.: The National Freedmen's Aid Union, 1867.

New England Freedmen's Aid Society. *New England Freedmen's Aid Society: Second Annual Report.* Boston: Office of the Society, 1864.

Pennington, James W. C. *The Fugitive Blacksmith; or, Events in the History of James W. C. Pennington, Pastor of a Presbyterian Church, New York, Formerly a Slave in the State of Maryland, United States.* London: Charles Gilpin, 1849.

Rawick, George P., ed. *The American Slave: A Composite Autobiography.* 19 vols. Westport, Conn.: Greenwood Press, 1972.

————. *The American Slave: A Composite Autobiography: Supplement, Series 1.* 12 vols. Westport, Conn.: Greenwood Press, 1977.

————. *The American Slave: A Composite Autobiography: Supplement, Series 2.* 10 vols. Westport, Conn.: Greenwood Press, 1979.

Reid, Whitelaw. *After the War: A Southern Tour, May 1, 1865 to May 1, 1866.* Cincinnati: Wilstach and Baldwin, 1866.

Report of a Committee on Freedmen in parts of Tennessee and the Mississippi Valley, To Friends' Board of Control, Third Month, 1865. Cincinnati: R. W. Carroll, 1865.

Report of the Proceedings of a Meeting Held at Concert hall, Philadelphia, on Tuesday Evening, November 3, 1863, to Take Into Consideration the Condition of the Freed People of the South. Philadelphia: Merrihew & Thompson, 1863.

Report of the Select Committee to Inquire into the Mississippi Election of 1875, with the Testimony and Documentary Evidence. 2 vols. Washington, D.C.: Government Printing Office, 1876.

Ripley, Peter, ed. *The Black Abolitionist Papers.* Vol. 5, *The United States, 1859–1865.* Chapel Hill: University of North Carolina Press, 1992.

Schurz, Carl. *Report on the Conditions of the South.* Reprint, New York: Arno Press and the New York Times, 1969.

————. *Speeches, Correspondence, and Political Papers of Carl Schurz.* Selected and edited by Frederic Bancroft. Vol. 1. New York: G. P. Putnam's Sons, 1913.

Simmons, William J. *Men of Mark.* Cleveland: G. M. Rewell, 1887.

Speech of Honorable Cassius D. Landon of Warren County on the Subject of Public Education June 14, 1870. Jackson, Miss.: Power & Barksdale, State Printers, 1870.

Statistics of the Operations of the Executive Board of Friends' Association of Philadelphia and its Vicinity, for the Relief of Colored Freedmen, As Presented to a Public Meeting of Friends, Held at Arch Street Meeting House, Philadelphia, 1st Month 19th, 1864. Philadelphia: Inquirer Printers Office, 1864.

Stone, Alfred, ed. *Mississippi's Constitution and Statutes in Reference to Freedmen and Their Alleged Relation to the Reconstruction Acts and War Amendments.* Oxford: University of Mississippi Press, 1901.

Taylor, Richard. *Destruction and Reconstruction: Personal Experiences.* New York: D. Appleton, 1879.

U.S. Bureau of the Census. *Negro Population in the United States, 1790–1915.* Washington, D.C.: Government Printing Office, 1918.

U.S. Congress. House. *Report of the Joint Select Committee to Inquire into the Conditions of Affairs in the Late Insurrectionary States, Made to the Two Houses of Congress, February 19, 1872.* 42d Cong., 2d sess., 1872. H. Rep. 22. Washington D.C.: Government Printing Office, 1872.

———. *Report of the Joint Select Committee to Inquire into the Condition of Affairs in the Late Insurrectionary States: Ku Klux Klan Conspiracy.* 42d Cong., 2d sess., 1872. H. Rep. 22, pt. 1. Washington, D.C.: Government Printing Office, 1872.

U.S. Congress. Senate. *Report of the Joint Select Committee to Inquire into the Condition of Affairs in the Late Insurrectionary States: Ku Klux Klan Conspiracy.* 42d Cong., 2d sess., 1872. S. Rep. 41. Washington, D.C.: Government Printing Office, 1872.

———. *Report of Carl Schurz on the States of South Carolina, Georgia, Alabama, Mississippi, and Louisiana.* 39th Cong., 1st sess., 1865. Exec. doc. 2. Washington D.C.: Government Printing Office, 1865.

Warren, Joseph. *Reports Relating to Colored Schools in Mississippi, Arkansas, and Western Tennessee, April 1865.* Memphis: Freedmen Press, 1865.

Yeatman, James E. *A Report on the Condition of the Freedmen in Mississippi, Presented by the Western Sanitary Commission, December 17, 1863.* St. Louis: Western Sanitary Commission, 1864.

SECONDARY SOURCES

Abney, M. G. "Reconstruction in Pontotoc County." *Publications of the Mississippi Historical Society* 11 (1910): 240–69.

Anderson, James D. *The Education of Blacks in the South, 1860–1935.* Chapel Hill: University of North Carolina Press, 1988.

———. "Race-Conscious Educational Policies versus a 'Color-Blind Constitution': A Historical Perspective." *Educational Researcher* 36 (2007): 249–57.

Bennett, Lerone. *Before the Mayflower: A History of Black America*. Reprint, New York: Johnson Publishing, 1988.

Berlin, Ira. *Generations of Captivity: A History of African American Slaves*. Cambridge, Mass.: Harvard University Press, Belknap Press, 2003.

Berthoff, Rowland. "Southern Attitudes toward Immigration, 1865–1914." *Journal of Southern History* 17 (1951): 328–60.

Bigelow, Martha Mitchell. "Vicksburg: Experiment in Freedom." *Journal of Mississippi History* 26 (1964): 28–44.

Bishop, Joseph. "Lynching." *The International Quarterly* 8 (1903): 199–208.

Blain, William. "Challenge to the Lawless: The Mississippi Secret Service, 1870–1871." *Journal of Mississippi History* 40 (1978): 119–31.

Bowman, Robert. "Reconstruction in Yazoo County." *Publications of the Mississippi Historical Society* 7 (1903): 115–30.

Braden, W. H. "Reconstruction in Lee County." *Publications of the Mississippi Historical Society* 10 (1909): 135–46.

Brown, Julia. "Reconstruction in Yalobusha and Grenada Counties." *Publications of the Mississippi Historical Society* 12 (1912): 214–82.

Bullock, Henry Allen. *A History of Negro Education in the South from 1619 to the Present*. Cambridge, Mass.: Harvard University Press, 1967.

Butchart, Ronald E. *Northern Schools, Southern Blacks, and Reconstruction: Freedmen's Education, 1862–1875*. Westport, Conn.: Greenwood Press, 1980.

Carroll, Thomas Battle. *Historical Sketches of Oktibbeha County*. Gulfport, Miss.: Dixie Press, 1931.

Cash, W. J. *The Mind of the South*. New York: Knopf, 1941.

Cimbala, Paul A., and Randall M. Miller, eds. *The Freedmen's Bureau and Reconstruction: Reconsiderations*. New York: Fordham University Press, 1999.

Cohen, Lucy M. "Entry of Chinese to the Lower South from 1864 to 1870: Policy Dilemmas." *Southern Studies* 27 (1978): 5–38.

Cohen, William. "Negro Involuntary Servitude in the South, 1865–1940: A Preliminary Analysis." *Journal of Southern History* 42 (1976): 31–60.

Cohn, David L. *The Life and Times of King Cotton*. New York: Oxford University Press, 1956.

Cornish, Dudley Taylor. "The Union Army as a School for Negroes." *Journal of Negro History* 37 (1952): 368–82.

Currie, James T. "Conflict and Consensus: Creating the 1868 Mississippi Constitution." M.A. thesis, University of Virginia, 1969.

———. "Freedmen at Davis Bend, April 1964." *Journal of Mississippi History* 46 (1984): 120–29.

Dabney, Charles W. *Universal Education in the South*. 2 vols. Chapel Hill: University of North Carolina Press, 1936.

Davis, Charles T., and Henry Louis Gates Jr. *The Slave's Narrative: Text and Context.* New York: Oxford University Press, 1985.

Davis, Ronald. *Good and Faithful Labor: From Slavery to Sharecropping in the Natchez District, 1860–1890.* Westport, Conn.: Greenwood Press, 1982.

DeBoer, Clara Merritt. *His Truth Is Marching On: African Americans Who Taught the Freedmen for the American Missionary Association, 1861–1877.* New York: Garland Publishing, 1995.

Dennett, John. *The South as It Is: 1865–1866.* New York: Harcourt Brace, 1965.

Drago, Edmund. *Black Politicians and Reconstruction in Georgia: A Splendid Failure.* Baton Rouge: Louisiana State University Press, 1982.

Du Bois, W. E. B. *Black Reconstruction in America: An Essay Toward a History of the Part Which Black Folk Played in the Attempt to Reconstruct Democracy in America, 1860–1880.* Reprint, Cleveland: World Publishing, 1964.

———. "How Negroes Have Taken Advantage of Educational Opportunities Offered by Friends." *Journal of Negro Education* 7 (1938): 124–31.

———. *The Souls of Black Folk.* Reprint, New York: Dover, 1994.

———. "Strivings of the Negro People." *The Atlantic Monthly* 80 (August 1897): 194–98.

Dunbar, Rowland. "The Rise and Fall of Negro Rule in Mississippi." *Publications of the Mississippi Historical Society* 2 (1898): 189–200.

Duster, Alfreda M., ed. *Crusade for Justice: The Autobiography of Ida B. Wells.* Chicago: University of Chicago Press, 1970.

Fleming, Walter Lynn, ed. *Documentary History of Reconstruction: Political, Military, Social, Religious, Educational and Industrial, 1865 to 1906.* Vol. 2. Reprint, New York: McGraw-Hill, 1966.

———. *Laws Relating to Freedmen, 1865–6.* Morgantown: University of West Virginia Press, 1904.

Foner, Eric. *Nothing but Freedom: Emancipation and Its Legacy.* Baton Rouge: Louisiana State University Press, 1983.

———. *Reconstruction: America's Unfinished Revolution, 1863–1877.* New York: Harper & Row, 1988.

———. "Reconstruction Revisited." *Reviews in American History* 10 (1982): 82–100.

Frankel, Noralee. *Freedom's Women: Black Women and Families in Civil War Era Mississippi.* Bloomington: Indiana University Press, 1999.

Franklin, John Hope. *Reconstruction after the Civil War.* Chicago: University of Chicago Press, 1961.

Franklin, Vincent P. *Black Self-Determination: A Cultural History of the Faith of the Fathers.* Westport, Conn.: Lawrence Hill, 1984.

Franklin, V. P., and James D. Anderson, eds. *New Perspectives on Black Educational History.* Boston: G. K. Hall, 1978.

Fuke, Richard Paul. *Imperfect Equality: African Americans and the Confines of White Racial Attitudes in Post-Emancipated Maryland.* New York: Fordham University Press, 1998.

Ganus, Clifford, Jr. "The Freedmen's Bureau in Mississippi." Ph.D. diss., Tulane University, 1953.

Garner, James. *Reconstruction in Mississippi.* New York: Macmillan, 1901.

Genovese, Eugene. *Roll, Jordan, Roll: The World the Slaves Made.* New York: Pantheon Books, 1974.

Gerteis, Louis S. *From Contraband to Freedman: Federal Policy toward Southern Blacks, 1861–1865.* Westport, Conn.: Greenwood Press, 1973.

Goodenow, Ronald K., and Arthur O. White, eds. *Education and the Rise of the New South.* Boston: G. K. Hall, 1981.

Gutman, Herbert. *The Black Family in Slavery and Freedom, 1750–1925.* New York: Pantheon, 1976.

———. "'Schools for Freedom': The Post-Emancipation Origins of Afro-American Education." In *Major Problems in African American History*, vol. 1 of *From Slavery to Freedom, 1619–1877*, edited by Thomas C. Holt and Elsa Barkley Brown, 388–401. New York: Houghton Mifflin, 2000.

Hardy, W. H. "Recollections of Reconstruction in East and Southeast Mississippi." *Publications of the Mississippi Historical Society* 8 (1904): 137–51.

Harris, William C. *The Day of the Carpetbagger: Republican Reconstruction in Mississippi.* Baton Rouge: Louisiana State University Press, 1979.

———. *Presidential Reconstruction in Mississippi.* Baton Rouge: Louisiana State University Press, 1967.

———, ed. *John Roy Lynch, The Facts of Reconstruction.* New York: Oxford University Press, 1970.

Holt, Thomas. *Black over White: Negro Political Leadership in South Carolina during Reconstruction.* Urbana: University of Illinois Press, 1977.

Holtzclaw, Robert Fulton. *Black Magnolias: A Brief History of the Afro-Mississippians, 1865–1980.* Shaker Heights, Ohio: Keeble Press, 1984.

Hunter, Tera W. *To 'Joy My Freedom: Southern Black Women's Lives and Labors after the Civil War.* Cambridge, Mass: Harvard University Press, 1997.

Jackson, Broadus B. *Civil War and Reconstruction in Mississippi: Mirror of Democracy in America.* Jackson, Miss.: Town Square Books, 1998.

Jones, Jacqueline. *Soldiers of Light and Love: Northern Teachers and Georgia Blacks, 1865–1873.* Chapel Hill: University of North Carolina Press, 1980.

Jones, J. H. "Reconstruction in Wilkinson County." *Publications of the Mississippi Historical Society* 8 (1904): 153–75.

Kaestle, Carl F. *Pillars of the Republic: Common Schools and American Society, 1780–1860.* New York: Hill & Wang, 1983.

Kendel, Julia. "Reconstruction in Lafayette County." *Publications of Mississippi Historical Society* 13 (1912): 223–72.

King, Wilma. *Stolen Childhood: Slave Youth in Nineteenth-Century America.* Bloomington: Indiana University Press, 1995.

Knight, Edgar W. *Education in the South.* Chapel Hill: University of North Carolina Press, 1924.

Kolchin, Peter. *First Freedom: The Response of Alabama's Blacks to Emancipation and Reconstruction.* Westport, Conn.: Greenwood Press, 1972.

Lacey, Nannie. "Reconstruction in Leake County." *Publications of the Mississippi Historical Society* 11 (1910): 271–94.

Litwack, Leon. *Been in the Storm So Long: The Aftermath of Slavery.* New York: Vintage, 1980.

———. *Trouble in Mind: Black Southerners in the Age of Jim Crow.* New York: Vintage, 1999.

Loewen, James W. *The Mississippi Chinese: Between Black and White.* Cambridge, Mass: Harvard University Press, 1971.

Lewis, David Levering. *W. E. B. Du Bois: Biography of a Race, 1868–1919.* New York: Henry Holt, 1993.

Magee, Hattie. "Reconstruction in Lawrence and Jefferson Counties." *Publications of the Mississippi Historical Society* 11 (1910): 163–204.

McCain, William D. "Education in Mississippi in 1860." *Journal of Mississippi History* 22 (1960): 153–66.

McLemore, Richard Aubrey, ed. *A History of Mississippi.* Vol. 1. Hattiesburg: University and College Press of Mississippi, 1973.

McMillen, Neil. *Dark Journey: Black Mississippians in the Age of Jim Crow.* Chicago: University of Illinois Press, 1989.

McMurray, Linda O. *To Keep the Waters Troubled: The Life of Ida B. Wells.* New York: Oxford University Press, 1998.

McNeily, J. S. "Climax and Collapse of Reconstruction in Mississippi." *Publications of the Mississippi Historical Society* 12 (1912): 283–474.

———. "The Enforcement Act of 1871 and the Ku Klux Klan in Mississippi." *Publications of the Mississippi Historical Society* 9 (1906): 109–71.

———. "From Organization to Overthrow of Mississippi's Provisional Government, 1865–1868." *Publications of the Mississippi Historical Society,* centenary series, 1 (1918): 9–403.

———. "War and Reconstruction in Mississippi." *Publications of the Mississippi Historical Society,* centenary series, 1 (1918): 165–535.

McPherson, James M. *The Negro's Civil War: How American Negroes Felt and Acted during the War for the Union.* New York: Pantheon Books, 1965.

Moore, Ross. "Social and Economic Conditions in Mississippi during Reconstruction." Ph.D. diss., Duke University, 1938.

Morris, Robert C. "Educational Reconstruction." In *The Facts of Reconstruction: Essays in Honor of John Hope Franklin*, edited by Eric Anderson and Alfred A. Moss Jr., 141–66. Baton Rouge: Louisiana State University Press, 1991.

———. *Reading, 'Riting, and Reconstruction: The Education of Freedmen in the South, 1861–1870*. Chicago: University of Chicago Press, 1981.

Nichols, Irby. "Reconstruction in DeSoto County." *Publications of the Mississippi Historical Society* 11 (1910): 295–316.

Nieman, Donald. G., ed. *African Americans and Education in the South, 1865–1900*. New York: Garland Publishing, 1994.

———. "The Freedmen's Bureau and the Mississippi Black Code," *The Journal of Mississippi History* 40 (1978): 91–118.

Noble, Stuart Grayson. *Forty Years of the Public School in Mississippi: With Special Reference to the Education of the Negro*. New York: Teachers College, Columbia University Press, 1918.

Oshinsky, David M. *"Worse than Slavery": Parchman Farm and the Ordeal of Jim Crow Justice*. New York: Free Press, 1996.

Peirce, Paul Skeels. *The Freedmen's Bureau: A Chapter in the History of Reconstruction*. Iowa City: University of Iowa Press, 1904.

Perkins, Linda M. "The Black Female American Missionary Association Teacher in the South, 1861–1870." In vol. 3 of *Black Women in American History: From Colonial Times through the Nineteenth Century*, edited by Darlene Clark Hine, 1049–63. Brooklyn, N.Y.: Carlson, 1990.

Perman, Michael. "Counter Reconstruction." In *The Facts of Reconstruction: Essays in Honor of John Hope Franklin* edited by Eric Anderson and Alfred A. Moss Jr., 121–40. Baton Rouge: Louisiana State University Press, 1991.

Plumpp, Sterling. *Blues Narratives*. Chicago: Tia Chucha, 1999.

Pollard, Edward A. "The Romance of the Negro." *The Galaxy* 12 (1871): 470–78.

Posey, Josephine. *Against Great Odds: The History of Alcorn State University*. Jackson, Miss.: University Press of Mississippi, 1994.

Puckett, E. F. "Reconstruction in Monroe County." *Publications of the Mississippi Historical Society* 11 (1910): 103–60.

Pyburn, Nita Katherine. "Public Schools in Mississippi Before 1860." *Journal of Mississippi History* 21 (1959): 113–30.

Ransom, Roger, and Richard Sutch. *One Kind of Freedom: The Economic Consequences of Emancipation*. New York: Cambridge University Press, 1977.

Rice, Elizabeth G. "A Yankee Teacher in the South: An Experience in the Early Days of Reconstruction." *Century Magazine* (May 1901): 151–54.

Richardson, Joe M. *Christian Reconstruction: The American Missionary Association and Southern Blacks, 1861–1870*. Athens: University of Georgia Press, 1986.

Sallis, William Charles. "The Color Line in Mississippi Politics, 1865–1915." Ph.D. diss., University of Kentucky, 1967.

Sansing, David. "The Failure of Johnsonian Reconstruction in Mississippi, 1865–1866," *The Journal of Mississippi History* 34 (1972): 373–90.

Schweninger, Loren. "Black Economic Reconstruction in the South." In *The Facts of Reconstruction: Essays in Honor of John Hope Franklin*, edited by Eric Anderson and Alfred A. Moss Jr., 167–88. Baton Rouge: Louisiana State University Press, 1991.

Singletary, Otis. *Negro Militia and Reconstruction*. Austin: University of Texas Press, 1957.

Southerner. "Agricultural Labor at the South." *The Galaxy* 12 (1871): 328–41.

Span, Christopher M. "'I Must Learn Now or Not At All': Social and Cultural Capital in the Educational Initiatives of Formerly Enslaved African Americans in Mississippi, 1862–1869." *Journal of African American History* 87 (2002): 22–31.

———. "Knowledge is Light, Knowledge is Power: African American Education in Antebellum America." In vol. 1 of *Surmounting All Odds: Education, Opportunity & Society in the New Millennium*, edited by Carol Camp Yeakey and Ronald D. Henderson, 1–29. Greenwich, Conn.: Information Age Press, 2003.

Sparks, Randy. "'The White People's Arms Are Longer than Ours': Blacks, Education, and the American Missionary Association in Reconstruction Mississippi." *Journal of Mississippi History* 54 (1992): 1–27.

Sterling, Dorothy. *The Trouble They've Seen: The Story of Reconstruction in the Words of African Americans*. New York, Da Capo Press, 1994.

Swint, Henry L. *Dear Ones at Home: Letters from Contraband Camps*. Nashville: Vanderbilt University Press, 1966.

———. *The Northern Teacher in the South, 1862–1870*. Nashville: Vanderbilt University Press, 1941.

Thorton, J. Mills. "Fiscal Policy and the Failure of Radical Reconstruction in the Lower South." In *Region, Race, and Reconstruction: Essays in Honor of C. Vann Woodward*, edited by J. Morgan Kousser and James M. McPherson, 349–94. New York: Oxford University Press, 1982.

Timberlake, Elise. "Did the Reconstruction Regime Give Mississippi Her Public Schools?" *Publications of the Mississippi Historical Society* 12 (1912): 72–93.

Trelease, Allen. *White Terror: The Ku Klux Klan Conspiracy and Southern Reconstruction*. New York: Harper & Row, 1971.

Vaughn, William P. *Schools for All: The Blacks and Public Education in the South, 1865–1877*. Lexington: University Press of Kentucky, 1974.

Vincent, Charles. *Black Legislators in Louisiana during Reconstruction*. Baton Rouge: Louisiana State University Press, 1976.

Walker, Vanessa Siddle. *Their Highest Potential: An African American School Community in the Segregated South*. Chapel Hill: University of North Carolina Press, 1996.

Wallace, Jesse Thomas. *A History of the Negroes in Mississippi from 1865 to 1890*. Reprint, New York: Johnson Reprint, 1970.

Watkins, Ruth. "Reconstruction in Marshall County." *Publications of the Mississippi Historical Society* 12 (1912): 155–213.

———. "Reconstruction in Newton County." *Publications of the Mississippi Historical Society* 11 (1910): 205–28.

Wayne, Michael. *The Reshaping of the Plantation Society: The Natchez District, 1860–1880*. Baton Rouge: Louisiana State University Press, 1983.

Weathersby, William Henington. *A History of Educational Legislation in Mississippi from 1796 to 1860*. Chicago: University of Chicago Press, 1921.

Webber, Thomas L. *Deep Like the Rivers: Education in the Slave Community, 1831–1865*. New York: W. W. Norton, 1978.

Wharton, Vernon Lane. *The Negro in Mississippi, 1865–1890*. Reprint, New York: Harper & Row, 1965.

Wiley, Bell Irvin. *Southern Negroes, 1861–1865*. Reprint, New Haven, Conn.: Yale University Press, 1965.

Williams, George Washington. *A History of the Negro Race in America, 1619–1880*. Vol. 2. Reprint, New York: Arno Press, 1968.

Williams, Heather Andrea. *Self-Taught: African American Education in Slavery and Freedom*. Chapel Hill: University of North Carolina Press, 2005.

Williamson, Joel. *After Slavery: The Negro in South Carolina during Reconstruction, 1861–1877*. Chapel Hill: University of North Carolina Press, 1965.

Woods, William Leon. "Travail of Freedom: Mississippi Blacks, 1862–1870." Ph.D. diss., Princeton University, 1979.

Woodson, Carter G. *The Education of the Negro Prior to 1861*. Washington, D.C.: Arno Press, 1921.

Work, Monroe N. "Some Negro Members of Reconstruction Conventions and Legislatures and of Congress." *Journal of Negro History* 5 (1920): 72–76.

Wyatt-Brown, Bertram. "Black Schooling during Reconstruction." In *The Web of Southern Social Relations: Women, Family, and Education*, edited by Walter J. Fraser Jr., R. Frank Saunders Jr., and Jon L. Wakelyn, 146–65. Athens: University of Georgia Press, 1985.

INDEX

Abney, M. G., 131

African American refugees: in Union army camps, 35, 49, 50–51, 53, 54, 55, 56–57, 87, 196 (n. 3); on former plantations, 36; black laborers' financial support for, 41; effects of war on, 55–56

African American schools: blacks' building of, 5, 11, 13, 25–27, 32, 34, 39, 41, 48, 80, 161, 186 (n. 5), 200 (n. 59); and American Missionary Association, 5, 27, 34, 38, 51, 58, 191 (n. 7); purpose of, 10; and Freedmen's Bureau, 13, 27, 38, 39–40, 51, 68–69, 81–82, 103, 109, 120, 202 (n. 84); private schools, 15, 27, 28, 29–34, 37, 38, 39–40, 67, 80–81, 82, 123, 129, 148, 200 (n. 59); white southerners' violent opposition to, 16, 107, 108, 110–13, 156, 158, 160–62; funds provided by southern blacks for, 27, 28, 32, 40, 41–42, 147, 186 (n. 1), 195 (n. 66); and Society of Friends, 27, 51, 58; and northern benevolent societies, 27, 51, 58–62, 73, 74–75, 82, 83, 103, 120, 200 (n. 59); Alvord's assessment of, 29–30, 32; in churches, 32, 33, 64–65, 110, 129, 160, 161, 177, 178; on former plantations, 32, 35–36,

103, 105, 106, 107; prohibition of, 37, 191 (n. 6); order and discipline in, 38; as self-supporting, 38, 39, 49; troops required for protection of, 49, 72, 73, 108, 110, 111; transformative potential of, 52; in Union army camps, 58–63; lack of space for, 59–60, 68, 110; white southerners' tacit opposition to, 60, 84–85, 108, 109–10, 129, 163; growth in, 64, 69, 103, 175; postwar increase in supplies for, 67–68; and presidential restoration policy, 68; and assenting local whites, 68, 69, 73, 76, 85, 103–4, 105, 106, 107, 108, 114, 117; accessibility of, 72–73, 78; and ambitions of freedpeople, 85, 154; funds provided by white southerners for, 104; Mississippi legislators' opposition to, 108; for public school system, 128–29, 131, 135, 215 (n. 42). *See also* Black education; Public school system

African Civilization Society of New York, 28

Alabama, 190 (n. 21)

Albright, George Washington, 3–4, 7, 18–19, 33, 34, 177, 185–86 (n. 1), 186 (n. 5)

Alcorn, James Lusk, 127, 132–33, 160, 167, 212 (n. 14)

Alcorn College, 133

Allen, Sarah, 159

Alvord, John W.: on freedpeople's educational initiatives, 29–32, 33, 38, 40, 41; on mass movement for literacy, 46; reports of, 84, 199–200 (n. 56); on white southerners' opposition to black education, 110; on public school system, 122, 153

American Missionary Association (AMA): African American schools established by, 5, 27, 34, 51, 58, 191 (n. 7); African American schools consolidated with schools of, 38; and roles of teachers, 59; and black teachers, 71, 82; and white southerners–freedpeople labor negotiations, 105; and public school teachers, 131; and normal school for African Americans, 132, 215 (n. 47); and university for African Americans, 132–33; and Sabbath school lesson plans, 201–2 (n. 79)

Ames, Adelbert, 153, 167, 176, 190 (n. 20), 214 (nn. 36, 40)

Ames, Charles B., 159, 214 (n. 42)

Amnesty oath, 68

Anderson, James D., 45, 208 (n. 62)

Apprenticeship law, 93

Archer, Jim, 52

Arkansas, 28–29, 221 (n. 53)

Arrests: and black codes, 93, 94; of Klansmen, 160

Asian Americans, 211 (n. 2)

Baker, Anna, 52

Bardwell, J. P., 37–38, 71, 106, 111

Berlin, Ira, 50, 85

Bible: and literacy, 47, 52, 65; as text in day schools, 64–65; as text in night schools, 65–66; as text in Sabbath schools, 67, 201 (n. 79); as text in public schools, 165

Bishop, J. N., 159

Black children: black parents' control of, 43; day schools for, 64–65; inadequate clothing for, 72; apprenticing of orphaned, 93; and public school system, 118–19, 120, 125, 134; enrollment in public schools, 120, 133–34, 135, 138, 143, 144, 152, 168–69, 216 (n. 58); shortage of teachers for, 131, 134; violence toward teachers of, 131, 159, 160, 161–62; attendance in public schools, 134–35, 143, 144, 147, 162, 169; educational opportunities for, 135, 142, 143, 147, 148–49, 152, 153, 159, 162, 166–67, 168, 175, 176, 177–80

Black codes: restrictions on freedpeople, 18, 74–75, 92, 93, 94, 95, 207 (n. 45); and role of literacy, 47–48; and white southerners' reaction to emancipation, 90; purpose of, 92, 95, 206 (n. 37); and regulations on black labor, 92–94; and economic rights of freedpeople, 93; enforcement of, 94–95; freedpeople's resistance to, 98; and white southerners' opposition to black education, 108

Black education: funding for, 3, 4, 27, 28, 40, 41–42, 185–86 (n. 1), 195 (n. 66); during Reconstruction, 5–6, 8, 187 (nn. 8, 9); postbellum evolution of, 5–6, 187 (n. 9); early histories of, 5–8, 187 (nn. 8, 9), 188 (n. 12); white southerners' opposition to, 6, 9–10, 11, 13, 14, 17, 31–32, 41, 46, 52, 85, 102–3, 107, 108, 109, 110, 156, 157–58, 178–

79; control of, 9, 10–11, 39–40, 75–76, 77, 80–82, 103, 104, 105, 107, 133–34; purpose of, 9, 10, 11–12, 13, 14, 17, 43–48; white education compared to, 15, 38, 111–12, 120, 125, 131, 138, 142–43, 147–48, 149, 152, 153, 178, 217 (n. 69); Du Bois on, 23, 191 (n. 7); Maryland convention on, 27–28, 192 (n. 15); role of Civil War in, 34, 35–37, 49; white southerners' support for, 103, 104, 105, 209 (n. 88); white southerners' acceptance of, 104–5, 106, 107; and demand for higher education, 132–33. *See also* African American schools; Public school system

Black families, and apprenticeship law, 93

Black inferiority: regiment schools challenging, 66–67; northern ideologies of, 75; white southerners' beliefs in, 84, 107, 154; and public school system, 123

Black labor: and labor contracts, 11, 12, 74, 79, 80, 88, 89, 90, 92, 93, 96, 98, 105, 107, 109, 112, 113, 205 (n. 17); and role of education, 11, 74, 76, 77, 79, 85, 102, 106, 107, 121, 158, 164; regulation of, 18, 92; blacks' requests for recognition of, 28–29; and role of literacy, 47–48; and Union army, 50, 56, 196 (n. 3); and black self-sufficiency, 76–77; and white property owners, 79, 85, 89–90, 98, 102, 109, 112, 162; effect of emancipation on, 87, 97; immigrant labor as replacement for, 90–92; and black codes, 92–94; and sharecropping, 95; and working hours, 97, 98; white southerners' control over, 97, 162; as contribution to white wealth, 157

Black laborers: and funding of schools, 40–41; and cotton industry, 40–41, 69–70, 85, 88, 89, 92; wages of, 42–43; and goals of northern benevolent societies, 51, 74; interest in education, 63; and regiment schools, 66; right of choice for, 88, 89

Black landownership: and citizenship rights, 9; role of education in, 11, 45; as symbol of freedom, 88; low percentage of, 88, 128–29, 157; labor contracts viewed as jeopardizing, 90; black codes prohibiting, 92–93; local antagonism toward, 122; and elections of 1875, 175; statistics on, 212 (n. 14). *See also* White property owners

Black militiamen, 40, 66, 201 (n. 73)

Black regiments, 35

Black self-sufficiency: opposition to, 6, 11; education's role in, 11, 28, 74; and African American schools, 38, 39, 106; and funding for schools, 41; and independent farming ventures, 76; and free-wage labor, 76–77; and northern-born teachers, 154

Black suffrage: white southerners' opposition to, 18, 99, 102; freedpeople's petitioning Congress for, 98–99; white southerners' acceptance of, 99–100, 104, 122, 153; and Mississippi constitutional convention of 1868, 100–101; Waddell on, 108; constitutional guarantee of, 113–14; Adelbert Ames's support for, 167. *See also* Citizenship rights; Voting rights

Black teachers: in Civil War era, 4, 5, 25, 33, 37; in African American schools, 29–30, 33, 177, 178; children as, 30; freedpeople providing salaries for,

32, 41; formerly enslaved African Americans as, 33–34, 38, 39, 71; free blacks as, 38–39; in rural areas, 69; and American Missionary Society, 71, 82; competence of, 80, 81; freedpeople's preference for, 81, 82; roles of, 81; white southerners' preference for, 106–7; white southerners' violent opposition to, 111–12, 161; freedpeople as, 131; normal schools for, 132, 133, 215 (n. 47); in public school system, 133, 138

Blake plantation, 35

Blanding (Freedmen's Bureau agent), 111

Brown v. Board of Education (1954), 178

Bruce, Blanche Kelso, 167, 173, 190 (n. 20), 212 (n. 14), 221 (n. 59)

Bruce, Frederick, 88

Bryant, John E., 78

Bullen, Claiborne, 52

Butchart, Ronald E., 61

Butler, Benjamin F., 196 (n. 3)

Cardozo, Thomas W., 166, 167, 190 (n. 20), 221 (nn. 53, 55, 59)

Carroll, Thomas Battle, 103

Caruthers, Belle, 33–34, 177

Chase, Mary, 26

Churches: formerly enslaved African Americans' establishment of, 5, 8, 25, 32, 34; African American schools held in, 32, 33, 64–65, 110, 129, 160, 161, 177, 178

Cincinnati Contraband Relief Commission, 36

Citizenship rights: formerly enslaved African Americans' exercise of, 8, 28–29; freedpeople's use of education for, 9, 12, 13, 16, 28, 32, 45, 48, 64, 74, 77, 81, 109, 124, 125, 158, 175; white southerners' control of, 10; and public school system, 15, 130, 176; disfranchisement of African Americans, 16, 19, 173; white southerners' opposition to, 18, 75, 98, 102; and literacy, 25, 31, 44, 46, 48; freedpeople's expectations of, 29, 96, 113; and formerly enslaved African Americans' associations, 32; and schools of northern benevolent societies, 51, 74; and regiment schools, 66; and expectations of Freedmen's Bureau officials, 77; and black codes, 92; and black suffrage, 100; and educational opportunities, 149, 152, 153, 167, 179

Civil Rights Bill of 1873, 167

Civil Rights Bill of 1875, 125

Coley, Annie, 52

Colonization movement, 28

"Colored," definition of, 211 (n. 2)

Color line: and northern-born teachers, 155; and teachers of black children, 161; and election of 1875, 172

Compton, C. E., 27

Confederacy: Mississippi's role in, 17; defeat of, 67, 68; and postwar Confederate guerrillas, 72; and disfranchisement of ex-Confederates, 101, 102, 214 (n. 36)

Congressional Globe, 99

Connecticut, 219 (n. 7)

Corliss, George, 102

Cotton industry: antebellum dominance of, 17; and black laborers, 40–41, 69–70, 85, 88, 89, 92; and school attendance, 65; effect on educational opportunities, 69–72, 164; effect of

Civil War on, 86–87; and immigrant labor, 91; effect of emancipation on, 97; and crop failure, 157–58; lack of postbellum recovery of, 172. *See also* Plantations

Crime rate, 166

Cultural imperialism, of northern benevolent societies, 75, 81

Daily Clarion, 104–5, 123–24

Daily Worker, 3, 4, 177, 185 (n. 1), 186 (n. 5)

Davis, Alexander K., 167, 190 (n. 20), 221 (nn. 53, 59)

Davis, Charles T., 185 (n. 1)

Davis, Jefferson, 17, 35

Davis, Joseph, 35–36, 88

Davis, Ronald K., 95

Davis Bend plantation, 35–36, 76, 88

Day schools, 64–65, 67

De Bow's Review, 91

Delaware, 28

Democratic Party: and elections of 1875, 14, 16, 172–73, 175; and black suffrage, 99, 100, 113–14; and public school system, 156, 164, 214 (nn. 36, 40); and Ku Klux Klan activities, 158; and elections of 1873, 167, 172, 173

Democratization, black schools as force for, 12

Dickerson, G. N., 164

Dorris, Johnny Mae, 177–80

Douglas, William K., 38

Du Bois, W. E. B.: on public education, 4, 117, 119; on propagandas of history, 7–8, 189 (n. 14); on subjugation of formerly enslaved African Americans, 18; on black education, 23, 191 (n. 7); on emancipation, 24–25; as

teacher of formerly enslaved African Americans, 25; on poor whites' view of education, 45; on mass movement for literacy, 46

Easom, P. H., 178

Eaton, John, Jr.: and camps for formerly enslaved African Americans, 24, 50, 54, 55, 56–57, 58; and freedpeople's support of African American schools, 28; on freedom-seeking blacks, 52, 55; and northern-born teachers, 61; on freedpeople's enthusiasm for education, 63; educational expectations of, 76; and Freedmen's Bureau, 194 (n. 56); and using formerly enslaved African Americans as laborers, 196 (n. 3)

Educational policy: and public school system, 6, 14; and development of black education, 10–11, 17

Egypt, 86

Eldridge, Stuart, 93

Elections of 1868, 112

Elections of 1873, 167, 172–73

Elections of 1875, 14, 16, 19, 172–75, 176

Emancipation: formerly enslaved African Americans' experience of, 14, 18–19, 24, 87; white southerners' opposition to, 17, 18, 72, 75, 85, 89, 95, 99, 107; rise of, 23–24; Du Bois on, 24–25; and mass exodus of enslaved African Americans, 55; white southerners' responses to, 85, 90, 94, 96–97; effect on black labor, 87, 97; and agency of freedpeople, 88; as threat to racial status quo, 89–90; black codes deterring, 95; effect on Mississippi society, 95–96, 97

Emmens, F. B., 160

Employment opportunities, and public school system, 149, 152, 153, 154, 176, 178

Enforcement Act, 160–61

Enslaved African Americans: population of, 17, 31, 55, 186 (n. 2), 190 (n. 21), 192 (n. 15), 198 (n. 23); literacy of, 33–34, 37; Union army as haven for, 53, 54–56, 197 (n. 22); deaths during flight from slavery, 55, 56–58, 197–98 (n. 23), 198 (n. 26); persistent flight of, 55, 86, 87; effects of war on, 55–56, 59; white southerners' authority over, 87; and white southerners' property losses, 87. See also Formerly enslaved African Americans; Slavery

Fifteenth Amendment, 125

Fines, and black codes, 93, 94

Fiske, R. W., 55–56

Fleming, Walter Lynn, 10, 92, 206 (n. 37)

Florida, 221 (n. 53)

Foner, Eric, 66, 77, 81, 87, 90, 113, 167, 201 (n. 74), 202 (n. 84)

Formerly enslaved African Americans: and public school system, 3–4, 15, 138; proactive demeanor of, 5, 8, 28, 85; role in establishing African American schools, 5, 13, 24–25, 27, 32, 36, 39, 48, 49, 187 (n. 9); historians' representations of, 7, 18, 188 (n. 12); and value of education, 8, 12, 13, 25, 44–46, 179, 187 (n. 8); perceptions of abilities of, 9; white southern elites' thwarting advances of, 14; expectations of, 18–19, 25, 45, 48; Union army camps for, 24, 50, 54, 55, 56–57, 58; Eaton's camps for, 24, 50, 54, 56;

and Maryland educational convention, 28; associations of, 32; literacy of, 32; as teachers, 33–34, 38, 39, 71; and autonomy of schools, 40; funding of schools, 40, 41–42; initiative in seeking freedom, 49, 50, 196 (n. 3), 197 (n. 22); as labor for Union army, 50, 56, 196 (n. 3); and Union army, 53, 54–55, 197 (n. 22); as black legislators, 201 (n. 74). See also Black labor; Freedpeople

"Forty acres and a mule," 79

Fourteenth Amendment, 98–99, 125, 208 (n. 62), 214 (n. 36)

Frankel, Noralee, 53

Franklin, John Hope, 172

Free blacks: and establishment of schools, 5, 27, 28, 39; population of, 11, 31, 38, 186 (n. 2), 190 (n. 19), 192 (n. 15), 202 (n. 80), 205 (n. 22); as teachers, 38–39; taxation of, 42–43; and black codes, 92, 93–94, 207 (n. 45); economic freedom of, 205 (n. 22)

Freedmen's Aid Commission, 51

Freedmen's Bureau: educational initiatives of, 5, 48, 82; opposition to, 6; and establishment of African American schools, 13, 103, 109, 120; departure of, 14, 131, 132; and maintenance of African American schools, 27; and freedpeople's desire for education, 29–30, 62–63; and consolidation of African American schools, 38, 39–40, 51, 68–69, 81–82; funding for educational activities of, 41, 202 (n. 82); sponsorship of African American schools, 69, 202 (n. 84); and effects of cotton industry on education, 71–72; progress made by, 73; and white southerners' control of black education, 75–76; and plantation-lease system, 76, 78; expectations of officials, 77, 79; and free labor ideology, 77, 78; and importance of education, 78; and agency of freedpeople, 79–80; and quality of education, 80; and black labor, 89; and white southerners-freedpeople labor negotiations, 105; and labor contracts, 105, 205 (n. 17); white southerners' opposition to, 109; and Pease, 118

Freedmen's Inquiry Commission, 26

Freedmen's Pauper Tax Law, 42–43

Freedmen's School Society, 28

Freedpeople: expectations of, 9, 29, 52, 68, 77, 80, 91, 96, 113, 175; ambitions of, 13, 28–29, 51, 59, 75, 85, 87–88, 152, 154; black codes restricting, 18, 74–75, 92, 93, 94, 95, 207 (n. 45); pursuit of freedom, 19, 25; and importance of education, 25, 30, 31, 33–34, 36–37, 41, 43, 45, 48, 59, 62–63; educational activities and initiatives of, 26–34, 33, 38, 40, 41, 73, 75, 102, 114; and autonomy of schools, 39, 40, 51, 75, 77, 80, 81, 82, 204 (n. 122); schools established by, 39, 103, 120; building of African American schools, 41, 80; funding for schools, 42, 70–71; taxation of, 42–43; northerners' attitudes toward, 51, 76–77; medical needs of, 57–58, 60, 198–99 (n. 39); white southerners' oppositional relationship with, 58, 85, 87, 88; living conditions of, 59; response to northerners' schools, 62–63; enthusiasm for education, 63–64; requests for teachers to remain during summer, 70–71; resistance to racism, 75; strategies to promote self-improvement, 75; and contractual plantation labor, 79; land acquisition aspirations of, 79, 80, 87–88; agency of, 79–80, 88; underrecognition of, 80; proactive attitude toward educational opportunities, 82; use of educational skills, 82–83; white southerners' challenges to initiatives of, 84; mobility of, 89; economic aspirations of, 89, 90, 95; migration to Union-occupied areas, 96, 97, 98; political opportunities of, 99–100; and white southerners' violent opposition to black education, 111–13; and public school system, 118; and white southerners' violent opposition to public school system, 121; migration for safety, 159. See also Black labor; Formerly enslaved African Americans

Free labor ideology, 77–79, 90, 95

Freeman, Clara, 71, 199 (n. 50)

Friends' Association of Philadelphia, 35, 47, 51, 53, 54

Fugitive African Americans. See African American refugees

Galaxy, The, 91–92

Galloway, Thomas S., 159

Ganus, Clifford, Jr.: on opportunities for black education, 34; on blacks' funding African American schools, 41, 195 (n. 66); on northern-born teachers, 61; on Freedmen's Bureau, 68; on white southerners' opposition to black education, 110; on medical needs of freedpeople, 198–99 (n. 39); on normal schools for African Americans, 215 (n. 47)

Garner, James, 5, 187 (n. 9)

Garrett, Phillip C., 53
Gates, Henry Louis, Jr., 185 (n. 1)
Gathright, Thomas S., 130
Genovese, Eugene, 96
Georgia, 17, 61, 190 (n. 21), 199 (n. 56), 204 (n. 122)
Gill, M. E., 112
Goodrich's Landing plantation, 106
Grandison, Lily A., 37, 71, 199 (n. 50)
Grand Junction, Tenn., 24, 50, 55, 56, 196 (n. 3)
Grant, Ulysses S., 24, 50, 53, 54, 196 (n. 3)
Green, Granville, 40
Gunn, Henry, 37

Habersham, Jackson, 38
Halleck, H. W., 196 (n. 3)
Hardy, W. H., 7
Harper, Annie E., 197–98 (n. 23)
Harris, Blanche V., 71
Harris, William C., 5–6, 172, 187 (n. 9), 201 (n. 73)
Harwood, Anne, 131
Hawley, J. A., 62
Hill, James, 190 (n. 20), 221 (n. 59)
Hinds County Gazette, 102, 105, 154
Holly, Calvin, 161
Holly Springs, Miss., 4, 23–24, 50, 54
Holt, Thomas, 205 (n. 22), 207 (n. 45)
Hooker, Charles E., 156, 218 (n. 6)
Howard, Merriman, 80
Howard, Oliver Otis, 75–76, 194 (n. 56), 202 (n. 82)
Huggins, A. P., 158–59, 215 (n. 47)
Humphreys, Benjamin G., 103

Illinois, 218 (n. 6)
Immigrant labor, as replacement for black labor, 90–92

India, 86
Indiana, 218 (n. 6)
Indiana Yearly Meeting of Friends, 215 (n. 47)
Industrial education, 165

Jacobs, Henry P., 101, 117, 125
James, Joshua, 87
Jamison, A. J., 160
Jim Crow, origin of term, 189 (n. 13)
Jim Crow Mississippi, 3, 4, 7, 179
Johnson, Andrew, 5, 68, 74, 92, 98, 188 (n. 12), 201 (n. 73), 202 (n. 82)
Johnson, George, 38
Johnson, Luke, 41
Johnson School and Church, 38
Jones, Helen M., 111
Jones, Jacqueline, 51
Jones, Mandy, 37
Jones, Thomas Jessie, 178

Kansas, 218 (n. 6)
Kirk, Edward N., 51
Knox, John J., 93
Ku Klux Klan: opposition to black education, 6, 112, 158–62; and opposition to outcome of war, 72; and intimidation of teachers of black children, 159, 160, 161–62; reinvigoration of, 173; black members of, 219 (n. 15)
Ku Klux Klan Act, 160–61

Lacey, Nannie, 131
Landon, Cassius D., 119, 211 (n. 5)
Landownership: and immigrant labor, 91. See also Black landownership; White property owners
Laurence, St. Clair, 159–60
Lincoln, Abraham, 26, 50, 55, 74, 167
Literacy: and northerners' view of

black education, 9; formerly enslaved African Americans' valuing of, 25, 30, 31, 43, 44–47, 48; mass movement for, 25–26, 44–45, 46; antiliteracy laws, 31; formerly enslaved African Americans' skills in, 32; opposition to, 33, 37, 38–39, 46; of enslaved African Americans, 33–34, 37; and books used for schools, 36; and psychological victory, 43–44; social purposes of, 46–48; and Bible, 47, 52, 65; and day schools, 65; and Sabbath schools, 67; rates of, 138, 142, 149, 165, 166, 217 (n. 61)

Litts, Palmer, 72–73

Litwack, Leon, 7, 8, 46, 207 (n. 45)

Louisiana, 190 (n. 19), 202 (n. 80), 205 (n. 22), 221 (n. 53)

Loyal Leagues, 100

Lucas, James, 89

Lynch, John, 106

Lynch, John Roy, 73, 125–26, 132, 167, 190 (n. 20), 213 (n. 31), 214 (n. 40), 221 (n. 59)

Lynchings, 112–13

Magee, Hattie, 215 (n. 45)

Maine, 219 (n. 7)

Maryland, 27–28, 61, 192 (n. 15), 199 (n. 56)

Matthews, James H., 96

Maxey, Thomas S., 127

Mayo, A. D., 54, 73–74

McBride, Cornelius, 160

McCain, William D., 119–20, 212 (n. 5)

McCuthehen, William, 33

McDonald, A. C., 132

McDonald Hall, 132, 133

McMillen, Neil, 185–86 (n. 1)

Merrill, Ayres P., 91

Mississippi: readmission to Union, 5, 102, 120; as economic and social leader of South, 17; postwar resistance in, 17–18, 190 (n. 22); military rule of, 24; Civil War in, 49, 53, 67, 86; hostility toward northern-born teachers in, 61, 72, 131; conditions in interior of, 72–73, 106; pre–Civil War economic prosperity of, 86; climate of, 91, 92; economic crisis in, 155. *See also* Cotton industry

Mississippi Constitutional Convention (1868): black delegates to, 4, 100, 118, 125, 186 (n. 5), 208 (n. 69); and public school proposals, 4, 117, 118, 121, 122, 123–26, 152; defeat of proposed constitution, 101–2; adoption of constitution, 214 (n. 36); Republican delegates to, 214 (n. 40)

Mississippi Historical Society, 7

Mississippi legislators: and public school system, 15, 117, 119–20, 128; and Thirteenth Amendment, 18, 190 (n. 22); blacks as, 66, 167, 181–83, 201 (n. 74); and Howard, 76; opposition to emancipation, 95; and opposition to African American schools, 108

Mississippi society: impact of African American schools on, 17; white southerners' resistance to changes in, 90, 97, 102–3, 107, 112; formerly enslaved African Americans excluded from, 92; emancipation's effect on, 95–96, 97; and effects of black suffrage, 99

Montgomery, Benjamin, 88

Moore, Ross, 109

Morality, 9, 51, 64–65

Morris, Robert C., 107

Natchez Democrat, 99, 100

National Freedmen's Aid Union, 90

National Freedmen's Relief Association, 58

Native Americans, 211 (n. 2)

Native schools, 32–33

Negro problem, 9, 74–75

New England common school model, 118, 129, 155

New England Freedmen Aid Society, 45, 56

New Jersey, 219 (n. 7)

Nicks, Josephine, 37–38

Nieman, Donald, 92–93

Night schools, 64, 65–66, 67, 129

Noble, Stuart Grayson: on educational policy, 6; on proposals for integration of public schools, 123, 124; on building schools, 128; on public school system bureaucracy, 129, 213–14 (n. 36); on white southerners' attitude toward public school system, 153, 218 (n. 5); on teachers of black children, 155; on textbooks for public schools, 166; biases of, 188 (n. 12)

North Carolina, 61, 200 (n. 56)

Northern benevolent societies, and African American schools, 27, 51, 58–62, 73, 74–75, 82, 83, 103, 120, 200 (n. 59)

Northern-born teachers: in Civil War era, 4, 35–36, 49; white southerners' opposition to, 6, 7, 13, 105, 107, 108, 110–11, 154–55; roles of, 13–14, 26, 59, 67, 199 (n. 44); and expectations of freedpeople, 31, 51, 67; freedpeople providing salaries for, 32, 41, 70–71; and autonomy of freedpeople, 40; on value of literacy, 47; schools established by, 49, 51; freedpeople's

appreciation for, 51–52; realities confronting, 52–53, 110; shortage of, 61; in Union army camps, 61–62; population of, 61–62, 69; and freedpeople's enthusiasm for education, 63; and day schools, 64–65; and Mississippi climate, 70; and opposition in interior of Mississippi, 72–73, 106; and violence and terror campaigns, 72, 159; progress achieved by, 73; competence of, 81; and freedpeople's citizenship, 109; for public school system, 131; and social relations with black students, 154

Northerners: and expectations of African Americans, 9, 31, 51, 52, 75, 76–77, 80–81; and control of black education, 10–11, 80–82; and formerly enslaved African Americans' literacy, 32; and autonomy of freedpeople, 40, 51, 75; educational activities of, 48, 114; schools established by, 49–50, 58–59, 85, 154; reactions to freedom-seeking blacks, 54; beliefs about Mississippi, 61; and free labor ideology, 77–78; white southerners opposition to, 85, 89, 107, 108, 109, 129; and labor contracts, 89; and white southerners' support for black education, 103, 104, 209 (n. 88); inability to protect freedpeople, 113

Northern ministers, 49, 59

Northwestern Freedmen's Aid Commission, 58, 59

Northwestern Freedmen's Association, 57

Northwest Ordinance of 1787, 191

Ohio Yearly Meeting of Friends, 215 (n. 47)

Olds, A. D., 67
Ord, E. O. C., 73
Oshinsky, David M., 89, 94–95, 112–13
Oxford Falcon, 104, 107
Ozanne, U., 101

Panola Star, 104, 209 (n. 88)
Paternalism, 75
Peake, Mary Smith, 26, 191 (n. 7)
Pease, Henry R.: on number of African American schools, 73; on control of African American schools, 82; on white southerners' attitude toward black education, 106, 109; as superintendent of public school system, 118, 128; and public school system bureaucracy, 129–30, 133–34, 163–64; hiring of teachers, 131; and literacy rates, 138; on goal of high school, 142, 178; and taxation for support of public school system, 155; and violence and terrorism campaigns against public schools, 159; on length of school term, 164; on compulsory attendance, 166; and normal schools for blacks, 215 (n. 47)
Pennington, James W. C., 43–44
Perman, Michael, 174–75
Pierce, Edward L., 196 (n. 3)
Pierrepont, Edward, 174
Plantation-lease system, 76, 78
Plantations: African American schools on, 32, 35–36, 103, 105, 106, 107; wartime transformation of, 35–36, 40, 53, 55–56, 87; infirmary farms established on, 58; and free labor ideology, 77; and contractual labor, 79; economy of, 86, 88; and immigrant labor, 90–91; wages of, 91, 206 (n. 34)
Plumpp, Sterling, 179

Political economy: racial segmentation of, 9; and expectations of white southerners, 14, 18; effect of black education on, 16, 67, 120; white southerners' acceptance of changes to, 84; race as factor of, 156
Pollard, Edward A., 84
Poll tax, and funds for public school system, 121–22, 135, 157, 214–15 (n. 42), 217 (n. 67)
Poor white southerners: attitude toward education, 45; and subservience of formerly enslaved African Americans, 85; and public school texts, 165
Powers, R. C., 127–28
Presidential restoration policy, 68
Private schools: for African Americans, 15, 27, 28, 29–34, 37, 38, 39–40, 67, 80–81, 82, 123, 129, 148, 200 (n. 59); for white children, 119, 130, 142, 147, 169, 215 (n. 42)
Property taxes: and public school system, 118, 121, 122, 123, 155, 156, 162, 164, 175–76, 214–15 (n. 42); higher postbellum rate of, 156–57, 218–19 (n. 7); and taxpayers' revolt, 158
Public school system: establishment of, 3, 14, 73, 114, 128; initiatives promoting, 3–4, 5, 13; Harris on, 5; educational policy related to, 6, 14; purpose of, 14, 152; capacity of, 15; racial segregation of, 15, 16, 117–18, 123, 125, 127–28; white southerners' attitudes toward, 15, 16, 120–21, 124, 126–28, 129, 130, 148, 155–56, 159–60, 166–67, 169, 214 (nn. 40, 42), 218 (n. 5); dual system of, 15, 123, 125, 126, 128, 153, 156, 162; and citizenship rights, 15, 130, 176; teachers for, 18, 128, 131,

133, 134, 159, 160, 162, 163, 164, 175, 218 (n. 7); day schools incorporated in, 65; grassroots African American schooling efforts incorporated into, 82–83, 128; proposals for integration of, 101, 123–24, 125, 126–27, 149; funding of, 118, 121–22, 128, 129, 135, 147, 155, 156, 176, 214–15 (n. 42), 217 (n. 57); laws governing, 118–19, 164, 165, 192 (n. 11), 217 (n. 70); pre–Civil War organization of, 119–20, 211–12 (n. 5); enrollment in, 120, 133–34, 135, 138, 143, 144, 147, 152, 166, 168–69, 172, 216 (n. 58); bureaucratic control of, 121, 128, 129–30, 133, 163–64, 213 (n. 31); expenditures on, 128, 130–31, 163, 213 (n. 31); buildings for, 128–29, 130, 131, 133, 138, 163, 218 (n. 7); in majority-black counties, 134–35, 138, 142, 143, 147, 148, 149, 157, 169, 216–17 (n. 59), 217 (n. 67); types of schools in, 138, 142–43, 148–49, 152, 178; educable to enrolled black student ratio, 138, 147, 217 (n. 69); in majority-white counties, 142–44, 147, 148–49, 169, 172, 217 (nn. 67, 70); and proportional distribution proposition, 156, 218 (n. 6); and length of school term, 163, 164; textbooks of, 163, 165–66; curriculum of, 164–66; and compulsory attendance, 166; and elections of 1875, 175; and petitions of parents for child to attend public school, 216 (n. 58), 216–17 (n. 59), 217 (n. 70)

Pyburn, Nita Katherine, 211–12 (n. 5)

Racial equality: and citizenship rights, 9; role of education in, 10, 11, 12, 28, 109, 110, 179; and public school system, 15, 121, 123, 154, 167; and edu-cational opportunities, 15, 166–67; freedpeople's expectations of, 29; freedpeople's use of education for, 45, 64, 74; and goals of northern benevolent societies, 74; and expectations of Freedmen's Bureau officials, 77; and northern-born teachers, 154; white southerners' lack of acceptance of, 154; violence and terror campaigns against, 159, 162, 173–74, 176; and Adelbert Ames, 167

Racial segregation, of public school system, 15, 16, 117–18, 123, 125, 127–28

Racism, 6, 75–76, 131

Ransom, Roger L., 69, 97, 98

Reconstruction Acts of 1867, 214

Reconstruction: status of African Americans during, 3, 8; and black education, 5–6, 8, 187 (nn. 8, 9); traditionalist perspective on, 10, 108, 120, 131, 156, 187 (n. 9), 188 (n. 12), 206 (n. 37), 215 (n. 45); resistance to, 14, 17, 162; and northern-born teachers, 52; and black legislators, 66, 167, 181–83, 201 (n. 74), 205 (n. 22); and regulation of black labor, 92; white southerners' belittling efforts of, 98; expenditures of, 158, 213 (n. 31); counterattack on, 172–73

Reformed Presbyterians, 58

Regiment schools, 64, 66–67

Reid, Whitelaw, 35–36, 87, 91

Republican Party: white southerners' opposition to, 6, 7, 14, 172, 173, 174, 214 (n. 40); and black suffrage, 98–99, 100, 113–14, 167; and public school system, 129

Revels, Hiram, 132, 133, 190 (n. 20)

Reynolds, George D., 79, 89

Rice, Thomas "Daddy," 189 (n. 13)

Richardson, Solomon, 41
Riley, Franklin L., 6, 7
Robb, J. W., 99
Rogers, Noah, 37
Rose Hill church day school, 64–65
Rowntree, Henry, 36–37
Rust University, 132

Sabbath schools, 64, 67, 201–2 (n. 79)
Sallis, William Charles, 121
Sansing, David, 92
Saxton, Rufus, 196 (n. 3)
Schurz, Carl, 108
Schweninger, Loren, 212 (n. 14)
Segur, Carrie, 131
Selma Times, 104–5
Shadd, I. D., 190 (n. 20)
Shannon, James J., 104
Sharecropping, 95, 143, 149
Shaw University, 132, 133
Sherman, William Tecumseh, 55
Shipley, Samuel, 35, 53, 57–58, 59
Slaveholders, population of, 17, 190
    (n. 21)
Slavery: compensation for, 9, 79, 80;
    and Thirteenth Amendment, 18, 44,
    190 (n. 22); Civil War highlighting
    conditions of, 34–35, 54; defenses of,
    36; abolition of, 37, 68, 85, 87; illiter-
    acy as vestige of, 43–44, 46; effects
    of, 44, 55, 67; and mission of Union
    army, 50; vestiges of, 52; enslaved
    African Americans' disapproval of,
    55, 57; freedpeople's attitude toward,
    89, 95. *See also* Enslaved African
    Americans; Formerly enslaved Afri-
    can Americans
Slavery to freedom transition: and
    African American schools, 9; critical
    nature of, 11; and literacy, 44; and

northern benevolent societies, 51;
    and Reconstruction policies, 74; and
    Freedmen's Bureau, 78; and expec-
    tations of freedpeople, 80; and white
    southerners' opposition to northern
    influence in, 85; and black codes, 92;
    and public school system, 152; and
    citizenship rights, 175
Smith, Edward, 132–33
Snider, William, 161
Society of Friends, African American
    schools established by, 27, 51, 58
Somers, Anna, 67
South: blacks' role in economic restora-
    tion of, 29; social order of, 43
South Carolina, 61, 190 (n. 19), 199–200
    (n. 56), 202 (n. 80), 205 (n. 22), 207
    (n. 45), 221 (n. 53)
Sparks, Randy, 37, 61–62, 67, 73, 82
Stevens, Thaddeus, 101
Stringer, T. W., 100–101
Subordination of blacks: education as
    threat to, 12, 102–3; and white south-
    ern elites, 14, 77, 201 (n. 73); formerly
    enslaved African Americans' experi-
    ence of, 18–19; and expectations of
    Freedmen's Bureau officials, 77; and
    poor whites, 85; and expectations of
    white southerners, 89, 102, 107; and
    black codes, 92; and white southern-
    ers' attitude toward public school
    system, 123; and elections of 1875, 175
Sumner, Charles, 98
Sunny South, 110
Sutch, Richard, 69, 97, 98
Swint, Henry, 51, 104, 108

Taylor, Richard, 113
Taylor, Tom, 40
Teachers: for public school system, 18,

128, 131, 133, 138, 159, 160, 162, 163, 164, 175, 218 (n. 7); white southerners as, 104, 105, 131; training for, 132, 215 (n. 47). *See also* Black teachers; Northern-born teachers

Tennessee, 27, 61, 192 (n. 11), 199 (n. 56)

Thirteenth Amendment, 18, 44, 98, 190 (n. 22), 214 (n. 36)

Thomas, Samuel, 78–79, 80, 97

Thornton, J. Mills, 157

Timberlake, Elise, 120, 212 (n. 5), 218 (n. 5)

Tougaloo College, 132–33, 215 (n. 47)

Trelease, Allen, 112, 122, 158, 219 (n. 15)

Trumbull, Lyman, 202 (n. 82)

Turner, Nat, 191 (n. 6)

Twenty-Seventh Ohio Infantry Volunteers, 50

Underclass, 48

Union army: and educational opportunities for African Americans, 13, 41, 82, 120; reports of African American schools, 34; camps of, 35, 41, 49, 50–51, 53, 54, 55, 56–63, 87, 196 (n. 3); and northern-born teachers, 49–50, 53; principle mission of, 50; and freedom-seeking blacks, 50, 53, 54–57, 197 (n. 22); and black labor, 50, 56, 196 (n. 3); destruction of railways and river blockades, 58; and regiment schools, 64, 66–67; property confiscated by, 64, 87; progress made by, 73; freedpeople's enlistment in, 98; as protection against violence and terror campaigns, 162

United Brethren of Christ, African American schools established by, 51, 58

U.S. Supreme Court, 188 (n. 12)

Universal education: African Americans laying groundwork for, 4, 5; rise of, 8–9, 121, 176; and formerly enslaved African Americans' associations, 32; debate over, 122; and centralized bureaucracy, 129; African Americans' attitude toward, 135; white southerners' attitude toward, 156. *See also* Public school system

Universal suffrage, 100–101, 153

University of Mississippi, 132

Vagrancy, and black codes, 93, 94

Vagrancy Act, 94

Vincent, Charles, 205 (n. 22)

Violence and terror campaigns: and political control of white southern elite, 14; and elections of 1875, 14, 19, 172–75, 176; and public school system, 16; and white southerners' opposition to African American schools, 16, 107, 108, 110–13, 156, 158, 160–62; and northern-born teachers, 72, 159; and white southerners' reactions to freedpeople, 85, 96; and white southerners' reaction to emancipation, 90, 96–97; and Constitutional Convention of 1868, 101–2; and labor contracts, 112; and freedpeople's voting rights, 112, 173–75; and lynchings, 112–13; and white southerners' opposition to public school system, 121, 158–61, 163; and teachers of black children, 131, 159, 160, 161–62; Alcorn's secret service team initiative, 160

Virginia, 17, 26, 61, 190 (n. 21), 191 (nn. 6, 7), 200 (n. 56)

Voting rights: white southerners' control of, 10; and blacks holding major state offices, 16, 100, 167, 190 (n. 20); freedpeople's expectations of, 29, 175; role of education in, 45; and intimidation of freedpeople, 101–2; and Ku Klux Klan's terrorizing of freedpeople, 112; and violence and terror campaigns, 112, 173–75; effect on educational opportunities, 168

Waddell, William, 108
Walden, Charles C., 135
Warren, Addie, 111
Warren, Joseph: and Freedmen's Bureau, 39, 194 (n. 56); on private African American schools, 39–40; on lack of space for African American schools, 60; on freedpeople's desire for education, 62–63; expansion of educational opportunities for blacks, 69; on black teachers, 71; and educated black labor initiative, 76; on white southerners' support for black education, 103, 105; on white southerners' opposition to black education, 107, 108; on white southerner's opposition to northern-born teachers, 110; report on African American schools, 200 (n. 59)
Washington, D.C., 28
Watkins, Daniel, 27, 192 (n. 11)
Watkins, Ruth, 132
Watson, J. W. C., 105
Wayne, Michael, 86, 88, 206 (n. 34)
Wealth: education as stepping stone to, 45, 46, 47; and white property owners' losses, 87; black labor's contribution to white wealth, 157
Weathersby, William Henington, 130
Webster, D., 161
Wells, Ida Bell, 23–26, 177

Western Freedmen's Aid Commission, 58
Western Sanitary Commission, 33, 57, 58
Wharton, Vernon Lane, 5, 53, 66, 73, 99, 174, 187 (n. 9), 201 (n. 74)
Whipple, George, 61
White children: private schools for, 119, 130, 142, 147, 169, 215 (n. 42); enrollment in public schools, 133–34, 135, 138, 166, 169, 172, 216 (n. 58)
White education: funding for, 3, 185–86 (n. 1); black education compared to, 15, 38, 111–12, 120, 125, 131, 138, 142–43, 147–48, 149, 152, 153, 178, 217 (n. 69); and history of public schools, 119, 120, 211–12 (n. 5)
White Leagues, 173
White militias, 96–97, 112, 158, 162, 173, 174, *See also* Ku Klux Klan
White property owners: and public school system, 15, 121, 122–23, 127, 130, 156, 166; and free labor ideology, 77–78; and black labor, 79, 85, 89–90, 98, 102, 109, 112, 162; and cotton industry, 86; losses of, 87, 90, 157; and immigrant labor, 90–92; and black codes, 92; and black children, 93; expectations of, 96; acceptance of African American schools, 106; opposition to African American schools, 109, 156, 163
Whiteside, Charles, 45
White southern elite: expectations of African Americans, 14, 16, 176; political control of, 14, 16, 156–57
White southerners: opposition to black education, 6, 9–10, 11, 13, 14, 17, 31–32, 41, 46, 52, 85, 102–3, 107, 108, 109, 110, 156, 157–58, 178–79; historians' ratio-

nalization of actions of, 7; on limitations of blacks, 7, 10; black education
as challenge to attitudes of, 8–9, 156;
expectations of African Americans,
10, 18, 77, 78, 85, 89, 95, 102, 105, 143,
148, 154, 178, 209 (n. 91); and control
of black education, 10–11, 75–76, 77,
82, 103, 104, 105, 107; population of,
11, 86, 186 (n. 2), 190 (n. 19), 204 (n. 9);
northerners' attitudes toward, 13; attitudes toward public school system,
15, 16, 120–21, 124, 126–28, 129, 130,
148, 155–56, 159–60, 166–67, 169, 214
(nn. 40, 42), 218 (n. 5); black education as protection from, 47; oppositional relationship with freedpeople,
58, 85, 87, 88; opposition to Union
army camp schools, 60; restoration
of property to, 68; and assenting
local whites, 68, 69, 73, 76, 85, 103–4,
105, 106, 107, 108, 114, 117; opposition
to northern-born teachers, 72–73;
and expectations of Freedmen's
Bureau officials, 77, 79; freedpeople's
attitude toward, 80; support for black
education, 103, 104, 105, 209 (n. 88);
as teachers, 104, 105, 131; acceptance
of black education, 104–5, 106, 107;
and control over African Americans,

109, 113; attitudes toward Ku Klux
Klan, 162; on black troops, 201 (n. 73)
White supremacy: challenges to, 6,
11; historians' validation of, 8; and
elections of 1875, 16, 172–73, 175, 176;
black codes reinforcing, 48; and black
suffrage, 99; and Democratic Party,
100

White vigilantes, 96, 160–61, 173
Wilder, C. B., 26
Wiley, Bell, 58
Williams, George Washington, 191
(n. 6)
Williams, Heather, 66
Wills, Nelson, 27
Wiseman, T., 109
Wood, Thomas J., 76, 107
Woods, William Leon, 5, 43, 93, 101, 187
(n. 8)
Wooley, R. B., 161
Works Progress Administration slave
narratives, 37, 52, 185 (n. 1)
Wright, S. G., 60, 62, 106
Writing materials, 64, 200 (n. 67)

Yeandle, William H., 164
Yeatman, James, 32–33, 57, 66
Young, Clara, 37
Young, George W., 54